Advance praise for
The Parents' Public School Ha

"This comprehensive volume offers a true gold mine of practical advice and information for those parents who appreciate that their own involvement is needed if their children are to reach their full potential in their journey through school. It tells how to give the help they need. It will also serve to make parents feel very much at home in the world of today's schools."
—Louise Bates Ames, Ph.D.,
    Associate Director and cofounder of the Gesell Institute of Human
    Development

"This book is a comprehensive look at the ins and outs of public schooling. As an advocate of school-based management, I find this book a most useful tool for helping parents become powerful agents in the educational development of their children."
—James P. Comer, M.D.,
    Maurice Falk Professor of Child Psychiatry, Yale Child Study
    Center; Associate Dean, Yale School of Medicine

"This handbook is a knowledgeable primer by an experienced educator for concerned parents on what parents can expect from the schools, from their children, and from themselves."
—Dr. Dorothy Rich, founder and president of the Home and School
    Institute and author of *MegaSkills: How Families Can Help
    Children Succeed in School and Beyond*

"Kenneth Shore has succeeded in achieving his goal of giving parents the knowledge and skills to become active partners in their child's education. His style is never didactic or pedantic. Not only does he provide the kind of factual, practical information parents need to participate effectively in the schools, but the book is filled with many useful suggestions of strategies and techniques for parents to utilize in their efforts to ensure the success of their child in school."
—Nancy Berla, coauthor of *Innovations in Parent & Family
    Involvement,* formerly with National Committee for Citizens
    in Education

THE PARENTS' PUBLIC SCHOOL HANDBOOK

*How to Make the Most of Your
Child's Education, from Kindergarten
through Middle School*

Dr. Kenneth Shore

A FIRESIDE BOOK Published by Simon & Schuster
New York London Toronto Sydney Tokyo Singapore

FIRESIDE
Rockefeller Center
1230 Avenue of the Americas
New York, New York 10020

Designed by Crowded House

Manufactured in the United States of America

1   3   5   7   9   10   8   6   4   2

Library of Congress Cataloging-in-Publication Data
Shore, Kenneth.
The parents' public school handbook : how to make the most of your child's
education, from kindergarten through middle school / Kenneth Shore.
p.   cm.
"A Fireside book."
Includes bibliographical references and index.
1. Education, Elementary—Parent participation—United States—Handbooks,
manuals, etc.   2. Parent-teacher relationships—United States—Handbooks,
manuals, etc.   3. Public schools—United States—Handbooks, manuals, etc.
4. Middle schools—United States—Handbooks, manuals, etc.   I. Title.
LC225.3.S56   1994
372.11'04—dc20   94-12658   CIP
ISBN 0-671-79498-1

The author gratefully acknowledges permission from the following sources to
reprint material in their control.
   The National Committee for Citizens in Education for the Parents Rights Card.
   Straight Arrow Publishers, Inc., for "Life After School," by Dr. Kenneth
Shore, from *Family Life* September/October 1993, copyright © 1993 by Straight
Arrow Publishers, Inc.
   World Book Publishing for an excerpt from *Getting Ready for School,* © 1987
World Book, Inc.
   Steven Zemelman, Harvey Daniels, and Arthur Hyde for "Chart of Educational
Practices," from *Best Practice: New Standards for Teaching and Learning in
America's Schools* (Heinemann, A Division of Reed Elsevier Inc., Portsmouth,
NH, 1993).

To my mother,
my foremost teacher

CONTENTS

INTRODUCTION

"Let's declare that—during the decade of the nineties—
our goal will be to have all parents become full partners in
the education of their children."
— Ernest L. Boyer, president of the Carnegie Foundation
for the Advancement of Teaching

The jury has returned and the verdict is unanimous: parent involvement works. Scores of studies over three decades have documented
what teachers have known all along—that children do better in school
when the adults who know them best are involved in their education.
It is not an exaggeration to say that parent involvement is the single
most important factor in a child's academic success.

This is hardly a new discovery. Researchers at the University of
Chicago documented in 1964 that the more parents valued education,
the better their children did in school. At about the same time, researchers studying the Headstart program were finding that parent
support was behind much of the program's success. Since then, study
after study conducted both here and abroad has found similar results,
namely, that students benefit in a variety of ways from their parents'
involvement—through higher grades, improved test scores, and increased motivation. And these gains are evident in children from
varying socioeconomic backgrounds. Parents also benefit directly
from involvement in their children's education. Not only do they better understand their children's educational programs, they also report
feeling better about themselves, getting along better with their children, and becoming more involved in other community programs.

Why do parents play such a key role? Quite simply, they have the greatest impact on their children's motivation to learn. This influence begins at birth and extends through high school and beyond. Parents are their children's foremost teachers, and home is their first school. They have given them five years' worth of lessons prior to kindergarten, following a curriculum shaped by their own knowledge and values. But their teaching role does not end once their children enter public school. It just enters a new stage, one in which they join forces with the school to formally educate their child.

Parents and educators must form a partnership in which they bolster each other's efforts and capitalize on each other's skills and knowledge. Parents, after all, are experts on their children. Nobody knows more about children than their parents. They know their likes and dislikes, their strengths and weaknesses, their moods and temperaments, and their areas of special sensitivity. And they usually have a good handle on what will work with their children and what will not. When schools work closely with parents, they can tap this gold mine of knowledge to better understand and work with their students.

The conclusion is inescapable: parents must become a crucial part of the educational process if their children are to make optimal academic progress. Educators cannot do the job alone. They need the support of parents who value education and convey its importance through word and deed to their children. A school may have a first-rate staff and top-notch facilities, but it cannot educate its students effectively without the active support of parents.

Yet at least one group of educators thinks that parents are not pulling their load. According to a 1993 survey of one thousand teachers conducted by Louis Harris & Associates, a substantial majority of teachers listed increased parent involvement in their children's education as their top priority. In another survey, 60 percent of teachers gave parents poor grades in supporting their children's schooling.

If parents are not doing their share to support their children's education, schools must assume part of the blame. Many educators, fearful that parents will want a say in the running of the school, place roadblocks in the path of parents seeking school involvement. School staff may pay lip service to the concept of parent involvement, but their actions often speak a different language. They may steer parents toward such traditional activities as attending parent-teacher conferences and raising funds and away from participating in substantive educational decisions. At the same time, many parents are content to relinquish responsibility for their child's education to the school. While some parents may have limited time to become actively involved, others may believe that education should be left to the educators. Some are intimidated by the prospect of dealing with principals and teachers or feel they have little to offer. Still others face obstacles in participating because they have difficulty bridging the gap between their own culture and that of the school. In reality, parents are the linchpin to their children's academic success. When educators discourage parent involvement and when parents choose not to participate, the schools are denied their most valuable tool for bolstering student achievement.

If the promise of parent involvement is to be fully realized, then parents and schools will need to learn to view each other as teammates rather than adversaries. Removing the barriers that continue to separate parents and schools will require considerable effort. Schools must reach out to parents, letting them know they value their involvement and providing opportunities for their genuine participation. At the same time, parents will need to shed their inhibitions and place school involvement near the top of their agenda. There are signs that this barrier is beginning to fall as states and school districts across the country experiment with different ways of involving parents in the academic life of their children. Even the federal government has gotten into the act. The Family School Partnership Act is a federal law that promotes family involvement in children's education.

Just what do we mean by parent involvement? Parents can participate in their children's education in a wide variety of ways—from helping them to learn multiplication facts to serving on the school board, from requesting a particular teacher for their child to helping interview candidates for principal. At the most basic level, parents can foster their children's academic achievement by helping them on the home front—by making schoolwork a priority, by monitoring their academic progress, by building their confidence, and by providing a variety of learning opportunities outside school. Secondly, parents can be involved in the life of their children's school—by attending school events, by going to parent-teacher conferences, by working with the teacher to resolve problems, and by volunteering in school.

And thirdly, parents can be involved by advocating for school change. This may take the form of speaking before the school board to argue for a change in the disciplinary policies, serving on a school committee to redesign the grading system, or lobbying lawmakers on behalf of specific legislation.

This book provides parents with the basic tools to become involved at all three levels. The reader will take a tour of public school education, exploring the rights and responsibilities of parents, the obligations of schools, the inner workings of a school system and its key players, the basics of academic instruction, the various educational options, and issues unique to middle school. The book will also help parents acquire the skills they need to negotiate the public school maze so that they can make their voices heard and their presence felt. The overarching objective is to give parents sufficient knowledge and skills so that they can understand the goals and methods of the teacher's instruction, talk knowledgeably with principals and teachers, and participate meaningfully in key educational decisions about their children. And at each step of the way parents will learn what they can do at home to promote their child's academic competence and confidence.

My hope is that this book will demystify public education and empower parents to become effective advocates for their children. Who better to serve in this role than parents? After all, nobody cares as much for your child as you do and nobody will fight as hard for your child as you will. While many principals and teachers care passionately about their students, in the final analysis you are your child's most important advocate. And there no doubt will come a time when your child will need a person to advocate on his behalf—to raise questions, to express concerns, to ask for information, to request changes, and if necessary to challenge school decisions. In their concern with the welfare of all students, schools sometimes overlook the needs of individual students. It is up to you to ensure this does not happen.

If you find that you are timid about assuming this role, remind yourself that education is the most important investment you will ever make in your child. And remember that this is *your* school. You may not be doing the hiring, but you, along with other taxpayers, are paying the bills. You may not be making the key decisions, but you and other parents are the backbone of the system. You have a right— some would say an obligation—to have a say in your child's education.

This book focuses on elementary and middle school issues. Some of the information presented applies to students through twelfth grade, but issues specific to high school students are beyond the scope of this book. There is also good reason for focusing on these early years. It is during this period that children develop the basic academic tools that will lay the foundation for future academic performance. In addition, parents generally have the most impact on their children's school achievement during the elementary years. During these years, when attitudes toward learning and study habits are still evolving, children are more receptive to parent support.

While I have offered a variety of practical strategies for promoting your child's school achievement, you should not feel compelled to pursue all of them. Indeed, that would be virtually impossible. Parents, especially those who work outside the home and single parents, have many other demands on their time. The point here is to pursue those strategies that are suited to your circumstances as well as your child's needs. The book is meant to be used as a resource guide to consult when a particular issue arises. I have also included a glossary and three appendixes that provide a list of useful organizations and suggested books for both adults and children on school-related issues.

A few words about style. I have tried to write with a maximum of clarity and a minimum of jargon. In some cases, I have used educational terms so that readers may become familiar with the terms they are likely to hear in their discussions with school staff. I have chosen to alternate the use of *he* and *she* when referring to students and school personnel.

I have many people to thank for their contributions to this book. First, I am indebted to the many parents and teachers with whom I have worked over the years who have provided me with the base of knowledge and experience on which this book is founded. I also want to express my appreciation to those who reviewed portions of the manuscript and provided valuable feedback, including Dr. Dennis Baiser, Susan Drucker, Susan Falatico, Dr. Katherine V. Goerss, Kimberlyn Montford, Dr. Rebecca Notterman, and Dr. Rima Shore. I also owe a special debt to a good friend and colleague, Dr. Constance Vieland, who over the years has expanded my understanding with her keen insights and thoughtful questions.

Two people deserve special mention for helping this book become a reality. With wisdom and good judgment, Anne Edelstein, my agent, guided me through the process of finding a suitable publisher. Sydny Miner, my editor at Fireside, showed confidence in this project and efficiently moved the manuscript through the various stages of production.

I am especially grateful to my family, who have been more than generous in allowing me the time to work on this project. My daughters, Melissa and Rebecca, deserve my thanks for being understanding during the times I was unavailable and for helping me learn about the finer points of parenting schoolchildren. Finally, my wife, Maxine, has given me encouragement, good cheer, and the gift of time. She not only reviewed the manuscript and provided helpful suggestions from the perspectives of both a professional educator and a parent but also did more than her share of chauffeuring our children, making lunches, and monitoring homework. I could not have written this book without her support.

CHAPTER ONE

PUBLIC SCHOOLS: AN OVERVIEW

When it comes to school issues, educators are rarely of one mind about anything. There is one point, however, on which almost all educators unite: children learn best when their parents work in close cooperation with the schools. Think of this relationship as a partnership, with both you and the school sharing equally in the education of your child. Each plays a critical role because each has important areas of expertise and influence. Educators know what to teach your child at what age in a way that promotes understanding and retention. You are no less of an expert but in different areas. After all, you are your child's most important teacher and no doubt a keen observer of his special qualities. Over the years you have learned your child's strengths and weaknesses, his motivation, his temperament, and his vulnerable spots.

You can help make the most of your child's education by understanding how public schools work and learning effective strategies for navigating through the system. This chapter provides an overview of the public school system, including its key players, the rules of the game, strategies for negotiating the school maze, and ways of evaluating your child's school.

UNDERSTANDING THE SYSTEM

To advocate effectively for your child, you must first learn how the system works. A school system is like any other institution. It has policies and procedures that determine how things are to be done. Individual schools typically have handbooks that tell about such matters as what to do if your child is absent or how to request a teacher conference. The school district also should have a policy manual describing policies for the entire school population (for example, criteria for promotion and retention, attendance standards, and school rule violations resulting in suspension). This manual is available for review by the public. If you wish to learn about the district's policies, contact the board of education offices and request to see the policy manual.

While these written policies and procedures are helpful in understanding the school's position on a variety of issues, they do not tell the whole story. Schools also have many unwritten rules that often determine how things are really done. You can learn about these invisible rules and procedures by talking with school staff and other parents as well as becoming involved in the school system. The more you know about the inner workings of your school district (for example, how decisions are made, who makes them, what factors influence the decision makers, what constraints affect school staff, what political issues stir strong feelings) and the more visible you are around school, the more effective you can be as an advocate for your child.

Who's Who in the Public Schools

Perhaps most important, you need to know the people in the system and their roles. It's all well and good to know how to communicate, but you also need to make sure you're communicating with the right person. This requires an understanding of the school's personnel structure, which will vary with the size and priorities of the district. The larger the school system, the more homework you will need to do and the more determined you will need to be to penetrate the system. The following is a description of the key players in a public school system.

The State's Role in Public Education

Education in the United States has always been a state and local responsibility. The federal government has granted states considerable power to enact educational policy (although, as you will see from federal laws in the areas of special education and school records, the federal government has not ceded its authority completely). Most states in turn have transferred some of this decision-making authority to local school districts. In recent years, however, states have become increasingly active in determining what goes on in public schools. States have established specific mandates that school districts must comply with in such areas as attendance, graduation, standardized testing, special education, teacher certification, curriculum, and length of school year. Local districts retain some latitude in how these mandates are achieved. Thus, while states may require that school districts teach certain subjects, the districts usually retain the right to choose which textbooks and teaching approaches they will use.

The state department of education, which is headed by a state commissioner or superintendent, is responsible for developing educational policy in the state. It writes the regulations that accompany education laws and ensures that local school districts are complying with the letter and spirit of these laws. The state department is also an important source of information for parents about legal issues, parent rights, special education, and gifted education.

Board of Education

The board of education, sometimes called the school committee, is the school district's governing body. It is typically made up of from three to fourteen community residents who are elected for terms of two to four years. (About 3 percent of school boards are appointed.) Through these board members, the community exercises control over what happens in the school. The board represents the voice of the public and thus should be responsive to parent concerns. The board's primary responsibilities are to set school policy and establish district goals. In practical terms, the board has the final say on a number of school matters, including hiring the superintendent, approving the budget, negotiating personnel contracts, approving curriculum guidelines, establishing disciplinary policies, and deciding whether to build a new school or close an old one.

While the role of the board is to determine the district's educational destination, the role of the superintendent is to navigate the course. But there is a fine line between setting and administering policy. And it is a line that boards and superintendents often cross. Because board members are typically not educators, they often defer to the superintendent and rubber-stamp his policies and practices. When this happens, the superintendent may wield too much power. Some boards veer off in the other direction and become involved in issues more appropriate for school administrators.

School boards usually meet at least once monthly. Most states have "sunshine laws" that require that these meetings as well as the board votes be open to the public unless the board goes into "executive session" to discuss confidential matters (for example, personnel decisions). Minutes of board meetings, including budget documents, are also available to the public. There will usually be a time during the meeting when residents have an opportunity to speak. Check your local paper or call the board office for details regarding board meetings, including the agenda. If you have time to go to only one or two meetings, consider attending when the board is discussing the school budget. Budgetary decisions can have a critical and enduring impact on the quality of education in a school district. And you can have a say in determining how money is spent in the schools by speaking up at board meetings and campaigning for the budget's passage.

Superintendent

The superintendent is the CEO of the school district. He is responsible for its day-to-day operations, although his responsibilities will vary with the size of the district. In larger districts, the superintendent will have assistant superintendents in such areas as curriculum and instruction, personnel, and business. The superintendent, who typically has worked his way up from being a teacher and principal, is often involved in matters of budget, curriculum, personnel, special programs, and transportation. He also plays a key role in hiring and evaluating principals. In recent years, superintendents have been increasingly occupied with financial matters as educational funding has been cut back and the public has been reluctant to accept tax increases. In this area, superintendents are responsible for submitting an annual budget to the school board and for ensuring that the school district gets its fair share of the federal and state money earmarked for education.

Superintendents in small or moderately sized districts may meet with parents to discuss concerns regarding their children although it is important that you try to resolve the problem at a lower level before approaching the superintendent.

Director of Special Services

A key administrator from parents' perspective is the director of special services. Sometimes called the director of student services or director of special education, this administrator oversees programs for students with special needs and supervises the district's evaluation teams. If your child is having problems in school, you may want to contact this administrator to learn what special programs are available in the district and whether your child might be eligible. He can usually be contacted by calling the district's central administration offices.

Principal

The school principal may have little contact with your child, but she likely exerts a large influence on his education. As the educational leader of your child's school, the principal sets the tone for what happens in the building and helps to establish the school climate. Teachers often reflect the standards and values of their principal. If the principal stresses academic achievement, teachers will be more inclined to present academically challenging lessons. If the principal is warm and upbeat, you will likely see an energetic and enthusiastic faculty. If the principal places a premium on discipline and order, you will probably see teachers who are intent on keeping control in the classroom. The bottom line is that good principals make for good schools. And what makes a good principal? A person who is firm but fair, kind but still in charge, encouraging but not excusing, consistent but not rigid. An effective principal commands the respect of teachers, students, and parents.

The principal wears many hats. At various times, she may assume the role of educational leader, disciplinarian, motivator, counselor, manager, and accountant. Her responsibilities may include ensuring that the school is properly maintained, devising the school budget, scheduling teachers, assigning students to classes, disciplining students, supervising and evaluating staff, consulting with teachers to solve problems, conferring with parents, and serving as a liaison to the community. While these activities may keep principals tied to their desk for much of the day, the effective principal is highly visible. She can be seen visiting classrooms, walking the halls, greeting students in the morning, and chatting with parents. And she might even teach a class. Schools, especially at the secondary level, may have one or more assistant principals who have designated responsibilities. Ask the school secretary which administrator can appropriately address your particular concern.

Teacher

The teacher is quite simply the most important person in your child's formal education. At the elementary level, the teacher is with your child for five or six hours a day, 180 days per year. While teachers are bound to follow the district's curriculum guide, they have considerable latitude in how the class is run, how the lesson is presented, and how the students are evaluated. And even though they must follow the disciplinary practices established by the principal, they have much leeway in how they motivate students, how they promote self-esteem, and how they deal with students with learning and behavior problems. Teachers must be certified by the state in which they teach. In most states, teachers must pass a standardized test (as well as take required courses) to become certified. While the requirements of teacher certification help to ensure at least a minimum level of competence, teachers vary widely in ability, experience, and devotion. Because of this disparity, it is worth taking the time to talk with other parents about the teachers in the grade your child will enter next year and then to request the teacher you feel may be best suited to your child (see chapter 3).

Guidance Counselor

You may remember your guidance counselor as the person who helped schedule your high school classes. Guidance counselors are still in the business of scheduling, but they do much more. Many spend time counseling students who are having problems either at home or at school. They may also consult with teachers and confer with parents. Recognizing the important role that guidance counselors can serve, school districts have increasingly assigned counselors to elementary schools where they counsel students individually or in groups and provide classroom instruction to promote social and emotional development. The ability of your child's guidance counselor to give him individual attention depends on the counselor's student caseload. The ratio recommended by professional associations of one counselor for every 100 students is rarely achieved.

School Psychologist

Almost all school districts have school psychologists. These are psychologists with masters or doctoral degrees who work with students having school-related problems. These problems may be academic, behavioral, or emotional. A major responsibility of the school psychologist is to evaluate students to determine whether they are in need of special education and, if so, to work with the parents and school staff to arrange educational programs to meet these special needs. The school psychologist may also counsel students and parents and consult with staff to resolve student problems. If you have concerns about your child's adjustment either in school or at home, you may find it useful to speak with your school's psychologist. She is also a good resource regarding psychological services in the community. Ask the school secretary how to contact her. The school district may also have a social worker and learning specialist who work with students with learning or behavioral problems.

School Nurse

If your child has a physical problem or is prone to illness, you will probably get to know the school nurse. She plays a key role in helping to ensure that health problems are not obstacles to learning. Her role has expanded in recent years, especially with the special education trend called "inclusion," in which students with disabilities are increasingly being integrated into regular classes. Today's school nurse does much more than tend to sick or injured children. She is also responsible for keeping track of immunization records, administering medication (with parent and physician approval only), screening students' vision and hearing, and arranging sports physicals. In addition, she may go into the classroom to discuss health issues with students and help students readjust to school after a long illness or hospitalization. If a school does not have a nurse or shares a nurse with another school, someone should still be assigned responsibility for caring for sick children and keeping medical records. If your child has a medical condition such as allergies, asthma, diabetes, or epilepsy, contact the school nurse and alert her to any information the school needs to know about your child. The school nurse is likely to be knowledgeable about medical and health resources in the community and may be especially helpful if you are new to the community.

Librarian

Most schools have librarians. The school librarian does much more than check books in and out. Her role is also to help students learn how to use the library and promote a love of reading. She decides which books the school should purchase and may even read stories to students. The librarian is a good resource for parents and is likely quite open to answering your questions. She will be able to recommend to you children's books in specific areas of interest or on family matters (for example, divorce), books at a specific reading level, or magazines on particular subjects. She may also be able to suggest books for parents on child-related or school issues. Many school libraries have sections devoted to parent concerns.

School Secretary

If there is one person other than the principal who has her finger on the pulse of what's happening in a school, it is the school secretary. She is an excellent source of school information for parents and an experienced problem solver. She may clarify for you school rules or procedures, inform you of whom to contact with a particular concern, get a message to your child, and even loan your child money for lunch. Most school secretaries are very cordial and approachable. Get to know them.

Parents

Last but not least are the adults with the greatest stake in how the school system is run: the parents. More than ever before, parents are becoming involved in school matters—and not just to bake cookies for a fundraising event or chaperone at a school dance. In communities across the country, parents are seeking out and being given opportunities to participate in substantive issues of education. Some school districts have even implemented parent councils that share decision-making responsibility for running the schools with principals and teachers. In some cases, parents are having a say in the hiring of the principal, selection of textbooks, and design of the curriculum. Whether or not parents are involved in helping to chart school policy, they exert their largest influence on the educational system by sending children to school who are ready and eager to learn. The next two chapters will take a closer look at ways that parents can become partners with school staff in the education of their children.

Negotiating the School Maze

Whom should you contact if your child has a problem? As a general rule, speak with the teacher first about any concerns regarding your child's education and then move to the next level—the principal—only if you are not satisfied with the teacher's response or she does not have the power to make the necessary change. Teachers have control over most of what happens in their classroom but lack the power to make changes in a school practice or policy. A principal is the school's gatekeeper and has control over most practices of the school but not school district policy. The principal may be inclined to back up the teacher, so be prepared to give compelling reasons for your request. For school problems outside the classroom (for example, on the playground or at the bus stop), seek out the principal or the guidance counselor.

If you are not satisfied after talking with the teacher and principal and want to pursue the matter further, consider talking with the superintendent (or assistant superintendent in a large district), but bear in mind that the superintendent is likely to support the principal's decision. (As a matter of courtesy, let the principal know of your plan to contact the superintendent.) At the local level, your ultimate recourse is the board of education. You can speak up at a board meeting at a "residents' forum," or you can contact a board of education member individually about your concerns. This is the time to take advantage of your connections. The board member may be willing to intervene with a school official or bring the matter to the attention of the full board. To pursue your concerns beyond the local level, contact county or state education officials or parent advocacy groups (see appendix A for a listing of organizations).

Going over the heads of school staff without speaking with them first may alienate the people with whom you will need to work cooperatively. So respect the school hierarchy in solving school problems and don't jump rank except in unusual situations. But you should not hesitate to climb this ladder one rung at a time to pursue serious concerns until you find somebody who has the power and willingness to solve your problem. You may lose the goodwill of the teacher or principal but you may gain an important change in your child's education. This may be a tradeoff worth making. And with time, you may be able to gain back their goodwill with some gestures of support. As you pursue your concerns, keep in mind the assertiveness strategies outlined in the next chapter.

If you have a problem with a districtwide policy, you may want to begin at the top—with the superintendent (or the appropriate central administrator). Find out the rationale for the policy. You may be able to persuade the district to grant you an exception to the policy (often called a variance), so be prepared to justify your request with a convincing argument and outside documentation, if necessary. Schools, like most institutions, are reluctant to grant exceptions to policies except under unusual circumstances for fear of inviting similar requests from other parents. If medical or emotional issues are involved, a letter from your child's physician to the school district can be influential. As an example, districts may be willing to grant parents' request that their child attend an elementary school other than the one in their attendance area if presented with a compelling reason for the change (for example, it is better equipped to deal with your child's special needs).

If the school agrees to take action on your request, follow up with a letter expressing appreciation as well as your understanding of the action to be taken. This letter will help to prod the school district to honor its agreement. The wheels of public school education can turn slowly and may even come to a grinding halt unless spurred by an insistent parent.

EVALUATING YOUR CHILD'S SCHOOL

Public schools are not all the same. They vary in what they teach. They vary in how they teach. And they vary in how well their students learn. Parents are often faced with the task of evaluating how successfully a school performs. They may be relocating and want to move to a community with a first-rate school system. Or they may live in a community that gives them a choice about which school their child can attend. Or they may want to transfer their child to another school district within the state, which some states such as Minnesota allow. Or they may want to identify the strengths and weaknesses of their child's present school in an effort to improve its quality. Whatever the reason, evaluating a school is a daunting task for even the most sophisticated of parents. This section will help parents figure out what areas to investigate and which questions to ask.

Parents who live in districts with "magnet schools" face the challenge of evaluating which school is best suited to their child. Magnet schools, so called because they draw students from the entire district, are public schools which specialize in a particular subject area or emphasize a specific teaching approach. They may offer programs in such areas as music, creative and performing arts, math and computers, science and technology, and even foreign language. Some magnet schools stress open education where students are given the freedom to chart their own academic course while other magnet schools focus on basic academic skills and even impose strict dress and behavior codes. Some magnet schools are designed for students who are gifted while others are for students alienated from school and at risk for dropping out. Magnet schools are founded on the premise that students have different strengths, temperaments, and learning styles, and schools are most successful when they adapt to these diverse needs. If your school district offers magnet schools, you will likely need to spend time evaluating the different options by talking with other parents, visiting the various schools, and speaking with staff. Students may not necessarily be accepted into the school of their choice since there may be entrance requirements and districts may consider other factors in making placements (for example, space availability, racial balance, geographical location, and schools attended by siblings).

If you are searching for a school for your child, your job is not simply to find a school with a good educational reputation but also one well suited to your child's needs and interests as well as your own educational values. So in weighing the strengths and weaknesses of different schools, keep in mind your child's educational profile and what you think will be best for him. Will he benefit most from the diversity of a large school or the intimacy of a small one? Will he do well in a system with a traditional, structured approach to academic instruction or will he fare better in a system that fosters exploration and self-discovery? Will your child be overwhelmed in a school that is highly competitive or will he thrive with the academic challenges? If your child is musically inclined, does the school have adequate opportunities and resources to promote growth in this area?

You should look at various factors and gather information from different sources in making a judgment about the quality of a school. You will of course want to talk with parents who have children in the system at various levels and go through back issues of the local newspaper and school newsletter. In addition, you will want to gather data that allows you to make objective comparisons among school districts. The following information should be available to you from your local school district (ask for a "school profile") or from the state department of education, although you will need to do some digging and be willing to wade through bureaucratic obstacles:

- money spent per student (annual district expenditures divided by total number of students in district)
- school size
- teacher-student ratio (this ratio can be misleading because of special education and remedial programs, so also look at class sizes)
- standardized test scores
- grade retention rates
- teacher salary scale
- teacher turnover rates
- income level of residents
- ethnic diversity of school population
- attendance rates of students and teachers
- dropout rates
- percent of students entering and leaving the district annually
- average Scholastic Aptitude Test (SAT) scores
- graduation rate
- percent of graduates entering four-year college

While the above information will help you to compare one school system with another as well as with the state averages, nothing can replace a visit to the school itself. It's best to visit when school is in session so you can get a feel for the tone of the school as well as an idea of its teachers and students. Call the school to arrange a time to tour the building and meet with the principal.

As you tour the school and talk with people, keep the following topics in mind and consider the following questions. No school will receive straight A's but the better the school's report card, the more confident you can feel that your child will get a good education.

BOARD OF EDUCATION AND THE SUPERINTENDENT: Start at the top in evaluating the school district by taking a look at the board of education, which sets school policies, and the superintendent, who carries out these policies. They exert considerable influence on the size of the budget, the allocation of resources, program development and key personnel decisions. By attending board meetings, reviewing school board minutes as well as newspaper accounts of its activities, and talking with informed people, you can gauge the quality of the board and the superintendent. The superintendent's office may even provide you with documents describing board members' views on a range of educational issues. Consider the following questions: Are board members knowledgeable? Do they concern themselves primarily with matters of education and avoid personal and political wrangling? Is the board responsive to parent concerns? Does it tackle controversial matters forthrightly and openly? Does the board defer to those with educational expertise on such matters as educational evaluation and textbook selection? Is it excessively concerned with athletic teams? Is the budget passed regularly? Is the superintendent well informed? Is he an advocate for *all* students? Is the superintendent independent from the board and willing to assert his own point of view?

SCHOOL PRINCIPAL: The principal sets the tone for most of what happens in a school. When you meet the principal and see her in action, keep the following questions in mind: Does she have clearly defined goals that guide the school's practices? Is she a strong and energetic leader who inspires dedication in teachers? Is she willing to fight to obtain the best possible services for the students? Does she value the expertise of teachers and respect and consider their ideas? Does she supervise instruction, participate in some educational activities, and on occasion even teach a class? Does she relate to students in a kind and respectful manner? Does she know most of the students by name? Does she run an orderly school where the focus is on learning without being overly concerned with discipline? Is she accessible to parents and attentive to their concerns?

TEACHING STAFF: Perhaps no factor is more crucial to the education of your child than the quality of his teacher. Judging the caliber of a teaching staff is no easy task, but there are some signposts to guide you. A desirable teacher salary scale signals a commitment by the board of education to attract first-rate teachers. Staff turnover is another clue. A relatively high number of teachers departing for other districts suggests problems of faculty morale. A history of recent labor strife between teachers and the board (for example, a strike) should raise questions about the level of teacher satisfaction in the district and the board's commitment to quality education. As you visit the school and talk with staff, consider these questions: Are teachers involved in curriculum development and textbook selection? What is the educational level of the teachers generally and in the subjects they are teaching? Does the school district recognize and reward good teachers? Are there sufficient teaching aides to give teachers time to plan their classes adequately? Does the district encourage teachers to stay current with new educational developments by having them attend workshops and conferences? Do teachers share ideas with each other? Are teachers available to students for extra help? (Chapter 3 lists questions to consider when observing a teacher in the classroom.)

SCHOOL FACILITIES AND EQUIPMENT: As a first priority, the school building must be safe and well maintained. As you tour the building, look for signs of peeling paint and leaking ceilings, and ask whether there is a problem with asbestos or radon. Note whether the school is well lit, orderly, and cheerful. And check the bathrooms to see if they are clean and well supplied. The appearance of a school reflects the pride and commitment of its staff. A school that is not clean and is marred by graffiti or vandalism suggests ineffectual leadership and a discouraged staff. Also consider whether the school is flexible enough to accommodate different kinds of programs. At the elementary level, there should be at least one large room that meets the needs of the physical education program and is adequate for assemblies and musical and dramatic performances.

Good equipment does not ensure good teaching but it can sure help. Some questions to ask: Do students have frequent access to computers? Are the computers used to their full potential? Are staff members trained in the use of the computers for educational purposes? Is there a television with a VCR? What other kinds of media are available (for example, films, records, and tapes)? Is there equipment to conduct science experiments? What kind of budget does the art teacher have? Does she have her own room? Is there adequate playground equipment?

SCHOOL CLIMATE: The personality of a school affects the mood and enthusiasm of its students. As you walk through the school, pay attention to your gut feelings. Is this a place you would like to be if you were a child? Do the children seem happy and enthusiastic? Do they relate to each other in a friendly, cooperative manner or is there a lot of pushing and shoving? Are the students actively engaged in schoolwork? Is there a spirit of friendliness and encouragement on the part of the staff (including the secretaries and custodians)? Do the teachers appear sensitive to their students' needs?

The school's appearance is a good barometer of the school's climate. Halls attractively decorated with students' work are visible evidence of the staff's efforts to promote student esteem. If permitted, take a peek in some classrooms. Ask yourself whether the physical settings inspire learning. Are the classrooms drab or inviting? Are there signs of "hands-on" activities?

Try to be in school during the morning or afternoon announcements. These announcements often speak loud and clear about the school's values and priorities as well as the range of activities available to students. Note whether children are giving the announcements. Are students' accomplishments highlighted? Are students involved in positions of responsibility (for example, is there a student council)? Is there an avoidance of frequent announcements during the day that interfere with instruction?

ACADEMIC INSTRUCTION: Some districts have adopted specific educational philosophies that guide the way the school is organized and the manner in which instruction is delivered. If this is the case in your district, find out if there is provision for the student who requires a different approach. For example, if the school is *open space,* are there closed classrooms for children who are prone to distractibility and inattention? Other questions to ask: Is academic excellence a high priority? Is the district willing to make necessary changes in its educational program while not embracing any and every innovation? Is the focus on learning during academic classes, with minimal interruptions for announcements or organizational matters? Is homework regularly assigned, checked by teachers, and returned to students? Does the district evaluate students' academic skills on a regular basis and, if so, report the results to parents? Does the school make use of community resources? Are the schools' field trips worthwhile learning experiences? Does the district rely solely on test scores to make educational decisions or does it wisely use other criteria as well? Find out whether the district employs tracking (grouping by skill level) and, if so, how these decisions are made. The following list, derived from the book *Best Practice* by Steven Zemelman, Harvey Daniels, and Arthur Hyde, describes educational practices which represent state-of-art teaching.

BEST EDUCATIONAL PRACTICES

The following is a summary of recommended educational practices agreed upon by experts from different educational fields.

- LESS whole-class, teacher-directed instruction, e.g., lecturing
- LESS student passivity: sitting, listening, receiving, and absorbing information
- LESS prizing and rewarding of silence in the classroom
- LESS classroom time devoted to fill-in-the-blank worksheets, dittos, workbooks, and other "seatwork"
- LESS student time spent reading textbooks and basal readers
- LESS attempt by teachers to thinly "cover" large amounts of material in every subject area
- LESS rote memorization of facts and details
- LESS stress on competition and grades in school
- LESS tracking or leveling students into ability groups
- LESS use of pull-out special programs
- LESS use of and reliance on standardized tests
- MORE experiential, inductive, hands-on learning
- MORE active learning in the classroom, with all the attendant noise and movement of students doing, talking, and collaborating
- MORE emphasis on higher-order thinking; learning a field's key concepts and principles
- MORE deep study of a smaller number of topics, so that students internalize the field's way of inquiry

---

- MORE time devoted to reading whole, original, real books and nonfiction materials
- MORE responsibility transferred to students for their work: goal-setting, record-keeping, monitoring, evaluation
- MORE choice for students, e.g., picking their own books, writing topics, team partners, research projects
- MORE enacting and modeling of the principles of democracy in school
- MORE attention to affective needs and the varying cognitive styles of individual students
- MORE cooperative, collaborative activity; developing the classroom as an interdependent community
- MORE heterogeneously grouped classrooms where individual needs are met through inherently individualized activities, not segregation of bodies
- MORE delivery of special help to students in regular classrooms
- MORE varied and cooperative roles for teachers, parents, and administrators
- MORE reliance upon teachers' descriptive evaluation of student growth, including qualitative/anecdotal observations

CURRICULUM AND EDUCATIONAL MATERIALS: A curriculum is a detailed description of the goals, methods, and materials to be used to guide the teacher. The United States, unlike many other countries, does not have a standardized curriculum, so the school curriculum will vary from state to state and even from district to district within the same state. Most schools have written curriculum guides that parents can review and use to compare programs at different schools. Some schools use curricula designed by the state. In assessing a district's curricula, look at the scope of the subjects taught. Does the district focus on basic academic skills at the expense of other subjects (art and music, for example)? Is there attention to understanding and applying concepts and not just memorizing facts? Do the curricula value student creativity? Do they follow logically from one grade to the next? Are the curricula reviewed and updated periodically? Try to find out how closely teachers follow the curriculum guides. Ask to look at the textbooks, making note of how recent they are, whether they are appropriate to the grade level, and whether they are free of ethnic and sexual stereotypes. Are there enough textbooks for all students?

DISCIPLINE: When it comes to disciplining students, a school needs to walk a fine line between being relaxed and being regimented. Check to see if the school has a written code of conduct. Review what the rules and consequences are but also try to find out what actually happens. Take a look at the playground during recess or the cafeteria during lunch. If you see numerous conflicts or hear staff frequently screaming at students, you should wonder about the staff's ability to manage students. Similarly, observe whether students are lined up outside the principal's office for disciplinary reasons. When students are disciplined, is it done in a firm but fair manner? Does the school have a system of incentives and rewards to encourage good school behavior?

CLASS SIZE: The research on class size can be summarized succinctly: the smaller the class, the better the education. A smaller class allows for more frequent teacher contact with individual students. An ideal class size is about fifteen students, although this ratio is rarely achieved in public schools. A small class size (fewer than twenty-five in public schools) is particularly important in the younger grades, namely kindergarten through third grade. As elementary classes approach thirty students, they lose their effectiveness. Teacher aides can help lessen the impact of a large class. Find out if your district has a class size cutoff that triggers either the creation of a new class or the hiring of an aide. Also ask about the size of the reading and math groups.

SPECIAL PROGRAMS: Special programs beyond special and remedial education are largely at the discretion of the local school district. (Special education is required by federal law for students with educational disabilities and remedial education is required by many states for students with academic weaknesses.) Keep your child's special needs in mind as you inquire about the available programs. You may want to find out what services are available for academically gifted students, for students with artistic or musical talents, for students with limited English proficiency, for students who are alienated from school and considering dropping out, or for students presenting behavior problems. How many guidance counselors does each school have? Are there any at the elementary level? Are there full-time nurses in each building? Does each school receive services from a school psychologist and a speech language pathologist? Is the school psychologist limited to testing or does she counsel students and consult with staff and parents? Is there an after-school tutoring program? A homework hotline? A before- and after-school child care program? Extracurricular activities? Check the school's monthly calendar to see what kinds of special events the school sponsors.

SCHOOL LIBRARY: The school library speaks volumes about the quality of a school. First of all, does it have one? Many schools do not. If there is no library, are students taken on trips to the public library? Second, is it well stocked? The American Association of School Librarians recommends that a school library have sixteen to twenty-four books per student (or forty items for each student if films and booklets are considered). Do some of the books complement the topics being studied in the classroom? Does the library have magazines for students and teachers? What about a section for parents? How often do students go to the library? Is the library available to students before and after school?

A school library, which may also be called a media center, should be staffed by a certified school librarian who does more than check books in and out or maintain quiet. She should also teach basic library skills and promote the enjoyment of reading by, for example, having a story time or inviting a children's book author to meet with students.

SCHOOL COMMUNICATION: An effective school keeps parents informed of the progress of their students as well as its educational activities. In assessing how well your school communicates, consider the following: Is there a school newsletter? Are you apprised of important policy decisions by the board of education? Are you told of upcoming board meetings? Do you receive frequent notices from the principal and teacher? Are parents informed of their child's placement in academic groups, problems with homework, or academic or behavioral difficulties? How many times a year are report cards given out? Is there a regular parent-teacher conference? Are teachers receptive to additional meetings if requested by parents?

PARENT INVOLVEMENT: Just as parents have an obligation to be involved in their child's education, schools have an obligation to promote parent participation. Some schools pay lip service to the idea of parent involvement, saying they want parents involved while subtly discouraging their participation. Note whether the school provides genuine opportunities for parent involvement. Is there a parent-teacher association? How active is it in school affairs? Are parents involved in key school decisions such as the screening of candidates for principal? Are parents allowed to observe a class in session? Does the district offer opportunities for parents to volunteer in school? Does it provide educational programs for parents (for example, speakers, workshops, or parent groups)?

Evaluating a school district is a tough job for parents living in or near the district. This task is even more formidable when you live far away. For parents who are considering moving to a community in another state, a service is available (for a fee) that can help you evaluate the quality of the district. Called SchoolMatch, this organization has information on all American public school districts as well as accredited private schools throughout the world. In addition to providing detailed information that allows parents to compare schools in a region or across the country, it advises parents about the district's special programs. For further information, call 800–724–6651 or write to SchoolMatch, 5027 Pine Creek Drive, Westerville, Ohio 43081. For parents who live in a state that allows leeway in the school their child attends, computer programs may be available to help parents match schools to children's and families' needs.

SCHOOL RECORDS

The school will begin a file on your child during his first year of school and maintain it until he graduates. These records help the school keep track of your child's year-by-year performance, provide teachers with information on his strengths and weaknesses, and allow you to evaluate his progress. The primary school file on a student, called a "cumulative file," is usually kept in the school's main office, although in some schools the teacher may hold on to the records. This file usually contains past and present grades, standardized test scores, and attendance records. Teacher comments and samples of your child's work may also be part of the file. The nurse will likely have a file on your child containing medical records and immunization information. At the secondary level, the principal or vice principal may also keep a separate file with disciplinary records. Increasingly, school records are becoming computerized.

Students receiving special education may have another file, often called a "confidential file," in the special education or special services department. This file will contain the referral for evaluation, evaluation reports, the Individualized Education Program (IEP), and correspondence.

Your child's school records may contain sensitive information about your child, and thus it is important that the records not be misused. In the past there have been abuses: parents were denied access to their child's school records; people were given access to school files without parental permission; and unsubstantiated and prejudicial comments were recorded about students in their file. Fortunately, these practices are illegal today because of the safeguards provided by the Family Educational Rights and Privacy Act of 1974, more commonly known as the Buckley amendment.

Your school district is obligated to inform parents annually of these legal rights and the district's school records policy. The Buckley amendment, which applies to all public schools nationwide (as well as other schools receiving federal funds), provides a variety of safeguards, which are described below.

WHAT ARE YOUR RIGHTS? Parents are entitled to review their child's school records. The school must comply within forty-five days of your request to examine the records. You may ask a school official to review these with you and interpret the contents or you may review them in private. You can also bring someone with you to review the records, and you are free to take notes. Most school districts will provide you with copies of the records, although you may have to pay a duplication fee. A natural parent without custody of his child can also examine these records unless a court order forbids it. The only records on their child parents are not allowed to see are those made by a staff member but not shared with anyone (for example, personal notes jotted down by a psychologist during an evaluation).

WHAT ARE YOUR CHILD'S RIGHTS? When students turn eighteen or begin attending a postsecondary school, they inherit their parents' rights regarding school records. They can review their records and must authorize their release before anyone outside the school can examine them.

WHO ELSE CAN SEE THE RECORDS? School records on your child may be reviewed by school staff members who are involved with your child's education. They may not be reviewed by anyone outside the school without parental consent except under special circumstances (for example, a court order or an emergency). Prospective employers therefore can only see your child's records upon your consent (or that of your child, if he is eighteen or over). The school district must keep a record of persons who have reviewed your child's records.

WHAT IF YOU DISAGREE WITH THE RECORDS? If you find statements in your child's file that you feel are inaccurate or inappropriate, you can request that the records be amended. You can also insert into the file a statement explaining your disagreement. Direct this request to the principal for a cumulative file or the director of special services or special education for a confidential file. While disputes about school records can usually be resolved in a nonadversarial manner, you are entitled to a hearing if you remain dissatisfied. In addition, the Family Policy Compliance Staff (listed in appendix A) will answer questions and investigate complaints regarding school records.

If you want to review your child's records, contact the principal or director of special services. Your district may require that this request be made in writing. It is especially important to review the records before you move to a new district, which will request these records. As you examine the file, be alert for subjective comments that unfairly prejudice your child (for example, "Susan is a strange child") and irrelevant statements (for example, "James has far-out political beliefs").

CHAPTER TWO

MAKING YOUR VOICE HEARD AND YOUR PRESENCE FELT

Your success in working with school staff hinges on your ability to foster a partnership. This requires mutual trust and support. It also requires good communication skills. Parents who assert themselves effectively not only gain the attention of the teacher and principal but increase the chance that their ideas will be respected, considered, and perhaps even implemented. Parents who communicate effectively also engender goodwill with school staff and perhaps even increased attentiveness to their child. This chapter offers strategies for making your voice heard and then moves on to discuss ways of making your presence felt through school involvement and advocacy. But first let's take a look at what rights you have as a parent of a public school student.

PARENTAL RIGHTS

Advocating for your child requires a knowledge of your rights as parents, namely understanding what you are entitled to do and what you have a right to expect from the school district. As you read the following list of parental rights, you may be surprised to learn how much power you have. These rights give you a potentially influential voice in your child's education.

This list of parental rights was compiled by the National Committee for Citizens in Education and is printed with its permission. The rights listed are granted by federal or state laws, regulations, and court decisions as of December 1992. States where the rights apply are listed in abbreviated form. The District of Columbia and Department of Defense Dependent Schools (DODDS) are also included. It is possible that a right may not apply throughout your state but still be granted by your local school board. Call the principal of your child's school or consult the policy manual to find out about additional rights parents have in your district. Decisions by school officials may be appealed to the local school board. The next step is either the state education department or court.

Student Discipline

You have the right as a parent in any of the states listed . . .

- To take legal action against a school official if your child has been disciplined with "excessive or unreasonable" physical force. (All states and DODDS)
- To appeal the suspension of your child. (All states and DODDS except KS, UT, and WI)
- To appeal an administrator's decision to place your child in a class for students labeled "disruptive." No placement can be made in an emotionally disturbed class without obtaining parental permission. (All states and DODDS except GA, KY, MI, MO, ND, SC, UT, VT, WA, and WI)
- To protest the physical punishment of your child because it is prohibited by state law or regulation. (AK, AR, CA, CT, DC, HI, IO, MA, ME, MI, MN, MT, ND, NE, NH, NJ, NY, OR, RI, SD, VA, VT, and WI)

Student Instruction

You have the right as a parent in any of the states listed . . .

- To see instructional materials used in research programs funded by the Department of Education and National Science Foundation. (All states except DODDS)
- To have your handicapped child placed in an "appropriate" public school program. Parents also must give written consent for the placement of their handicapped child. (All states and DODDS)

- To appeal an administrator's decision prohibiting your daughter from trying out for and playing in male-dominated sports. (All states and DODDS except AR, CO, IL, IN, KS, KY, MN, MO, ND, TN, WI, and WY)
- To visit your child's classroom(s) at any time during the day, providing you first notify the school office. (AK, AL, AZ, DC, DODDS, FL, IA, IN, LA*, MD, ME, NC, ND, NH, NM, NV, NY*, OH, OK, SC*, TX, UT*, and VA*)
- To attend a minimum number of conferences with your child's teacher(s). (AK, AL, AZ, DC, DODDS, FL, LA, MD, MS, MT, NC, NH, NV, OH, OK, and TN)
- To educate your child at home, providing you meet conditions and standards set by your state. (All states and DODDS)
- To request that your child be excused from studying subjects you object to on religious, moral, or other reasonable grounds. (AK, AZ, CA, CT, DC, DODDS, FL, IA, ID, IL, IN, LA, MD, ME, MI, NC, NH, NV, OH, PA, SC, UT, VA*, WA, and WV)
- To request that your child be excused from reading assigned books you object to on religious, moral, or other reasonable grounds. (AK, AL, AZ, CA, CT, DC, DODDS, FL, ID, IL, IN, LA, MD, ME, NC, NH, NV, NY, OH, SD, UT, VA*, WA, and WV)
- To request that your child be excused from school activities you object to on religious, moral, or other reasonable grounds. (AK, AL, CA, CT, DC, DODDS, FL, ID, IL, IN, KS, LA, MD, ME, MI, MS, NC, ND, NH, NV, NY, OH, OK, PA, RI, SD, UT, VA*, VT, WA, and WV)

Student and Other Records

You have the right as a parent in any of the states listed . . .

- To look at all your child's school records. You may challenge any record you believe is untrue or unfair. School officials must respond to your challenge within a "reasonable time." If still dissatisfied, you may request a hearing. (All states and DODDS)
- To look at all official school policies. (All states and DODDS)

* Local policies may prevail.

- To look at other official school records such as research and planning reports (but not personnel records). (AK, AL, AR, CA, CO, CT, FL, HI, ID, IN, KS, KY, LA, MD, MO*, ND, NH, NM, NV, NY, OR, SC, SD, TX, UT, VA, VT, WA, and WI)

Other Rights

You have the right as a parent in any of the states listed . . .

- To appeal a school policy or decision that prevents your child from expressing controversial views, so long as they are not obscene, slanderous, or libelous, and do not cause serious disruption. (All states and DODDS except AR, CO, KY, MI, MN, MO, NM, TN, VT, and WI)
- To speak at all public meetings of the local school board (CA, HI, IL, MI, MT, ND, UT, VT, and WV). In other states, many local school boards make provision for parents to speak at all public meetings.
- To attend all meetings of the school board (except for executive sessions on personnel and property issues) and be present at the voting on all school board decisions affecting the school district. (All states)
- To appeal some local board decisions to a higher state authority (other than a court). (AL, AZ, CO, CT, DE, DODDS, FL, GA, IA, IL, IN, LA, MA, MD, ME, MS, MT, NE, NH, NJ, NM*, NV, OH, OK, RI, SC, TX, VT, WA, WI, and WV)
- To appeal a policy or decision that prevents your child from joining a club or activity that is controversial but otherwise lawful. (AL, CA, CT, DC, DE, DODDS, FL, GA, HI, IA, ID, LA, MD, ME, MO, MS, MT, NC, NE, NH, NJ, NV, NY, OH, OK, OR, RI, SC, SD, TX, WA, WV, and WY)
- To be a member of any parent/citizen group and have your group recognized and heard by school officials. (AK, AL, AZ, CA, CT, DC, DODDS, FL, HI, ID, IN, KY, LA, ME, MN, MS, MT, NC, NE, NH, NV, NY, OH, RI*, SC, VT, WA, and WY)
- To appeal an action, policy, or decision permitting an unreasonable search of your child or his/her property by school employees. According to the Supreme Court Decision of January 1985 *(New Jersey v. T.L.O.)*, school officials must have reasonable

* Local policies may prevail.

suspicion to believe that a school rule or a law has been violated before searching your child, and the manner of conducting a search must be reasonably related to its valid objective and circumstances. (All states and DODDS)

- To challenge the removal of books from a school library based on school officials' personal dislike of ideas they contain. (All states and DODDS)

GETTING YOUR MESSAGE ACROSS

To begin with, it is important to keep in mind that communication is a two-way street. Your message must not only be conveyed clearly, you must also listen attentively to the person with whom you are communicating. Careful and attentive listening not only enables you to understand what another person is thinking, it also conveys respect for the speaker and her message.

Listening is an active process requiring sensitivity and responsiveness. The more actively you listen to your child's teacher and principal, the more it is likely that they will give your views a respectful and attentive hearing. The active listener

- looks directly at the person who is speaking
- does not interrupt
- encourages the speaker (for example, through a nod of the head or a simple "uh-huh")
- listens for the feeling behind the message
- observes the speaker's body language
- tries to understand the speaker's perspective

Understanding the essence of what the speaker is saying may require digging beneath the spoken words. This is particularly true with educators, who are often reluctant to speak candidly to parents for fear of their reactions. Their comments may be vague, or they may sugarcoat what they say. A teacher who says that a student "is trying" may really mean that she is having difficulty but has not given up. A principal who says to a parent that her child is "all boy" may really be saying that he is misbehaving in school. You need to listen for the underlying message and, if necessary, clarify the person's meaning by asking specific questions and focusing on observable behavior.

Asserting Your Point of View

Your job when meeting with school staff involves more than just listening. You also need to express your views. The purpose of this is not just to vent your feelings but to let school staff in on key information that can help them work more effectively with your child. More on what kinds of things schools need to know in the next chapter. For now, let's focus on how you can get your message across.

Asserting their point of view with teachers or principals does not come easily to many parents. The prospect of speaking to a teacher may stir up old anxieties connected with their own experiences as students. Similarly, making a request of a principal may dredge up fears of dealing with a person in authority. Additionally, parents may believe that school staff have little interest in knowing their views. In reality, teachers are usually eager to hear your concerns. Most understand that they can be more successful with your child and their job can be made easier if they know what's on your mind.

How you express your views is just as important as your willingness to express them. It may be true in schools that "the squeaky wheel always gets the grease," but it is also true that some squeaky wheels get more grease than others. The response you get from school staff will depend in large part on your style of communication. Parents often fit into one of three categories of communication styles: aggressive, nonassertive, and assertive.

Aggressive parents express their views in a hostile, dominating, sometimes sarcastic manner and insist that the listener accede to their demands. This approach is rarely effective with educators and may even make them more determined not to budge. Even when aggressive parents succeed in obtaining their short-term demands, they risk losing the rapport with school staff that is important to their long-term working relationship. They may win the battle but the victory will be short-lived. Moreover, a teacher who has been the victim of a verbal assault from parents may react by being less attentive to their child.

Nonassertive parents express their views in a tentative or hesitant manner or may not express them at all. Lacking confidence in their views or fearful of rocking the boat, they often agree to whatever the school proposes. In so doing, they deny the school and their child the benefit of their own wisdom and increase the chances of a wrong decision. Nonassertive parents often end up feeling frustrated, powerless, guilty, and even angry.

Adopting an assertive manner with school staff is a far more effective approach. Assertive parents express their views and feelings in an honest, straightforward, and calm manner while respecting the rights of others. When you speak assertively, you have a greater chance of being heard, understood, and respected, and your ideas are more likely to be implemented.

Parents who assert themselves effectively on behalf of their child are more likely to

- recognize that they have an important role to play
- gather key information before a meeting
- ask questions when confused or uncertain
- elicit observations rather than defensive reactions
- use body language that matches their message
- offer their own ideas about how to solve a problem
- state their views as opinions rather than facts
- restate their viewpoint when necessary to ensure understanding
- respect others' viewpoints
- maintain their focus on understanding the problem and looking for solutions
- express appreciation to school staff when appropriate or acknowledge the difficulty of their task
- convey a sense of cooperation
- avoid faultfinding or name-calling
- avoid starting sentences with the word "you"
- disagree, when necessary, with the school's viewpoint
- not accept vague reassurances when they have genuine concerns
- confront school officials in a nonthreatening manner if they do not fulfill their promises or obligations
- follow up a school meeting with a letter summarizing what was agreed upon

Give thought to your own style of communication when dealing with people in authority. Do you become angry and demanding when you do not get satisfaction? Or do you tend to cave in quickly when your ideas are rejected? If asserting yourself does not come easily, rest assured that you are like many other parents. Speaking your mind to figures of authority while maintaining your poise and confidence can be a formidable challenge. Fortunately, this is a skill that can be learned. People can learn to engage in assertive behavior and unlearn their more aggressive or nonassertive behavior.

If you think your style of communication could use some fine-tuning, consider taking an "assertiveness training" course. This may be offered in your local adult school, university, or mental health center. Or you might borrow a book from your public library on becoming more assertive (see appendix B: "For Further Information"). Developing these skills will help you advocate more effectively not only with school staff but with other persons as well.

Parents and teachers are particularly prone to miscommunication when talking about a child's problem. The parent may become distressed or angry and say something that the teacher interprets as criticism and reacts to defensively. Communication breaks down, the likelihood of cooperation decreases, and confrontation increases. Future communication is characterized by distrust and suspicion. Parents have a far better chance of engaging in a cooperative problem-solving discussion if they react in a supportive way to what the teacher is saying. This may not come easily to a distressed or angry parent, and you may have to swallow hard, but it is necessary to keep lines of communication open. As an example, if a teacher talks about your child being out of her seat all the time, you might say, "That must make it hard for you to teach." Or if the teacher tells you that your child is speaking disrespectfully, you might say, "Teachers shouldn't have to put up with that." Comments like these make the teacher feel supported and more willing to work with you to solve the problem.

Keeping Records on Your Child

As your child goes through school, you will attend many meetings, make and receive numerous phone calls, and accumulate a myriad of documents. By keeping careful track of these communications, you can enhance your ability to advocate for your child. A comprehensive, well-organized file can help you monitor her progress (or lack of progress), recognize patterns of performance, identify strengths and weaknesses, and prepare for meetings. The file's contents may even provide you with the documentation to justify your requests for educational services and hold the school district accountable for its promises.

This file, best kept in chronological order, might include
- developmental history of your child (for example, age at reaching various milestones)
- relevant medical information
- report cards, progress reports, and samples of schoolwork
- standardized test results
- your observations of your child's strengths and weaknesses
- notes about prior school problems and helpful responses
- notes of contacts with school staff or other professionals
- names and addresses of useful organizations or individuals
- letters sent and received
- relevant articles that you have clipped

Keeping careful records is especially crucial for parents of special education students. If your child is in special education, you will receive a variety of documents related to her education; the most important is the Individualized Education Program (IEP). Issues related to special education are discussed in chapter 9.

GETTING INVOLVED IN YOUR CHILD'S SCHOOL

If recent surveys are any guide, teachers want parents to participate more actively in their child's education. One way that you can accomplish this is to become more involved in the life of your child's school. Your school involvement is another way of saying to your child that school is a high priority. In addition, she will likely take pride in your participation, whether it be chaperoning on a trip, helping out at the book fair, or serving on a committee to evaluate the district's grading system. These and other activities give you an opportunity to find out about the school and its staff as well as meet other parents. If you help out in your child's classroom, you can free the teacher to spend more time teaching, learn about approaches for working with your child, develop a better understanding of the curriculum, and observe your child in an academic setting. And you may even find it rewarding.

As a bonus, your visibility in school may earn you the goodwill of the school staff. There will likely come a time when you will want to cash in on this goodwill (for example, if you request a specific teacher for your child for the following year). Even if you don't, your child's teacher may be a little more attentive to your child if she knows of your school involvement.

Making Schools Parent-Friendly

Despite the benefits of school involvement, many parents remain disconnected from their child's school. Schools share part of the responsibility for parents' limited involvement. Fearful that parents will want to help run the school, school staff often steer parents toward such activities as fund-raising or chaperoning and away from matters of education. Administrators may also worry that parents will key into negative aspects of the school and report to other parents. As a result, many principals send mixed messages to parents. They pay lip service to the concept of parent involvement but are slow to draw parents into participating in school affairs beyond book fairs or bake sales.

Parents may be reluctant to become involved for other reasons. While some parents have limited time to offer the schools because of work or family commitments, many others have the time but back off because they are intimidated by the prospect of dealing with teachers or principals. Some feel that they have little to contribute. In reality, parents offer schools a rich source of information and support, especially important in today's climate of diminished funding for public education. Yet if schools are to gain the full measure of what parents can offer, they must reach out to parents and make them feel wanted. The following are some steps that schools might take to open the doors to parent involvement:

- creating an office in the school for the parents' organization and a bulletin board for posting information for parents
- posting and distributing parent involvement information, including class observation practices, volunteering opportunities, and procedures for contacting principals and teachers
- assigning a coordinator of volunteers who matches the talents and interests of parents with the needs of the school

- hiring a parent liaison to reach out to parents and involve them in school-related activities
- training parents to enhance their effectiveness as school volunteers
- communicating with parents through a newsletter about school news and events
- implementing a parent information hotline with prerecorded messages from the principal about school activities and from teachers about classroom activities and assignments
- reviewing the proposed school budget with parents and seeking their input
- explaining the curriculum to parents and discussing how they can supplement and extend teacher instruction at home
- giving assignments that require children to work with their parents (for example, interviewing their parents)
- allowing parents to observe their child's class
- arranging flexible hours for parent-teacher conferences and providing child care services
- providing interpreters so that non-English-speaking parents can be more involved in conferences
- offering teachers time and resources to work with parents and to keep them informed of their child's progress (for example, placing telephones in classrooms for teachers to contact parents)

Parents may want to suggest to the school district that they adopt some of these strategies, or others, as a way of encouraging parent involvement. This might be done through the PTA.

Volunteering in Your Child's School

In most districts parents have the opportunity to volunteer in some capacity in their child's school. Volunteering need not require a large commitment of time. The concept of quality time applies to volunteering just as it does to parenting. Your involvement might range from a one-time-only basis to a once-a-day basis. Consider whether you have special skills that the school can use. The chart on the next page lists various opportunities for volunteering in school.

If you are interested in volunteering, give the principal a call. She may recommend opportunities for helping out in school or suggest that you talk with the teacher directly about assisting in the class-

OPPORTUNITIES FOR SCHOOL VOLUNTEERING

- serve as room parent
- tutor students in the classroom
- read stories to students during recess
- assist at a class party
- speak to your child's class or school on a topic of student interest
- start an after-school computer club
- supervise children in an after-school recreational program
- prepare school bulletin boards
- serve as an aide on a school bus
- photograph students at school activities
- work as an aide in the library, main office, cafeteria, nurse's office, or on the playground
- develop or work at a homework hotline
- organize teacher appreciation activities
- prepare food for an ethnic festival
- help write a school newsletter or design a flier
- help run the book or science fair
- arrange assembly programs
- develop and help run a "guardian angel" program where parents are called if their child has not shown up for school and they have not notified the school of her absence
- develop a list of community resources for parents and children
- recruit other parents as school volunteers
- help construct a playground
- donate plants, books, carpeting, or other items
- help plant trees

room. If your school district has a volunteer coordinator, you may need to go through her to try to match your skills and interests to the school's needs.

A few words about volunteering protocol. Do not overextend yourself. Make sure that you are able to be there when you say you can. The school will be relying on you to show up. If you are assigned to a classroom, remember that you are there to assist the teacher, so take your cues from her. It may take a while for the two of you to develop a working chemistry. The teacher may be insecure about having someone observe her, so avoid giving her advice or constructive criticism. Also, do not distract the teacher while she is conducting a lesson. In your interactions with students, be positive, encouraging, and respectful.

School involvement is more difficult for parents who work outside the home or are single parents. Their limited time or energy may keep them from helping out in school. While this may engender feelings of guilt, it is understandable if parents are unable to be very involved in school affairs—and it need not hamper their child's education. A parent does not need to volunteer at a book fair or chaperone on a class trip to demonstrate the importance of education. This message is conveyed most importantly at home in the way parents talk about matters of education and the priority they place on schoolwork. For parents who are occupied during the day and wish to contribute, opportunities are available to help out during nonschool hours. You might offer to take care of the class rabbit during school vacation, manage the school booth at a weekend community fair, send in materials needed by the teacher, or sew costumes for the school play. If you are employed during the day, check whether your employer will give you release time to share your skills with students in school or allow you to arrange a class visit to your place of work. In Massachusetts, state employees are given release time to volunteer in their children's schools and to meet with teachers. And many companies are following suit, adopting parent-friendly policies.

A good starting point for becoming involved in your child's school is to join the parent-teacher association (PTA). Some school districts have a parent-teacher organization (PTO), which has no state or national organization as the PTA does but which serves the same purpose as the local PTA. The national PTA, of which local PTA members are automatically members, is the largest parent group in the country, with about seven million members. It uses its power to lobby on behalf of issues related to children (for example, asbestos in the schools or the nutritional value of school lunch programs).

Joining the PTA and participating in its activities is a good way for mothers and fathers to meet people, gain specific information, and obtain the perspectives of other parents. Many parents join their local PTA, but few participate. They may view the PTA as primarily a social organization. While PTAs may arrange social activities for parents and teachers to foster a spirit of cooperation, these organizations are more action oriented than in years past. Most go beyond raising funds, although this function remains important, especially in light of the decreased funding for public education. They may also develop programs, provide speakers, offer forums for discussion of parent concerns, arrange activities to honor teachers, and sponsor student activities. Some PTAs also act as forces for change by rallying parent support on behalf of a particular issue.

Parents as Partners on the Educational Team

It used to be that parent involvement was limited to baking cookies for school meetings or decorating the gym for a party. But today parents are becoming involved in school affairs in ways that were unthinkable a couple of decades ago. And some school districts are welcoming parents into roles that were previously reserved for school staff only. In some cases, parents are being included in substantive educational matters such as interviewing candidates for principal, drafting the school budget, developing school improvement plans, charting attendance areas, and reviewing curriculum.

A growing trend in public education is to involve parents in the actual running of the schools. Many school districts across the country have developed what are called community schools, in which parents have a large voice in school decisions. These schools not only give parents a say in how the school is run but provide families with social services right in the school such as after-school child care and adult education. Hundreds of schools across the country have embraced this model.

Kentucky is one state that is sold on the merits of substantive parent involvement. By 1996, all schools in the state will be run by a school council consisting of parents and teachers. This is currently happening in Chicago, where parents have broad governing authority in all of the city's 551 public schools. The idea behind this "school-based management" approach is to give the adults most directly affected by school decisions, namely parents and teachers, a voice in such matters as hiring the principal and teachers, developing the budget, buying new equipment, writing the curriculum, and developing school disciplinary policies. While some see this team-based approach as a blueprint for chaos and inefficiency, others view this broadening of ownership of school decisions as a way of increasing accountability and enhancing the motivation of decision-makers to run the schools well.

ADVOCATING SCHOOL CHANGE

Parents can be an important voice for school change if they organize and speak with a united voice. A board of education is much more likely to respond to a large, organized parent group than scattered individual voices. Parents who have carefully planned and diligently organized have been able to exert considerable influence on a range of school issues. The following are examples of concerns that parent groups have taken on:

- developing an after-school child care program
- revising the disciplinary code
- barring corporal punishment as a form of school discipline
- developing alternatives to tracking
- modifying the system of grading students
- placing a school guard at a dangerous school crossing
- reviewing textbooks to ensure they are current and free of stereotypes
- demanding elimination of asbestos from school buildings
- retaining educational programs being considered for elimination
- ensuring comparable resources in the district's various schools

If parents are to make headway with issues that require board of education approval (which changes in school policy do), they will need to convince the superintendent and the board of the importance of the issue and the breadth of public support. This does not require a degree in education, but it will demand effective organization and communication. Rallying parents on behalf of an issue requires considerable time and energy, but if the issue is important, it is time well spent. Once you and other parents have identified your core concern, give your group a name to enhance its visibility.

The communication might take the form of a presentation before the board. This presentation can be made by one person or a few but it is essential that many parent supporters attend the meeting. Recruit parents to the meeting by sending out fliers, posting notices, obtaining mention in the local newspaper, and setting up a phone chain. The school may even give you names of parents with similar concerns if it supports your cause. Contact the board secretary in advance of the meeting and try to be put on the agenda. If that is not possible, parents can always speak during the period reserved for public comment. The presentation should be grounded in facts and research, should be forceful but not hostile in tone, and should offer some solutions to the problem. Make sure you have done your homework, if necessary reviewing the district's policy manual, consulting the state department of education about applicable state regulations, and checking with other districts to find out how they handle the same issue. If you need information from your school district, it should be made available to you in accordance with your state's public records law or the federal Freedom of Information Act.

Parents have other tools at their disposal that they can use to marshall support for their cause. They can conduct a parent survey. If you go this route, make sure to let the school district know. Keep the survey brief and the questions neutral. You can distribute a petition. You can conduct a letter-writing campaign, targeting board of education members. You can obtain media attention by writing letters to the local newspaper, giving interviews, and distributing press releases. These and other strategies are discussed in greater depth in *Parenting the Schools,* by Jill Bloom.

If these strategies are unsuccessful in convincing the board to adopt your position, you can always take a long-range view and work to change the composition of the board. Given that school board elections usually attract a very low voter turnout, a well-organized parent group can greatly influence a board election. You might even consider running for the board yourself. Having a background in education is not a prerequisite for serving on a board, but a willingness to devote considerable time is. Check with the board office to find out about filing dates and nominating procedures.

CHAPTER THREE

THE PARENT-TEACHER CONNECTION

A key ingredient to the formula for academic success is a close working relationship between the most important authority figures in a child's life: parents and teachers. By forging an alliance founded on mutual respect, open communication, and an understanding of each other's pressures and constraints, you and the teacher can fine-tune your child's program and help resolve problems at the earliest stages. This chapter will discuss what you can do to build this kind of relationship with your child's teacher.

WORKING WITH YOUR CHILD'S TEACHER

Your relationship with your child's teacher may stir a mix of emotions. In addition to perhaps feeling anxious about dealing with the teacher due to emotional baggage you carry from your own school days, you may also feel a rivalry with her for your child's attention and even affection. Indeed, on school days your child may spend more time in his teacher's presence than in your own. Parents may also fear that their views will be discounted by teachers. After all, most parents were brought up with the belief that when it comes to education, teachers know best.

What Teachers Want from Parents

What teachers do know best is that they cannot go it alone in their effort to educate students and that they need help from parents.

Teachers want parents' trust and support, but perhaps what they want most is that parents convey respect for the teacher to their child. And for good reason: children generally perform better in school when their parents encourage respect for the teacher's authority and competence and when children see their parents and teacher as a united team working toward the same goals. The parents' vote of confidence in the teacher endows her with some of their authority and enhances student responsiveness.

Practically speaking, this means supporting the teacher's authority and decisions, speaking positively of the teacher to your child, not criticizing or second-guessing the teacher in your child's presence, and not providing frequent excuses for his failure to meet teacher requirements. If a child feels that his parents do not respect the teacher, he is placed in the awkward position of having to choose sides. Most children resolve this dilemma by adopting their parents' perspective. The result is that they are less likely to comply with the teacher's requests and respond to her instruction.

This approach is fine if you genuinely support what the teacher is doing, but what if you disagree with the teacher's methods or your child is having difficulty adjusting to the teacher? Simply giving the teacher a vote of confidence may not be enough, or may not be warranted. Let your child know you understand his concerns and, if justified, that you will try to resolve the problem. But don't promise what you can't deliver. Some problems are unlikely to go away, while others may go away on their own without your intervention. Deciding what course to follow is discussed later in this chapter in the section "When the Teacher Is the Problem."

In summary, teachers are more likely to feel supported if parents do the following:

- treat teachers with respect
- convey respect for the teacher's authority to their child
- not criticize the teacher in their child's presence
- appreciate the demands and constraints of the teacher's job
- monitor their child's schoolwork (but not do it for him)
- understand that the teacher cannot individualize instruction for all students in all classes
- support the teacher if she takes disciplinary action
- keep the teacher informed of family events that may affect a child's school performance

- contact the teacher with any classroom concerns before going to the principal
- not blame the teacher for school policies they dislike

As you go down this list, ask yourself how well you perform each of these tasks and whether your teacher relationship skills are in need of a tune-up. There are very practical benefits to mastering these skills: a supportive relationship with the teacher will pay large dividends if your child runs into difficulties in school.

Communicating with the Teacher

Communication between parent and teacher helps keep each informed of relevant information. You may find it useful to know about the teacher's academic expectations, homework routines, testing policies, and grading criteria. Teachers also need information from you to help them work with your child and understand his special needs. Your child's teacher will benefit from knowing about his physical and psychological needs, any interests or talents that she may want to highlight, and school-related programs in which the child is participating (for example, tutoring or counseling).

If your child has a medical problem, help the teacher understand the related behaviors she may see in the classroom and any implications for instruction. (Apprise the school nurse as well.) Also let the teacher know of events at home that may influence your child's school performance, including the illness or death of a family member, a divorce or separation, remarriage, the birth of a sibling, parental job loss, even the death of a pet. There is no need to go into detail or violate your family's privacy. The point is to give the teacher information that will enable her to be more sensitive to your child and provide an emotional safety net. You may also want to inform the teacher about areas of sensitivity for your child, for example, his self-consciousness about his speech impediment or his absent father. Knowing a student's vulnerable spots allows the teacher to be more understanding and perhaps avoid embarrassing situations.

Parents are also entitled to some consideration from teachers. You have the right to expect that teachers will apprise you of any problems with your child, will consider your views and suggestions, will respond to your concerns in a timely manner, and will be sympathetic to your family's special circumstances. Many parents do not expect teachers to be sensitive to their concerns and consequently may not share them. Bear in mind, however, that many teachers are also parents and may have had similar experiences. Most will be understanding and make an effort to be accommodating.

Most schools schedule parent-teacher conferences once or twice a year. While you will probably meet with the teacher sometime in the fall, an issue may arise that warrants earlier contact with the teacher. If the teacher calls you in for a conference prior to the regular meeting, inquire on the phone about its purpose and the people who will be there.

You can also contact the teacher prior to the regular conference. Minor problems can usually be resolved with a phone call. More serious problems (for example, chronic resistance to attending school, frequent difficulty in completing homework, reports by your child of taunting by other children, a marked change in behavior at home) require a face-to-face meeting with the teacher. Also, contact the teacher in the beginning of the school year if there is information about your child she should know from the first day or if there is information you need to know.

If you are not sure whether your concern merits a teacher contact, err on the side of calling. Teachers are frustrated when parents don't express concerns to them, since many are easily resolved. At the same time, do not contact the teacher for every single concern. Teachers can become aggravated with parents who seek them out daily about the smallest of matters. Let common sense be your guide.

If you call the teacher during school hours, keep in mind that she will probably be unable to come to the phone. Try calling fifteen minutes or so before or after school or find out from the school secretary when the teacher's free period is. Another option is to send in a note asking the teacher to call you before or after school. If you want to meet with the teacher, do not consider a chance meeting in the supermarket or a three-minute chat outside the school door adequate. Set up a formal meeting. Consider letting the teacher know of your concern ahead of time so she can reflect on your child's situation. Do not call the teacher at home unless she has given you permission or the situation is urgent. Prior to meeting with the teacher, review the section in this chapter entitled "Parent-Teacher Conferences."

Students experiencing school problems may benefit from regular contact between parent and teacher. This not only ensures that parents are kept informed of their child's progress but lets the child know that the teacher and parent are working together, making it more difficult for a child to play parent against teacher. Devise a communication system that meets your needs and respects the constraints on the teacher's time. You might call the teacher every Friday afternoon to find out whether your child is completing seatwork. Or you might meet with the teacher once a month to review your child's progress in reading and coordinate the help you are providing at home. Or you might communicate with the teacher through a homework pad or sheet that is reviewed and signed by both parent and teacher daily and that has space for comments (see chapter 7).

Not all problems require teacher contact. With a one-time incident that is not serious (remember, though, that what may be trivial to you may be serious to your child), consider waiting to see if the problem is resolved before you contact the teacher. Also, encourage older children to handle the problem on their own. Children whose parents are always intervening on their behalf don't learn to solve their own problems. Moreover, they get a message that their parents lack confidence in the child's problem-solving skills. If your child wants to deal with the situation on his own, let him, although you might role-play with him about what to say. Stay on top of the more serious problems to make sure they are resolved.

Showing Appreciation to the Teacher

Teachers are no different from others in wanting to feel appreciated. They value the hugs and kind words from their students, but they also need validation from parents. Yet when it comes to teachers, parents are often quick to criticize but slow to praise. It should not come as a surprise that many teachers feel underappreciated and overburdened. We have no doubt come a long way since the 1930s when teachers in the South were required to agree "to get at least eight hours of sleep while maintaining a healthful diet, and to consider herself at all times a willing servant of the school board and the townspeople." But we still have a way to go before teachers receive the recognition and status they deserve.

Perhaps what parents fail to appreciate most of all are the demands and pressures of teaching. If you need convincing of the rigors of teaching, try placing yourself in the teacher's shoes. Think of some birthday parties you have given for your child and then imagine being responsible for twenty-five children, six hours a day, 180 days a year.

If you are pleased with the efforts of your child's teacher, let her know. A short personal note of gratitude describing specifically how your child has benefited from the teacher will likely be far more appreciated than one more bottle of perfume. For parents who wish to give something tangible to the teacher, consider a gift made by your child such as baked goods, a pencil holder, a papier-mâché pin, or a bookmark. You might even wrap the gift in artwork done by your child. Another option is to buy something the teacher can use in her class, such as a special book, a poster, or an educational game.

Don't necessarily stop there. Consider sending a note to the principal lauding the teacher's efforts or if warranted submit the teacher's name to the principal for consideration as school district teacher of the year. You might even send a letter to the local newspaper praising the teacher or highlighting a particular school activity. Such actions will in small measure help restore the respect that educators enjoyed in the past but feel is lacking today—and will in large measure reinforce your relationship with the teacher and perhaps even the teacher's relationship with your child.

Requesting a Teacher

The quality of your child's teacher is the key to the quality of your child's education. And the teacher's influence may extend beyond education. As American historian Henry Adams wrote, "A teacher affects eternity." Given that a teacher can have a lasting and significant impact on your child, you may want to influence which teacher he receives. Yet schools are often reluctant to grant parental requests for specific teachers. There is good reason for this. If parents were allowed to select their child's teacher, some teachers would have too many students and others too few. If your school is like many, it has a policy that the principal will not honor parent requests for teachers. This is one of those cases where the unwritten rule often speaks louder than the written one. Principals sometimes grant these requests under special circumstances. This may be the time to cash in on the goodwill you generated as a result of your volunteer efforts in the school.

Don't assume, however, that goodwill will suffice. Make this request in writing to the principal during the spring and provide a specific reason why your child should be assigned a particular teacher. Make the case that this teacher's style is well suited to your child's educational needs but be sure not to criticize other teachers. If this is the first time you are requesting a teacher, let the principal know this. Reinforce your request with a supporting letter from a professional such as your child's pediatrician. Call during the summer to find out what action has been taken on your request.

Your child's current teacher may help you in deciding which teacher to request and may even make this recommendation to the principal. Other parents are also key sources of information on teachers. You may want to observe the prospective teachers before the end of the year (see "Observing Your Child's Classroom," later in this chapter). As you observe the teachers and talk with other parents, ask yourself what kind of teacher is best suited to your child. Does he need a teacher who is very structured or one who is looser in style? Will he do better with a teacher who is discipline oriented and runs a tight ship or one who is more nurturing and low-key? Will he respond better to a male or female teacher? to an older or younger teacher?

WHEN THE TEACHER IS THE PROBLEM

Volumes of research are devoted to examining the critical variables in education. When all is said and done, the most important factor in your child's formal education is his teacher. Fortunately, most public school teachers are competent, dedicated, and caring. At some point, however, your child will have a teacher who falls short in some aspect of teaching. A poor teacher, particularly at the elementary level where your child will have one primary teacher every year, is cause for parents' concern.

Teachers are not expected to be paragons of educational virtue. With the pressures on teachers to raise test scores and deal with an increasingly diverse student population, instruction understandably may fall short of expectations on occasion. But some teachers have styles that present significant and persistent problems for students. Some teachers are overly strict with their students, engendering anxiety and fear. Others are disrespectful to children and treat them in a demeaning and humiliating fashion. Others have difficulty managing their students' behavior, resulting in more chaos than learning. Still others are ineffective communicators and rely on busywork or films to instruct rather than teacher-student interaction. These and other teacher problems are not without consequences for students. Their anxiety may rise while their enthusiasm for school may fall. The issue for parents is when to take action—and when not to.

When Not to Act

What is a parent to do whose child is complaining about his teacher? Sometimes the best response is no response at all. You don't want to ignore your child's complaint but you also want to bear in mind that complaining about and blaming teachers is a favorite pastime of students. If your child is mastering the skills being taught, is going to school eagerly, and seems generally positive about the teacher, a one-time minor incident probably does not warrant follow-up. Time will probably take care of the problem. In some cases, an older child can handle the problem on his own.

If the teacher's style is not well suited to your child, your best approach may be to help him learn to adapt to the teacher. Children must learn to accommodate to teachers with different styles, standards, and expectations. It is not helpful for them to believe that their parents will rescue them from every discomfort or disappointment. You should, however, acknowledge your child's concerns and feelings while at the same time expressing confidence that he will learn to adjust. Offer your child some coping strategies and help him understand the reason for the teacher's decision or action. You may want to let your child know that teachers have shortcomings like everybody else but try to give the teacher a vote of confidence and find some positive qualities to highlight. If your child persists in his dislike of the teacher, do not try to talk him into liking her. Let him know that it is okay not to like a teacher but that he must still comply with her rules.

Diagnosing the Problem

Your child's distress with the teacher may not necessarily reflect a teacher failing. Consider these other possibilities: the teacher's reprimand or action was justified; your child's complaints reflect a learning problem rather than a teaching problem; the schoolwork is very easy for your child and he is bored; the teacher is academically demanding; or your child is distressed about something (for example, a peer problem) and is transferring his distress to the teacher. Also, children often complain about their teacher early in the school year. They may feel loyalty to their previous teacher and need time to make the transition. Their concerns usually fade as they develop trust and confidence in their new teacher and settle into a routine. The essential point here is to make sure your diagnosis is correct before you consider a remedy.

Gathering information about the teacher and the classroom helps to ensure an accurate diagnosis. Taking a teacher to task without finding out her perspective will be harmful to your relationship with the teacher and perhaps to the teacher's relationship with your child. Begin by talking with your child during a calm moment. Ask specific factual questions but try not to convey criticism of the teacher. If your child responds vaguely or has difficulty putting his thoughts into words, don't push the issue. Factor in your own knowledge of your child's reactions to teachers and situations in evaluating what he says and keep in mind that young children are not always the most reliable reporters. (My daughter's first-grade teacher struck a bargain with parents: she would not believe everything she heard about us from our children if we would not believe everything we heard about her.)

Other parents, especially those serving as classroom volunteers, can provide additional perspectives. Find out if their child is making similar complaints. Try to see the teacher in action for yourself by volunteering in class, chaperoning on a trip, or observing the class. Most school districts will allow parents to observe their child's class if arrangements are made in advance (see "Observing Your Child's Classroom," later in this chapter).

Whether you choose to pursue the matter, make sure to listen to your child and respond in a patient, sympathetic manner. He may not be seeking a solution but rather an opportunity to talk about his feelings. If warranted, help him understand the teacher's action and avoid criticizing her in his presence. Otherwise, you may foster his disrespect for the teacher and give him an excuse for not working. Young children have particular difficulty reconciling parents' negative feelings for a teacher with their obligations to cooperate with her. Older children can better handle your disagreement with the teacher and may even benefit from seeing two adults who disagree learn to resolve their conflict cooperatively.

Taking Action

At what point should you take action? If your child is coming home distressed or discouraged about school, is bringing home work that is either much too hard or much too easy, is resisting going to school, is visiting the school nurse often, or describes an incident suggestive of humiliation or gross insensitivity, it is time to make your concerns known. Begin by scheduling a face-to-face meeting with the teacher. This meeting may be awkward for you, so do some advance planning and perhaps even rehearse with your spouse or friend.

Keep the discussion on a constructive level. Most important, stay calm, avoid accusations, and do not make sweeping generalizations. Express your point of view but do so respectfully. Keep the meeting focused on what your child needs rather than what the teacher did wrong. For example, rather than state that the teacher's directions are confusing, say that your child often needs clarification about what to do. If you think that the teacher's style might be causing stress to your child, you might say, "I am concerned because Sarah seems worried about something in school and I'm wondering how we can work together so she seems more relaxed." You may want to describe specific incidents in school that upset your child, but be sure to give the teacher a chance to offer her perspective. The teacher might not have realized your child was upset or having difficulty. Offer strategies that you have found effective with your child. After all, you are the expert on your child. The more constructive the meeting, the greater the chance that the teacher will be responsive to your suggestions and the less chance there is that she will bear ill will toward you or your child.

Give the teacher some time to remedy the problem. Most teachers are eager to please parents and will respond to their concerns. But if there is no sign of progress after two or three weeks and you still have serious concerns, consider meeting with the principal in the hope of getting her to apply pressure to improve the situation. The principal may invite the teacher and other school staff members to this meeting (for example, the guidance counselor or the school psychologist). While this meeting may impair your relationship with the teacher, she is unlikely to take out her displeasure on your child, especially if she knows you are monitoring closely. If a plan of action is decided on, let the principal know you will contact her in a week or so to find out how the plan is progressing. At the end of the meeting, express your gratitude to the principal and the other meeting participants.

You may conclude that the problem is serious enough to warrant a midyear teacher change. While principals are even more reluctant to grant requests for midyear teacher changes than requests for specific teachers for the following year, they may accede to the wishes of an insistent but respectful parent. Some principals will tell you in the fall that more time is needed before a change can be considered but come the winter tell you that it is too late to make a change. Do not accept this. A student's teacher can be changed at any time during the school year and should be if the problem with the teacher is serious and persistent. Changing the teacher may not be the answer, however, and may even give rise to other problems. Moreover, such a change may give a message to your child that something is wrong with him or that the way to deal with a problem is to run from it. Use this strategy as a last resort. In most cases, parents can improve their child's classroom situation by working cooperatively and constructively with the teacher.

But if you view the situation as intolerable or abusive, stay the course and do not worry about being labeled a troublemaker. You may need to pursue this concern beyond the principal. If so, request a meeting with the superintendent and invite other parents with similar concerns. Schools are much more responsive to groups of parents. Be prepared to discuss specific examples. Do not expect that you will be able to have an incompetent teacher removed from her position if she has tenure (which is typically granted after a person has taught in a school district for three to five years, depending on the state). Teacher contracts provide strong protections to tenured teachers, and teacher removal only occurs under extraordinary circumstances. But if the school recognizes a problem with a teacher, it should be able to find some way to improve or remedy the problem short of teacher removal (for example, extra supervision, submission of lesson plans for review, provision of an aide, rearrangement of the teacher's schedule or class roster, or teacher reassignment).

OBSERVING YOUR CHILD'S CLASSROOM

Conferences give you a limited picture of what is happening in your child's classroom. And children are notoriously poor reporters of school activities. To obtain further understanding of your child's school performance as well as the quality of the classroom instruction, you can request to observe his class. About half of the states guarantee this right to parents by law. Many school districts invite parents to observe their child's class during American Education Week, but you may also wish to observe at other times. Most school districts will honor this request. Keep in mind that it may be hard to get a true picture of your child's classroom performance when you are observing since he will be keenly aware of your presence and thus may either put on a show or withdraw. You can get a truer picture if you're in the classroom on a periodic basis as a volunteer. The teacher too may put on a show for you during your observation, but you still should get a good sense of how she relates to students and communicates the lesson.

The following are examples of situations where you may want to observe a classroom:

- you want to decide which teacher to request for your child for the following year
- you are concerned that your child has a learning or behavioral problem
- you want to learn how to work more effectively with your child by learning about the curriculum and observing the teacher's technique
- you have doubts about the appropriateness of your child's class placement or the quality of teacher instruction
- your child has been recommended to skip a grade or stay back
- you want to observe a special education class recommended for your child
- you have heard that the teacher is doing an exciting project and wish to see it

If you wish to observe, do not show up unannounced. Call the principal two or three days in advance to request permission. The school may not be enthusiastic about this request. The teacher or principal may fear that you will be critical of what you see and demand change. Try to ease their concerns, but be persistent in your request, especially if the observation is crucial to a decision you are making. If approval is granted, let the principal or teacher select the day. Certain days may be atypical (for example, the day before a holiday or a Friday) because the students are unusually excited. Try to observe during a time that spans two subjects so you can see what the class is like during unstructured time. During the observation be as unobtrusive as possible and avoid making suggestions or providing assistance to the teacher. Remember that you are there to observe and not participate. Find something positive to say to the teacher and express your appreciation before leaving.

You do not need to be an educator to gain useful information from a classroom observation. The purpose of your observation should guide what you look for. The following list should help you identify what questions you may want answered. You will not be able to answer all these questions, nor will you need to, so focus on those of greatest concern to you and if necessary return for a second observation.

WHAT TO LOOK FOR IN A CLASSROOM OBSERVATION

- Is the classroom decorated cheerfully? Does the atmosphere seem conducive to learning? Is work from students of all ability levels displayed?
- Are there learning centers that students can go to for different activities (for example, a reading corner or listening center)?
- Are the teaching materials interesting?
- Do the students appear eager and motivated? Do they seem to take pride in their work?
- Is the teacher warm, enthusiastic, and cheerful? Does she have a sense of humor? Does she seem to enjoy teaching?
- Does she treat children with respect and take their questions and comments seriously?

continued

- Is she positive, encouraging, and free of sarcasm? Does she highlight students' strengths and not dwell on their weaknesses? Does she look for ways for students to succeed? How do students react when the teacher speaks with them?
- Is the teacher patient in dealing with children who have difficulties? Does she provide extra help? Is she sympathetic to students who are distressed?
- Does she try to draw out the more reluctant students to participate in class?
- Does she seem to have comparable expectations for boys and girls? Is she as encouraging of girls as she is of boys?
- Do the students treat each other with respect and do they interact cooperatively?
- Has the teacher established and posted classroom rules? Is the focus on positive behavior? Do the students seem to know the rules and routines of the classroom?
- Does she set and stick to reasonable limits? Do the students respect them? Can she be firm without screaming? Can she give reprimands quietly without disturbing others? Does she deal with misbehaving students without humiliating them? Does she try to rechannel their behavior in a positive direction?
- Does the teacher seem to have a mastery of the material?
- Does the teacher communicate clearly? Is the goal of the lesson clear to students? When given an assignment in class, do the students seem to know what to do? Does she write down assignments on the board?
- Does the teacher monitor their understanding of the assignment? Does she walk around class to check the students' work and offer help?
- Does she teach at a level appropriate to the students? Does she try to adapt the instruction and assignments to the needs of individual students?
- Is there more than one reading and math group to accommodate students of different skill levels? Are students moved to different groups when appropriate?
- Does the teacher use a variety of teaching methods and not just rely on lecture or the use of media? Do students work in groups? Does she provide hands-on experiences?

- Does she relate the lessons to the students' own interests and concerns?
- Does the teacher encourage questions and comments from students and respond supportively?
- Does she help students learn to think critically and draw meaningful conclusions? Does she ask thought-provoking questions?
- Does the teacher give helpful feedback to students on their written work? Does she go over homework from the previous night?
- Does she use her time wisely? Does she spend too much time engaged in noninstructional activities (for example, taking roll call, distributing papers, or collecting money)?

PARENT-TEACHER CONFERENCES

It used to be that parents only met with teachers if their child was having a problem. Today schools typically invite all parents of elementary students to teacher conferences once or twice a year to discuss their child's progress. This is an important opportunity for parents and teachers to exchange information as well as develop a working relationship. Your regular attendance at these conferences also demonstrates to your child your commitment to the school. If your school district does not have regularly scheduled conferences with teachers, call and request one even if your child is doing well. A report card or a written description cannot replace a meeting with your child's teacher.

The conferences are usually scheduled twenty or thirty minutes apart and typically consist of the teacher talking about the student's class performance, showing the parents examples of his work, and answering a couple of questions. This may be adequate for parents who have been talking with their child's teacher periodically or have few concerns. For some parents, however, this conference is not sufficient to answer all their questions. If you find this to be the case, request a follow-up conference. Teachers will likely agree to this request.

Some parents have trepidations about these conferences. Simply entering the classroom may resurrect painful memories from their own days as a student. They may worry about not knowing what to say. And they may be anxious about what they will hear, especially in the early elementary years. After all, the teacher conference is one of the only occasions parents hear a report from a professional on their child's skills and abilities. For parents who tend to see their child's triumphs and defeats as reflections of their own success as parents—and this includes most parents—negative comments by the teacher can be unnerving. They may worry that something is wrong with their child and may fear that the teacher will see them as blameworthy.

It may ease your worries if you keep in mind that many teachers are parents too. There is a good chance that your child's teacher has been in your shoes and is sensitive to your anxieties. Indeed, she may be just as nervous as you, fearing that parents will judge her negatively or challenge her teaching decisions.

If the teacher has some concerns about your child, there is no need to press the panic button. It is the rare student who goes through school without encountering some problems. Most are resolved with time or with some fine-tuning of the educational program. Whatever the problem, progress will be faster if you work in concert with the teacher to resolve it. The teacher is not looking for someone to blame but rather some support from you.

Given the likely brevity of your conference (the teacher may have as many as twenty conferences in one day), you need to use the time efficiently so that the meeting is as productive and informative as possible. The following strategies should help achieve that goal.

Before the Conference

RESCHEDULE IF NECESSARY: If you cannot attend at the assigned time, call the teacher to find a mutually convenient time. Remember that the teacher also has various demands on her time, so be prepared to be flexible. If possible, schedule a conference early in the day when the teacher is likely to be less tired and more responsive. If you cannot find a convenient time to meet, talk with the teacher by phone.

CONSIDER WHO WILL ATTEND: Try to arrange for both you and your spouse to attend and if possible leave the children home. If your children must come, bring snacks, toys, or books to keep them occupied. You want to be able to devote your full attention to the conference. If your spouse cannot attend, talk with each other before and after the conference. You may also bring a friend or relative with you to the conference. It is rare that children attend these conferences, but it may be warranted in some cases. The older the child, the more likely he will be able to participate and benefit. A child who attends can profit from seeing his parents and the teacher working together and may feel more of a sense of ownership of decisions— that is, that they are *his* decisions—if he has a say in the outcome. If your child participates, make sure not to bombard him with questions. Be positive, and if there are problems, focus on identifying solutions rather than on finding fault with your child. Sensitive matters may be better discussed apart from your child.

TALK WITH YOUR CHILD BEFORE THE CONFERENCE: Find out if he has any concerns about school. If he answers vaguely, ask some specific questions. Are any subjects causing you problems? Do you understand the homework? Do you feel you are called on enough? Can you see the board adequately? What subjects do you like? dislike? Are any children distracting or bothering you?

REQUEST AN APPOINTMENT WITH SPECIAL TEACHERS: Parent-teacher conferences are typically held with the primary teacher. If you wish to meet with a special teacher (for example, the art teacher), you may need to request this in advance.

WRITE DOWN YOUR QUESTIONS AND CONCERNS: Reviewing your child's schoolwork and textbooks may generate questions. Bring to the meeting notes with your questions as well as information you want to share with the teacher. You may be interested in asking some of the questions listed on the next two pages. Select those appropriate to your child's grade and situation. Arrange your questions in order of importance just in case time keeps you from asking them all. If there are issues you want to discuss that require some preparation or thought by the teacher, send her a note a week or so before the meeting to alert her to your concerns.

QUESTIONS PARENTS MIGHT ASK AT THE CONFERENCE

- What is the homework routine? How much time should be spent on homework? What role do you expect parents to play with homework? Is my child handing in homework regularly?
- What major projects will be assigned to students this year?
- Are tests given on a regular basis? If so, when? How has he done on classroom tests and quizzes?
- Which reading and math groups is he in? What is the procedure for moving into another group?
- What topics will my child be studying in science and social studies?
- Is he putting forth optimal effort? Is he working up to his ability?
- What are his academic strengths and weaknesses?
- Is he below, at, or above grade level in reading? writing? spelling? math? How does he compare with his classmates academically?
- Are there any signs of a learning disability? If so, should he be considered for remedial or special education?
- Does he show evidence of special talents or abilities? If so, what can be done to cultivate this talent?
- Are there other school programs that he can benefit from (for example, gifted and talented or enrichment program, after-school tutoring program, instrumental music, homework hotline, group for children of divorce)?
- Does he participate in class discussions?
- Does he work well independently?
- Does he seem anxious about any aspect of school?
- How does he get along with his classmates? Does he have any problems on the playground?
- Is he having any behavioral or social difficulties? How unusual are these difficulties for this age-group? Have there been any sudden changes in his behavior or mood that may suggest physical problems? Is there any evidence of vision or hearing

problems (for example, squinting or frequently asking for directions to be repeated)?

- How can we help our child at home? Are there any skills in need of reinforcement? What materials, activities, or strategies would you suggest that we use?
- When is the best time to contact you during school hours?

During the Conference

ARRIVE ON TIME. The conference schedule is usually very tight. Arriving late may lessen the amount of time you spend with the teacher. Do not stay much beyond the assigned time. Another parent is probably waiting. If necessary, arrange another time to meet with or phone the teacher.

ESTABLISH RAPPORT WITH THE TEACHER. Begin by saying something positive to the teacher about what's happening with your child (for example, "Justin is really excited about the dinosaur project"). But don't wait too long to get down to business, since time is limited. Maintain a respectful tone. End the conference with a positive comment to the teacher.

ASK FOR CLARIFICATION. Your child's teacher may use educational jargon that you do not understand and should not be expected to understand. Don't hesitate to request an explanation, ask for examples, or inquire how often he displays a certain behavior. Be aware that teachers may be vague or upbeat in their descriptions to avoid touching a nerve with you about your child. Rather than saying that your child is getting into fights on the playground, the teacher might describe your son as a "real challenge." Or the teacher may say that your child "is progressing" but neglect to tell you that he is working below the level of the rest of the class. Follow this simple dictum: *If you are not clear on the teacher's meaning, ask.*

ASK TO SEE SAMPLES OF YOUR CHILD'S WORK. Your teacher will probably show you some without your asking. Review of these work samples (work sheets, workbooks, handwriting samples, creative writing assignments, art projects, and so on) will help you understand what your child is doing and his level of progress. They may also give you ideas about how to help your child at home. You may want to ask the teacher to show you the textbooks and other materials she is using with her students.

SHARE YOUR VIEWS AND CONCERNS. Your role is not limited to nodding your head as you listen to the teacher. The conference is intended to be a dialogue. Let the teacher know of your child's special abilities and interests as well as events at home that may be affecting his school performance (see "Communicating with the Teacher"). If your child is having difficulties in school, share your observations about what works with him at home (for example, that he does better when the top of his desk is uncluttered or that he is more likely to remember information if he writes it down). If the teacher's description of your child is predominantly negative, help shape her perceptions by offering some positive qualities you have observed at home. Research shows that teachers are generally more responsive to students whom they perceive as capable and cooperative. You might also reframe some of the teacher's descriptions to help her view your child in a different and more positive light (for example, that he is "overly eager to participate" rather than "inconsiderate" or "very curious" rather than "hyperactive").

KEEP THE DISCUSSION ON A CONSTRUCTIVE, BLAME-FREE LEVEL. State your concerns in a calm, nonadversarial manner and avoid expressions of anger. This does not mean you should back off from expressing your opinion but do so respectfully. If you have a concern, focus on what can be done to help rather than what the teacher is doing wrong. Convey that you are willing to do your share with such questions as "How can we help?"

ASK FOR SUGGESTIONS. Ask what you can do to support or supplement the teacher's instruction. The teacher may also be able to answer questions about a range of school-related issues such as tutoring, summer school, and special school programs. It is okay to take notes.

SUMMARIZE THE KEY POINTS. Because conferences can be anxiety provoking, it is easy to miss or misinterpret what the teacher has said. Summarize the teacher's comments and suggestions and then ask whether your understanding is correct. If a plan of action is agreed upon, clarify who will do what when. Arrange a follow-up conference, if necessary.

After the Conference

SEND A FOLLOW-UP NOTE. A short note expressing your gratitude will be greatly appreciated. If you and the teacher have agreed on some course of action, convey in your note that you are hopeful that this plan will yield results. This will alert the teacher that you are monitoring the plan and focused on results.

TALK WITH YOUR CHILD. Your child will no doubt be eager to hear what you discussed at the conference. Tell him what you think is appropriate for him to hear. Highlight the positive comments made by the teacher about your child and make sure to say something complimentary about the teacher. In discussing problem areas, suggest specific ways of improving and avoid a critical tone. Also, elicit ideas from your child. Inform him of any changes the teacher will be making and let him know that you support these changes. If you will be talking with the teacher on a regular basis, let your child know this as well.

DO YOUR PART. Make sure to follow through on what you agreed to do at the conference. If the teacher described some concerns at the meeting, check with her a couple of weeks later to see if there has been progress and if your actions have been helpful.

BACK-TO-SCHOOL NIGHT

Most school districts invite parents to school in the fall to meet their child's teacher and see the classroom. This open house is a good opportunity to learn about your child's program and the teacher's expectations. It is a chance to see where he spends most of his day and how he spends his time. As with parent-teacher conferences, attendance at these meetings demonstrates to your child your seriousness about school. Try to arrange your family schedule so that both you and your spouse can attend. As you enter the class, you will probably be asked to sit at your child's desk, where you may find a note from him. Write a note back to him with some positive comments about the class.

The purpose of back-to-school night differs from that of the parent-teacher conference. While the conference is intended to be a discussion of your child's individual performance, back-to-school night is designed to offer you information about the teacher's goals, methods of instruction, expectations, and routines. Feel free to ask questions but stick to program and classroom issues. You may want to inquire about the homework and test routine, the amount of time your child should be spending on homework, procedures for absences, early dismissal policies, disciplinary methods, and curriculum. This is not the time to talk about your child. If you have concerns specific to your child, arrange a meeting with the teacher at another time or speak with her on the phone. At the end of the evening, consider going up to the teacher to introduce yourself and offer some kind words. Small rapport-building gestures such as this can help solidify the parent-teacher connection.

CHAPTER FOUR

GETTING A GOOD START

Jill can't stop thinking about September 7. That is the day she begins kindergarten. She has been attending a preschool program for two years, but kindergarten has a special feeling for her. It's the school her older brother attends. It's the "big time." Her excitement, though, is tinged with worries and questions. Will she like her teacher? Will the other kids like her? Who will she sit with on the bus? Will the teacher yell at her if she makes a mistake? Will she be able to find her classroom? What about the bathroom?

These and other concerns occupy the thoughts of many children like Jill who are about to enter kindergarten. Whether or not they attended a preschool program, kindergarten is a landmark event in their lives, one that promises many changes. First and foremost, it means separating from their parents, which can engender anxiety and even dread in some children. It means adapting to a new authority figure and adjusting to a new setting, with its own rules and routines. Children may be asked to engage in unfamiliar behaviors, such as waiting their turn, raising their hand, taking care of their possessions, and sitting quietly for a long period. For some children, especially those without preschool experience, these changes are daunting; for others, such changes are less unsettling. It is the rare child, however, who does not begin kindergarten with some apprehension.

This is also a rite of passage for many parents, especially those who have not had a child attend kindergarten previously. You may be unsure whether your child is ready for the demands of kindergarten. You may also wonder whether the school is ready for your child and can adequately meet her needs. Just as your child may be experiencing some pain at the thought of being apart from you, so too you may feel separation pangs. Letting go of a child even in small steps is not easy for most parents. You may find yourself going through periods of anxiety or sadness and recalling your own experiences with separation. If this describes you, rest assured that this is a common reaction.

Fortunately, children's fears of kindergarten are largely unfounded, and their worries usually exaggerated. Kindergartners often show a resilience that defies parental expectations and typically adjust well to their first year in public school. Their worries usually fade as they find that their teacher is quick with a smile and a kind, encouraging word, as they learn to fit in with other children, as they get to know the layout of the school, and as they master the routines of the school day.

Kindergarten is a critical year in a child's education. It represents her introduction to the public schools. What happens during this year helps to lay the foundation for what comes after and shapes her attitude toward school and her feelings about herself. While kindergarten teachers are usually attuned to the need to foster confidence and a positive attitude toward school, parents can also take steps to help their children get off to a good start in school. This chapter will help parents achieve that goal. It will also provide an overview of the kindergarten program. Given that kindergarten has undergone many changes in recent years, parents need to understand the various issues and stay tuned to the developments in their own districts. In this way, parents can play a key role in shaping their own district's kindergarten program.

TODAY'S KINDERGARTEN

The kindergarten of today is not quite what it used to be. It was not too long ago that the first year in public school consisted of mostly play activities. Children would attend for two to three hours a day and engage in such activities as building with blocks, playing with dolls, finger painting, and climbing on the monkey bars. They would have a snack, visit the bathroom, rest a bit, and perhaps listen to a story or practice tying shoes. By then it was time to clean up and go home. Many of these activities still go on, but today's kindergarten often resembles other elementary grades in its length and academic focus.

Many of today's kindergarten programs are full-day programs embracing the same hours as other elementary grades. Kindergarten curricula vary but it is not unusual for kindergarten teachers to have their students doing work sheets, completing workbook pages, and even participating in reading groups. For those more familiar with past school practices, it might seem as if the first-grade program has been moved down the hall to the kindergarten room. In some respects, today's kindergarten no longer lives up to the origin of its name as the "children's garden."

When the kindergarten movement swept the nation in the 1920s, the program served as a transition year between home and school. Social and cognitive goals were pursued in a relaxed, pressure-free setting. With the large number of children today in some kind of child care program before kindergarten, the need for a transition program is less important. The focus of kindergarten now rests on laying the cognitive foundation for the academic tasks of first grade. Fortunately, most kindergarten teachers have not forgotten the importance of stimulating their students' curiosity in the world around them and promoting feelings of confidence as learners.

These changes in the kindergarten program mirror changes in the larger society. As our world has grown more complex and technologically demanding, success in the workplace has placed a premium as never before on educational achievement. In their eagerness to give their children a head start in this race for achievement and success, many parents expressed impatience with a kindergarten program that differed little from their children's preschool programs. They wanted a program that was more challenging and built upon rather than a repeat of the preschool program. Educators in many districts responded with a "curriculum pushdown": what was taught in first grade was now taught in kindergarten and what was done in kindergarten was now done in preschool.

The Full-Day Kindergarten

This trend is especially evident in the decision of many districts nationwide to implement full-day kindergarten programs. Instead of attending school for two to three hours either in the morning or in the afternoon, students in full-day programs attend school the same length of time as other elementary students.

The full-day kindergarten is the school's response not only to this desire for a more intensive program but also to the needs of the contemporary American family. With the large number of families with either two working parents or a single parent, the need for good and inexpensive child care has become paramount with parents. Many districts have also tried to meet this need with before- and after-school child care programs in the school (see chapter 11).

Proponents of the full-day kindergarten contend that it allows the teacher to cover a wider range of topics and engage in a greater diversity of activities at a more relaxed pace. Teachers in half-day programs tend to be clock-watchers and have little time to work on academic skills or to pursue art, music, or other creative activities. Supporters maintain that students in full-day programs will receive a better academic foundation than those in half-day programs and thus will have less need for remediation or special education in later grades. They add that teachers in full-day programs get to know their students better, enabling them to more effectively identify and respond to children with learning problems.

Educators who question the value of the full-day program argue that more is not necessarily better, that twice as much is not necessarily twice as good. This point is well taken. The essential issue is less the quantity of the kindergarten program than its quality. The challenge for educators is to provide an enriching kindergarten program well suited to the developmental needs of five- and six-year-olds that does not become a boot camp for first grade. If school districts can resist the pressures to make full-day programs mini–first grades and instead can blend appropriate academic and creative activities (as well as nap time) in a relaxed setting, full-day kindergarten programs can work well. They are especially valuable to children with a poor academic foundation. The initial fear that a full-day program would be too long for five- and six-year-olds has not been borne out by experience.

School districts nationwide have experimented with other kindergarten arrangements. Some have implemented an extended-day program in which students stay for more than half the day but less than a full day so that students in both the morning and afternoon sessions have lunch at school. Other districts begin the year with a half-day program and gradually increase the length of the kindergarten day to a full-day program. Another option that has not gained wide acceptance because of the bureaucratic obstacles is to give parents a choice between a half-day and full-day program.

Kindergarten for Four-Year-Olds

Some districts have considered having students begin kindergarten at the age of four rather than five. Part of the impetus for this change comes from research documenting the success of the Headstart program with three- and four-year-olds from economically disadvantaged backgrounds. The research results are indeed impressive in showing that early education for children from poor homes had the following positive effects later on: less need for remedial help, less likelihood of dropping out, greater likelihood of college attendance and adult employment, and even less likelihood of criminal behavior. Researchers also concluded that the early instruction enhanced children's confidence and coping skills.

Few districts have actually implemented kindergarten for four-year-olds, and its effectiveness remains an open question. Other questions are unanswered as well: Are four-year-olds ready for public school instruction and capable of performing traditional kindergarten tasks? Can kindergarten teachers adjust their expectations and practices to the needs of four-year-olds? Are we pushing children into formal instruction too early and running the risk of alienating them from school? Can schools accommodate the wide disparities in abilities and maturity levels likely with four-year-olds? Are we depriving children of part of their childhood?

Most educators recognize the importance of providing early education to children who are disabled, from bilingual families, or from poor backgrounds. Indeed, many states have passed laws mandating education for disabled children from ages three to five. It is less clear that formal instruction is an educationally sound practice for four-year-olds who are not disadvantaged. Louise Bates Ames of the Gesell Institute of Human Development is among those who argue that four-year-olds are not mature enough to perform most kindergarten tasks. Moreover, some of what they may learn (for example, how to count to twenty) may be superficial learning without real understanding (as evidenced by the child asking "What's a twenty?"). It may be that these resources would be better spent by implementing parent education programs, as states such as Minnesota and Missouri have done.

Providing kindergarten to four-year-olds is part of a recent trend in education to try to speed up the development of children. This trend originated in the 1950s when Americans reacted to the Soviet Sputnik space program with an effort to intensify American education. The last decade has witnessed the proliferation of books, toys, and methods designed to accelerate learning. Many argue persuasively that educators cannot appreciably speed up children's development by exposing them to more at a younger age. The research of Jean Piaget, noted Swiss psychologist, tells us that children have built-in limitations to what they can learn and when they can best learn it. In short, cognitive development cannot be rushed. There are also risks to teaching children tasks for which they are not ready. Premature instruction can result in a child's being taught at too high a level or too hurried a pace and can engender frustration and discouragement.

WHAT TO LOOK FOR IN A KINDERGARTEN PROGRAM

There are different schools of thought about what makes a good kindergarten program. While most agree that kindergarten is designed to lay the groundwork for the more academic curriculum of first grade, there is disagreement about how to accomplish this. Some believe that kindergarten should be a relatively unstructured program in which children are free to explore activities of their choosing. At the other end of the spectrum are those who maintain that kindergartners should follow a prescribed curriculum with specific goals and objectives. (Some states have even passed laws setting forth specific goals for kindergarten instruction.) Most kindergarten programs fall somewhere between these two extremes.

While almost all kindergarten teachers now provide academic instruction, they differ in their emphasis and manner of presentation. Some may move slowly in presenting skills and concepts; for example, each week may be devoted to a different letter of the alphabet. Others may move at a faster pace and make greater use of traditional teaching tools utilized in first grade (for example, work sheets, workbooks, and reading groups).

A good kindergarten teacher adjusts her program to the developmental needs of her students and instructs at a level appropriate to their abilities. Given the wide array of abilities and maturity levels of kindergarten students, this is no easy task. Some children enter kindergarten already reading while others may not know the alphabet. Some children enter kindergarten with two years of preschool experience while others have never attended a formal educational program. Some enter kindergarten able to follow directions with little guidance while others need assistance every step of the way.

Even the most experienced teacher will have difficulty meeting her students' needs in a large group. Kindergarten classes should have no more than twenty-five students and hopefully less. Small classes are most important in the early elementary grades when children need frequent monitoring of their understanding and assistance with tasks. Because of the importance of this issue, you may want to contact your child's school during the summer to find out the size of the kindergarten classes. If you find the classes unacceptably large, you will need to rally other parents' support to have any chance of convincing the district to hire another teacher to lessen the teacher-student ratio. If the school district refuses, present as an alternative the hiring of paraprofessionals to assist in the classroom.

Some parents are disturbed to find that their children are spending part of their kindergarten day engaged in "play" activities at the expense of "real" educational tasks such as dittos and work sheets. What these parents fail to understand is that for five- and six-year-olds, play is an educational task. As kindergarten teachers are fond of saying, "Play is the child's form of work." Dr. Benjamin Spock, an authority on children, agrees wholeheartedly: "Play is the most important way children learn." The choice is not between play and work but between effective and ineffective means of learning.

Play is an active process in which children are using their senses —all their senses, not just hearing and vision—to learn about the world around them. Through play with their classmates, children also learn to solve problems and resolve conflicts without adult assistance. Kindergartners learn best when they are actively engaged, when they direct their own learning, and when concrete activities are used to reinforce concepts. For example, children are less likely to grasp the concept of part-whole relationships by hearing that two halves make a whole than by the teacher cutting the apple in half and having the children put them together. Using these apples to make apple sauce is also instructive: they learn new vocabulary when they make a list of ingredients, math when they measure, and science when they mix the ingredients together.

The good kindergarten teacher recognizes that children learn best from experience and provides concrete activities to foster genuine understanding. The good teacher not only provides structured activities but also offers children freedom to explore and discover. She provokes thought and promotes understanding by asking questions rather than just offering information. She fosters students' natural instinct to learn and encourages their curiosity. And she stimulates their use of language through a variety of activities requiring them to listen and express themselves.

Much of the debate about kindergarten academics centers on reading instruction. Parents are particularly eager for their children to develop a good foundation for reading in kindergarten and in some cases start formal reading instruction then. But reading well is more important than reading early. In addition, most kindergartners, while more sophisticated and knowledgeable than in the past, are not ready for formal reading instruction. For most, the focus should be on skills that are prerequisite to reading, which are called reading-readiness skills. These include listening attentively to a story, recognizing letter shapes and sounds, understanding basic concepts of sequence (for example, first and last) and position (for example, above and under), and learning vocabulary. Activities such as listening to books being read, singing songs, having discussions, and doing puzzles help to prepare kindergartners for formal reading instruction. If reading instruction is offered in kindergarten, the materials must be appropriate for five- and six-year-olds, and the teacher should include active experiences.

Some children enter kindergarten able to read with fluency and comprehension, the so-called spontaneous readers. The wide discrepancy in reading abilities among kindergarten children poses a real challenge for the teacher. While it is not harmful for the early reader to work on reading-readiness skills, the teacher should also give her some reading activities that are enriching and challenging and still developmentally appropriate. For example, the teacher might have the student read a story to the class, read a book from the school library and then describe the story to the teacher, or write her own book (perhaps dictated to the teacher) and then read it to the class.

Other children are late bloomers when it comes to reading. Just as some children are shorter than their peers in kindergarten but eventually catch up, so too children may be delayed in learning to read. They too usually catch up. Teachers and parents must learn to respect this timetable and avoid placing undue pressures on children to read through tedious drills. While many children are ready to "break the code" and learn how to sound out words at age six, some children are not ready until age seven or eight. We do these delayed readers a disservice by pushing them to read before they are able. The experiences of other countries are instructive. In Denmark, where formal reading instruction begins at age seven, there are few cases of illiteracy. In France, formal reading instruction begins at age five but approximately 30 percent of children have reading problems.

Some teachers have incorporated writing into the kindergarten curriculum. In an effort to take advantage of children's eagerness to write, teachers may encourage children to express themselves on paper in whatever way they are able, even if the result is a paper with "invented spelling" (for example, writing "ba" for "ball") and sloppy printing. Most kindergarten teachers prefer not to dwell on the spelling or sloppy writing lest they dampen their students' enthusiasm for writing. There will be plenty of time for emphasizing spelling and handwriting in later grades.

IS YOUR CHILD READY FOR KINDERGARTEN?

As kindergarten approaches, you may worry that your child is not prepared for public school and may have difficulty making the grade. These worries may be prompted by signs that your child is lagging behind other children of the same age. She may have difficulty expressing herself, have problems following directions, have poor motor skills, or have difficulty sitting still. If your child is immature or delayed in her development, you may face the dilemma of whether to postpone her kindergarten entry one year. You will likely receive much advice on this issue. Remember that the final decision belongs to you.

Kindergarten eligibility is based on the child's chronological age. This practice dates back to the late nineteenth century, when states established age requirements to counter the trend of parents sending children as young as two or three to public school. Today school districts typically require that a child turn five by a certain date to qualify for kindergarten although districts vary in the date they use. Whatever date districts use, the result is usually a kindergarten composed of children with widely varying abilities. If your child just missed the district cutoff date and must wait a year before entering kindergarten, take heart in the research that indicates that older children generally do better in school.

Critics of the chronological-age standard claim it relies more on the law of averages than sound educational principles. They advocate sending children to school when they reach a certain level of maturity and skill development. Proponents of this approach believe that a child's "developmental age"—a rough estimate of her cognitive and behavioral maturity—better predicts kindergarten success than her chronological age does. They contend that some children who are chronologically eligible are not ready for the demands of a public school and may suffer problems of low self-esteem and confidence if they begin school before they are ready. Research supports this contention. The Carnegie Foundation for the Advancement of Teaching estimates that one out of three children nationwide is not ready to begin school on their first day of kindergarten. Conversely, they argue that some children who are chronologically ineligible are ready for public school and are losing ground by being held out.

While there is no evidence that school districts are planning to abandon the chronological-age standard, parents have the option of delaying their child's entry into kindergarten for one year. School districts strongly resist, however, enrolling children in kindergarten before they are chronologically eligible. (Some parents get around this by enrolling their child in a private kindergarten and then in a public first grade the following year.)

The following guidelines may help you in making the decision whether to delay your child's kindergarten entry one year:

IS YOUR CHILD AT RISK FOR HAVING DIFFICULTY IN KINDERGARTEN? As a general rule, younger children are more prone to problems in kindergarten although they tend to catch up by third grade. (Children who were born prematurely should be considered somewhat younger than their chronological age.) Boys also tend to be slower to develop than girls although they too gradually catch up. In addition, children prone to illness as preschoolers may be delayed in their development. For example, frequent ear infections as a preschooler may lead to a delay in language development.

WHAT DOES YOUR CHILD'S PRESCHOOL TEACHER RECOMMEND? If your child went to preschool, her teacher will have a good sense of how your child's abilities and maturity level compare with those of other children about to enter kindergarten. Parents know their child well but often lack the knowledge of what behaviors and skills are typical of their child's age. Preschool teachers have a keen sense of age-appropriate norms. You might wish to observe your child in preschool to reach your own conclusions. Keep in mind that preschool attendance is not necessary for a child to be successful in kindergarten, especially if the parents have provided a variety of enriching activities at home.

WHAT ARE THE RESULTS OF THE KINDERGARTEN SCREENING? Many districts will test entering kindergarten students to identify those in need of special help. If your district does not conduct these tests routinely, you may still request that the district assess your child's readiness for kindergarten. Schedule a meeting with the evaluator (who may be a kindergarten teacher) to elicit her perceptions of your child's readiness.

ARE YOUR CHILD'S SKILLS ON A PAR WITH THOSE OF OTHER CHILDREN ENTERING KINDERGARTEN? The chart on the following pages lists 105 desirable skills for a child to have upon entering kindergarten. This list is based on a survey of three thousand kindergarten teachers by the editors of *The World Book Encyclopedia*. Your child need not have mastered all these skills to be ready for kindergarten. Children develop at different rates and some are late bloomers. But failure to know or be able to do most of the items on this list by the summer before kindergarten entry should raise questions about your child's school readiness. Pay particular attention to your child's ability to get along with other children, to attend to a task, to follow spoken directions, and to perform activities requiring eye-hand coordination. You might also request to see your school district's kindergarten curriculum to assess whether the goals and objectives are within your child's reach. Keep in mind that the list is intended to help you gauge your child's school readiness, not to serve as a program of instruction.

WHAT KINDERGARTEN TEACHERS WOULD LIKE YOUR CHILD TO KNOW

Size
Understands big and little
Understands long and short
Matches shapes or objects based on size

Colors and Shapes
Recognizes and names primary colors
Recognizes circles
Recognizes rectangles
Matches shapes or objects based on shape
Copies shapes

Numbers
Counts orally through ten
Counts objects in one-to-one correspondence
Understands empty and full
Understands more and less

Reading Readiness
Remembers objects from a given picture
Knows what a letter is
Has been read to frequently
Has been read to daily
Looks at books or magazines
Recognizes some nursery rhymes
Identifies parts of the body

Identifies objects that have a functional use
Knows common farm and zoo animals
Pronounces own first name
Pronounces own last name
Expresses self verbally
Identifies other children by name
Tells the meaning of simple words
Repeats a sentence of six to eight words
Completes incomplete sentence with proper word
Has own books
Understands that print carries a message
Pretends to read
Uses left-to-right progression
Answers questions about a short story
Tells the meaning of words heard in a story
Looks at pictures and tells a story
Identifies own first name in manuscript
Prints own first name

Position and Direction

Understands up and down
Understands in and out
Understands front and back
Understands over (on) and under
Understands top, bottom, middle
Understands beside and next to
Understands hot and cold
Understands fast and slow

Time

Understands day and night
Knows age and birthday

Listening and Sequencing

Follows simple directions
Listens to a short story
Listens carefully
Recognizes common sounds

continued

Repeats a sequence of sounds
Repeats a sequence of orally given numbers
Retells simple stories in sequence

Motor Skills
Is able to run
Is able to walk a straight line
Is able to jump
Is able to hop
Is able to alternate feet walking down stairs
Is able to march
Is able to stand on one foot for five to ten seconds
Is able to walk backward for five feet
Is able to throw a ball
Pastes objects
Claps hands
Matches simple objects
Touches fingers
Is able to button
Builds with blocks
Completes simple puzzles (five pieces or less)
Draws and colors beyond a simple scribble
Is able to zip
Controls pencil and crayon well
Cuts simple shapes
Handles scissors well
Is able to copy simple shapes

Social-Emotional Development
Can be away from parents for two to three hours without
    being upset
Takes care of toilet needs independently
Feels good about self
Is not afraid to go to school
Cares for own belongings
Knows full name
Dresses self
Knows how to use a handkerchief or tissue
Knows own sex

Brushes teeth
Crosses a residential street safely
Asks to go to school
Knows parents' names
Knows home address
Knows home phone number
Enters into dinner table conversation
Carries a plate of food
Maintains self-control
Gets along well with other children
Plays with other children
Recognizes authority
Shares with others
Talks easily
Likes teachers
Meets visitors without shyness
Puts away toys
Is able to stay on task
Is able to work independently
Helps family with chores

DOES YOUR CHILD SEEM APPREHENSIVE ABOUT KINDERGARTEN? Your child may give you cues that she is not ready. If she seems unusually clingy or fearful or is not sleeping well, she may be telling you that she doesn't feel prepared for the challenges of public school.

WHAT PROGRAMS ARE AVAILABLE FOR KINDERGARTNERS HAVING DIFFICULTY? Is there a developmental kindergarten (sometimes called a prekindergarten) that students attend for one year and then go to a regular kindergarten the next, or first grade if they have made dramatic strides? Are there programs where your child can receive help in a small group for part of the day? Does the school district have a transition class (sometimes called a pre-first class) for students who have gone through kindergarten but are not ready for the academic demands and pace of first grade? (Students who attend transition classes may go to either first or second grade the following year, depending on their progress.) Is there a guidance counselor at your child's elementary school? The availability of one or more of these programs may lessen your concern about placing your child in kindergarten.

WHAT ARE THE ALTERNATIVES TO KINDERGARTEN? Consider what your child will be doing if she does not go to kindergarten. Will she go to a preschool program that will help prepare her for kindergarten? Will you (or your child's baby-sitter) have the chance to engage in some school readiness activities with your child without overdoing it? Will your child be part of a play group with other children?

If you conclude that your child is significantly behind her same-aged peers in a variety of areas, consider holding your child back from kindergarten for a year. Giving your child the gift of a year to get ready for kindergarten will help her feel more competent and confident when she does enter school. Research supports this approach: children voluntarily held back from kindergarten one year generally receive better grades and higher test scores and are less likely to have learning problems. Researchers attribute these gains to greater self-discipline and maturity. While others may see this delay as the theft of time, placing a child in kindergarten who is not quite ready may give rise to problems of self-esteem and confidence. Even bright, verbally deft children who are young for kindergarten can experience stress and pressure, especially if they demand perfection of themselves.

If you choose to enroll your child in kindergarten despite concerns that she is lagging behind her peers, watch for signs of stress with your child, including

- resistance to school attendance
- frequent stomachaches or headaches on school day mornings
- complaints that school is boring, the work is too hard, or the children are unfriendly, or that she dislikes the teacher
- unusual crankiness or irritability before or after school
- increased clinginess or crying
- reoccurrence of thumb-sucking, bed-wetting, or immature speech
- sleeping problems
- reports from school of difficulty interacting with other children

If you are seeing some of these signs at home, check with the teacher to see if she is observing similar behaviors in school (for example, frequent visits to the school nurse). If you conclude that your child's stress is not likely to ease with time and the school year is not too far along, talk with her teacher about the merit of removing your child from kindergarten and placing her in a preschool program. This may come as a relief to your child and allow her to get a better start in kindergarten the following year.

KINDERGARTEN TESTING PROGRAMS

Most school districts conduct what are called kindergarten screening programs to identify children about to enter kindergarten who may be in need of special help. These results are also used to assess the strengths and weaknesses of incoming kindergarten students and thus guide teachers in designing appropriate programs. In addition, school districts may use the results to recommend that low-performing children be held out of kindergarten for a year. Using tests in this manner is the subject of intense debate.

If your district has a kindergarten screening program, you and your child will likely be invited to school during the spring prior to kindergarten entry. A school staff member, perhaps even a kindergarten teacher, will chat with your child briefly, observe how she relates with others, and then give her a relatively anxiety-free, twenty- to thirty-minute test in an effort to gauge her academic readiness, language development, and visual-motor skills. For example, she may be asked to draw a picture of a person, name different colors, build with blocks, identify "What barks?" and name objects that you ride. Do not prep your child for this test. To do so may not only engender anxiety in your child but may also invalidate the results.

While there is no universal screening test to assess entering kindergartners, the most commonly used measure is the Gesell School Readiness Screening Test. Screening tests generally yield a developmental age score. If your child receives a developmental age of four years, six months, this means that her school readiness skills are comparable to that of an average four-and-a-half-year-old child. Advocates of kindergarten screening maintain that a child's developmental age is a better measure of her readiness for kindergarten than her chronological age.

These screening tests have been attacked as invalid and unreliable measures of a child's abilities. Critics maintain that important decisions about a child's schooling—for example, when a child should start kindergarten—should not be based on tests that are prone to inaccurate or misleading results. They also contend that these test results may lower teacher expectations of student performance and engender feelings of failure with those who have difficulty. The weight given to these results in some districts has led to the unfortunate trend of some parents actually helping their children "study" for these tests.

Whatever test is used, the results should be interpreted with extreme caution when administered to four- and five-year-olds. Young children are especially vulnerable to distraction or distress while taking a test, and thus the results are often not a fair measure of their true ability. Moreover, children this young are going through spurts of development, cognitive as well as physical, so that the results obtained in the spring may not accurately represent the child's skills and abilities in the fall. The results can provide useful information about a child's present developmental level but they should never be used as the sole barometer of a child's ability. More important, they should never serve as the sole determinant of a child's school placement, in effect as an admission test. That decision should be based on parent and teacher observations in conjunction with the test results. And you should be a key member of this decision-making team.

PREPARING YOUR CHILD FOR KINDERGARTEN

Parents can enhance their child's adjustment to kindergarten by taking some steps ahead of time. You should not feel obligated to follow all the suggestions below, but some may suit your child's particular needs.

VISIT THE SCHOOL IN ADVANCE. Consider visiting the school with your child in the spring prior to kindergarten entry. (Some districts arrange these visitations as a matter of course.) If your child will be walking to school, walk with her, following the route she will take. Point out some landmarks and emphasize the importance of not taking shortcuts, but beware of arousing fear in your child with cautions about potential dangers. Also introduce yourself and your child to the crossing guard. If you would like to meet with the principal or tour the school, make sure to call in advance. Have your child drink from the water fountain, visit the school library, try out the playground equipment, and if possible take a peek in the kindergarten room. This visit should help her feel more familiar and comfortable with the school.

TEND TO SCHOOL BUSINESS. Make sure you have registered your child for school and completed the necessary documents. Your school will require proof of your child's birth date and evidence of immunizations. It may also ask you to provide proof of residency in the school district; a tax bill, rental agreement, or utility bill should suffice. If your school requires a physical examination, schedule a doctor visit as soon as possible to avoid the school rush. Even if an examination is not required, it is useful to have one anyway to check your child's vision and hearing. (The school nurse may also do these examinations.) Some school districts even require proof of a dental examination. While at school, inquire of the policies regarding inclement weather, early closing, and leaving school with your child early.

ARRANGE PLAY DATES WITH CHILDREN IN YOUR CHILD'S CLASS OR SCHOOL. You and your child will feel more comfortable as kindergarten approaches if she knows someone attending the same class or school. Just knowing one other child in the same class will help give her a sense of security.

HAVE YOUR CHILD SPEND TIME WITH ADULTS OTHER THAN PARENTS. A visit with grandparents, an aunt and uncle, or family friends will help to ease the upcoming separation for you as well as your child and will help her learn to adjust to different adult styles. This is especially beneficial if your child has not been in a preschool program or is not used to being supervised by other adults.

HELP YOUR CHILD LEARN TO ENJOY BOOKS. Every kindergarten teacher stresses to parents the importance of reading to their child. And with good reason. This will help to foster an appreciation for the joys of reading as well as promote language development. Introduce your child to your public library and have her get her own library card. Many public libraries have "story time" programs for young children. While at the library, ask the librarian to find some books you can read to your child about the first day of school. See appendix C for some suggestions. Other language activities—playing word or rhyming games, reading nursery rhymes, playing tapes, having your child describe her pictures, making a scrapbook with pictures of items beginning with a specific letter—also help lay the foundation for reading.

HELP YOUR CHILD LEARN BASIC SKILLS, INFORMATION, AND EXPRESSIONS. Buttoning, zipping, and tying (or fastening Velcro) are helpful but not essential skills for your child to know. (Make sure she wears clothes that she can put on and take off on her own.) By kindergarten, your child should be expected to know her full name, address, and telephone number. If she is having difficulty retaining this information, try teaching it through a nursery rhyme (for example, "Everything is fine and neat at 9 Willow Street"). If necessary, teach her the proper expressions for asking to go to the bathroom as well as requesting help without whining, demanding, or interrupting. Encourage good pronunciation and discourage baby talk. And be sure your child can care for herself in the bathroom.

DON'T DWELL ON THE SUBJECT OF SCHOOL. If you frequently talk about school, it may suggest to your child that it is worrisome for you, which may arouse anxiety in her. At the same time you don't want to avoid the topic. Rather, try to talk about it as part of the normal course of family events. A week or so before school begins, explain to your child what will happen in school. Talk about the beginning of school with enthusiasm and make sure not to use terms suggesting that school attendance is optional.

ALLOW YOUR CHILD TO EXPRESS FEARS OR WORRIES. It is natural for children about to enter kindergarten to be apprehensive. Your child's worries may seem small and trivial to you but in her mind they may loom large. Some of her worries can be relieved through your attention and reassurance. Spending some extra time with her before school starts may reassure her that the closeness with you will not end when school begins. Some of her worries can be relieved through information and discussion of the enjoyable activities she will be doing in kindergarten. Other worries may only abate as your child begins school and sees that her fears are without foundation. Giving permission to your child to share these feelings enables you to reassure and comfort her. You might talk with her about your own nervousness as you were beginning school (or another new situation), and how these feelings soon went away, to help her realize that her reaction is not out of the ordinary. You might also remind her of other new situations she has faced and mastered. Be careful about making comments to your child which generate anxiety (for example, "In a few weeks you'll be entering a school for big kids"). Keep in mind that older children can also arouse fear in a child about to enter school with exaggerated tales or school horror stories. If so, put an end to this quickly.

TAKE CARE OF YOUR OWN NEEDS. You may be so wrapped up in helping your child prepare for school that you neglect your own needs. Parents who do not work outside the home may feel a sense of emptiness during the first few weeks their child is in school. Give thought in advance to how you will use the time in a way that is constructive or fulfilling. Consider an activity unrelated to your child to give you another focus.

THE FIRST DAYS

As the first day of kindergarten approaches, your child will be filled with excitement and anticipation. And, most likely, so will you. These positive feelings will be tempered with worries by both parent and child about what might go wrong. There may well be some rocky moments during the first days as your child adjusts to a new setting, a new authority figure, and new rules and routines.

Signs of your child's struggle with these changes may surface in the form of difficult behavior. If so, there is no need to panic. This is a common reaction to the stress of beginning school. Your child may become more clingy and dependent. She may throw some tantrums. Sleeping or toileting problems may even emerge. Some children have a delayed reaction, exhibiting difficulties a few weeks into school as it dawns on them that school is a permanent arrangement. These problems are likely to be short-lived. As your child settles in to the routines of school, makes some friends, and learns to trust the teacher, these behaviors will probably fade.

Parents may find some of the following suggestions useful in making their child's first days in kindergarten as hassle-free as possible.

REVIEW THE FIRST-DAY PROCEDURE WITH YOUR CHILD. Go through the first day of school, step by step. Make sure your child is clear how she will get to and from school, what will happen when she arrives, and how long school lasts. Reassure her that her teacher will answer any questions she has as well as guide her about where to go at the end of the day. Let your child know that things may seem strange and confusing for the first few days but with time kindergarten will feel more comfortable.

RECORD THE MOMENT. Take a picture of your child at the bus stop or at the front door on the first day. Make this a first-day ritual, taking her picture in the same spot every year. You will treasure these pictures and be able to see your child's growth from year to year.

GIVE YOUR CHILD A SECURITY ITEM. To help your child cope more easily with the separation, place a favorite toy, book, or doll in her book bag or knapsack. You might also put a picture of the family in the bag (reinforce it by attaching it to an index card). Writing your home and work numbers on the back might help to reassure her of your accessibility. And if your child is an early reader, enclose a note in her lunch box with a loving and encouraging message.

RESTRAIN YOUR EMOTIONS WHEN YOUR CHILD LEAVES. Avoid overreacting as your child steps onto the bus (allow her to board by herself). Expressions of emotion may trigger distress or sadness in your child and make departing more difficult. If you are walking your child to school, do not linger outside class. At the same time, don't sneak out on your child. Rather, give her a hug, say good-bye, and leave! If your child begins to cry, remember that kindergarten teachers are very experienced with first-day jitters. Let the teacher take the lead. She will likely have the children busy with an enjoyable activity soon after entering class. If your child is extremely distressed, work with the teacher to develop a plan which is comforting to your child. For example, you may want to stay in a designated area of the school for the first hour or so during the first few days.

BE AVAILABLE THE FIRST FEW DAYS. If you are working, see if you can arrange some time off for the first day or two to see your child off or welcome her home. If that is not feasible, be available by phone after school. Let your child's caretaker know how to handle her if she is upset or acting out.

AVOID GRILLING YOUR CHILD ABOUT WHAT HAPPENED IN SCHOOL. Your child may not wish to elaborate on the school day and is unlikely to give kindergarten rave reviews. After all, it is not easy to give up the familiarity, coziness, and security of home. Be prepared for responses such as "fine" or "okay." Questions such as "What was the most exciting thing that happened today?" or "What was the best part of the day?" may trigger conversation more successfully than yes or no questions. If you're still having little luck and are eager for information, talk with the parent of a more verbal child to find out what is happening in school or contact the teacher.

AVOID OVERSCHEDULING YOUR CHILD. Kindergarten, especially a full-day program, is quite an adjustment for most five-year-olds. You may want to postpone decisions about after-school activities such as ballet or gymnastics until you see how your child is adapting to kindergarten.

IF YOUR CHILD BALKS AT GOING TO SCHOOL, STAY THE COURSE. It is not unusual for kindergartners to resist going to school during the first few days. Don't argue with your child or yell at her. Rather state in a calm, matter-of-fact manner that all children must go to school and she has no choice but to attend. Let her know that you understand that it can be hard to go to a strange place with people you don't know, but emphasize that it will feel a little more comfortable each day. If your child is crying as she gets on the bus or enters the class, rest assured that the tears are likely to cease almost as soon as you leave. Each day should get a little easier as your child settles into the school routine, becomes more trusting of the teacher, and learns to view the school as a safe and secure place.

CHAPTER FIVE

THE ABC'S OF INSTRUCTION

Virtually all parents are eager to help their children learn, but few are comfortable in this role. They may not understand what the teacher is trying to accomplish, they may lack confidence in their ability to teach their children, or they may fear confusing them. Yet both research and experience tell us that children learn better and retain more when their parents help them to practice and apply what they have learned. This chapter attempts to narrow this gap by providing parents with the basics of academic instruction so they can support and extend the teacher's lessons. The purpose is not to give parents the skills to teach their child—that is the teacher's job. Rather the aim is to help parents learn why teachers do what they do and what parents can do to reinforce these lessons at home. You can do this most effectively not by giving your child more work sheets or extra workbook pages but rather by incorporating these lessons into your child's everyday life so that he comes to understand their relevance and value their importance. You do not need an educational background to do this, just a basic understanding of the subject, a sensitivity to your child's needs, and a willingness to take some risks.

This chapter examines various approaches to teaching the core academic subjects and offers practical strategies for reinforcing academic skills at home. Because teachers vary in their educational philosophy and teaching approach, it is important that you understand what your child's teacher is trying to accomplish so that your help dovetails with her instruction. This chapter will also highlight effective teaching practices to help you gauge the quality of instruction your child is receiving in each subject.

READING: THE FIRST AND FOREMOST "R"

Reading is the most important skill that children will learn in school. It is, in the words of former Secretary of Education William Bennett, elementary school's "most solemn responsibility." Reading is the gateway to learning and basic to the mastery of other subjects. If students are to succeed in social studies, science, and even math, they will need good reading skills. Because reading is the key to unlocking the door to a world of knowledge, parents must pay special attention to how their child is progressing in this subject.

And judging by recent test results, many students are progressing slowly. According to a 1992 report issued by the Federal Department of Education, nearly 31 percent of eighth-graders and 41 percent of fourth-graders could not read with understanding passages suited to their grade level.

How Schools Teach Reading

Learning to read is a complex task. It involves two abstract skills: (1) the ability to translate written symbols into words—called decoding, and (2) the ability to gain meaning from those words—called reading comprehension. The purpose of reading is to gain meaning, and thus comprehension is essential. Learning to decode words without understanding is not reading but rather just word calling.

There are different schools of thought about how to teach reading. Some teachers emphasize phonics, where students learn how to sound out letters and combinations of letters, thus learning to connect the words they hear with the words they see. Phonics instruction, which is mostly completed by the end of second grade, enables students to break words into parts when reading or assemble them when writing. Other teachers stress a whole-word approach (sometimes called the look-say or sight method) in which students memorize whole words as well as their meaning. A third approach, which is gaining increasing popularity, is called whole language. The guiding principle of this approach is that reading is a language activity closely related to speaking and writing so that enriching a child's language skills aids in reading comprehension. Rather than drilling students with phonics or using work sheets or basal readers, teachers using whole language emphasize reading for understanding and provide a variety of language experiences. Students being taught with this approach are encouraged to talk and write about their thoughts and feelings as well as read books of their own choosing.

In practice, most teachers do not use one approach exclusively but rather decide where to place the emphasis. Whatever reading approach is favored, teachers should provide students with a good grounding in phonics. Knowing how to sound out a word allows students to read most words without hesitation. Studies have documented the importance of phonics to learning how to read. In addition, the Federal Department of Education endorsed phonics as essential to the teaching of reading in its 1986 publication *What Works*.

Yet phonics alone cannot teach a child to read competently. The English language has many words that defy the rules of phonics. While there are 166 rules of phonics, there are also 45 exceptions. Words such as *school, would, knife, phone,* and *psychologist* do not conform to these rules. To read and write these and other irregular words, students must retain their visual image. In sum, an effective reading program teaches students to sound out words that adhere to the rules of phonics and memorize the visual images of those that do not. Because children have different learning styles, no one approach to reading is right for all children. Some learn better memorizing sight words, while others are more successful learning the sounds of letters and blending them together. Ideally the reading program should be adapted to the child's learning style.

Just as children differ in when they are ready to walk and talk, so it is with reading. Some children enter kindergarten able to read. Others are not yet ready for formal reading instruction in first grade. A child who is ready to read at age five is not necessarily more intelligent than five-year-olds who are not. Rather, it means that the student has mastered the skills necessary for reading—what are called reading-readiness skills. Girls are as a general rule ready to read before boys. Highly active children and those with short attention spans may be slower to read than their peers. The key is to tailor instruction to students' reading development rather than their chronological age, to where they are rather than how old they are. Successful reading is far more important than early reading.

Some schools introduce reading as early as kindergarten even though many kindergartners are not yet ready for formal reading instruction. These programs run the risk of frustrating children who are not ready to read and engendering negative feelings about reading. This negative association can take time to overcome. It is instructive to note that in some Scandinavian countries children are introduced to reading at a later age than in the United States but are not disadvantaged by their later start. They reach the same skill level in reading by mid–elementary school as American children who started reading instruction earlier.

Most kindergarten programs aim to develop reading readiness skills—shapes, concepts of sequence (for example, first and last) and position (for example, up and down), letters, sounds of letters, and beginning sounds in words. By kindergarten's end, a child should have learned most if not all of the letters of the alphabet as well as their accompanying sounds. He should also be able to read some sight words.

Formal reading instruction generally begins in first grade. Reading is usually taught in small groups, although some teachers prefer to work with students individually. A typical first-grade class will have three or four groups. Students will be assigned to a group based on the teacher's observation of their reading and language development and their attention span, performance on teacher-administered and standardized tests, and the recommendations of previous teachers. The teacher may use the same reading book for different groups but move at a different pace for each group or use a different reader for each group. While teachers will try to disguise the level of the groups by giving them names such as the hawks and the falcons, children learn quickly whether they are in the high or low group.

If your child is placed in the middle or low group, don't panic. Many children take time to break the code but go on to become proficient readers. Most children who are slow to develop in reading eventually catch up to the early readers. Reading progress does not happen evenly. Rather, it tends to occur in sudden bursts following periods of little growth. It is not always easy to know whether your child is simply a late reader who will catch up with time or whether he is showing signs of a reading disability. Third grade is a critical year. If your child is not reading with fluency by this time, you have reason for concern and should contact your child's teacher.

Most schools use a nationally published reading series to teach reading. A typical series includes an instructional book geared to the students' level called a basal reader, a workbook, and a teacher's manual. A first-grader will usually begin with a short basal reader with few words—what is called a preprimer. After reading two or three preprimers, he will graduate to a primer and then a first reader. Beginning in second grade, students will generally go through two basal readers per year. Typically, they will read the story aloud in a reading group, discuss it with the teacher, and do follow-up activities. Basal readers may continue to be used throughout elementary school and in some cases into middle school. Each reader increases in difficulty and builds on the skills taught in the previous one.

By the end of third grade your child should be a competent reader. He should have a firm grounding in phonics and be able to sound out most words of three syllables or less. In addition, he should be able to use context clues to deduce the meaning of more difficult words. The focus of reading instruction begins to change in fourth grade. Whereas up until third grade students were learning to read, in fourth grade the accent is more on reading to learn. Reading becomes a tool for gaining information. A basal reader and reading groups may still be used and exercises may be employed to expand vocabulary, but the focus is on reading for meaning. Students will be challenged to probe beyond the literal contents of a story for its deeper meaning. They will read longer, more complex books with richer plots and the reading selections will include nonfiction as well as fiction. They will discuss the thoughts and feelings of the characters, speculate on cause and effect, and learn to distinguish fact from opinion.

The ultimate goal of reading instruction is to teach students to gain meaning from what they read. Unfortunately, because of the focus on standardized test scores, many programs emphasize reading skills at the expense of reading for meaning. Students may spend considerable time learning to read but not much time actually reading. When this happens, students learn to equate reading with filling in work sheets. Reading may come to be seen as a tedious, joyless activity. While phonics is no doubt an essential building block of reading, reading is more than a set of discrete skills. Children need to learn to understand what they read. Comprehension comes from learning specific skills—using context clues, drawing inferences, understanding sequence—but it also comes from reading books they enjoy.

Basal readers are better at teaching reading skills than comprehension. They are often dull and lifeless and do not actively engage children's minds. Publishers have been trying to breathe some life into basal readers by making the stories more exciting and relevant —and some of the results are promising—but there simply is no substitute for good children's literature. By fourth grade, if not before, teachers should be supplementing basal readers with children's classics or current children's books of high quality.

The following are characteristics of an effective reading program. Bear in mind that a reading program need not meet all the following criteria to do its job effectively.

- Reading is taught on an individual basis or in small groups, with each child having a chance to participate. The reading groups have no more than ten students (and ideally less).
- Students spend a minimum of one hour per day in reading instruction in first and second grades.
- Students receive instruction in the basic rules of phonics. Teachers help students learn sounds by having them read stories that use those sounds.
- The classroom has a variety of reading materials geared to the students' interests and ability levels. In addition to books and magazines, the classroom may have headsets for listening to taped stories. A reading corner with a rocking chair or beanbag chair is particularly inviting.
- The teacher closely monitors the progress of students in the reading groups and moves them to different groups when appropriate.
- The teacher spends time with each student to review his progress in reading and offer specific strategies if warranted.
- The teacher reinforces reading for comprehension by conducting discussions, asking probing questions, and giving explanations.
- The teacher presents many language activities, both written and oral, on the premise that reading comprehension is fostered by language development. Children have a chance to write about the story they have read without being graded or evaluated. This helps crystallize their thinking about the story.
- Teachers not only teach children how to read but motivate them to want to read. They stimulate their students' interest in reading by involving them in enjoyable activities related to reading. Students may write about what they have read, do art projects inspired by the story, or act out the story.

- Students are given time during the week to visit the school library as well as time during the day to read for pleasure. Some districts have DEAR periods—"Drop Everything and Read"—during which students and staff read a book of their choice.
- Seatwork done while other students are in reading groups is tailored to the students' individual needs and abilities and is reviewed by the teacher. This seatwork goes beyond work sheets to include enjoyable and instructive language activities. Students doing seatwork spend minimal time waiting for instructions.
- Students with significant problems in reading are referred to a remedial program or considered for special education.

As your child progresses through school, keep a close watch on his reading. Review the work he brings home and note any problem areas. Also have him read a story to you from his classroom reader, noting the fluency of his reading and the frequency of errors. Have him then read another story silently and ask him some questions to assess his understanding. This is especially important in the upper elementary grades where a child's good decoding skills may mask poor comprehension. You might request to observe your child's reading group to help you judge whether your child is keeping pace with his classmates. Also observe his enthusiasm for reading at home. Does he shy away from reading or does he eagerly seek out books?

If you conclude that your child has a reading problem, contact his teacher. She may reassure you that your child is progressing as expected or she may agree with your assessment, in which case you will want to discuss possible steps to take, including the following: a change in his reading group; modification of his homework; referral to a remedial reading program; consideration for special education; specific help to be provided by the parents; or tutoring.

Promoting Your Child's Reading Skills

What can you as parents do to improve your child's reading? The following strategies may be helpful, but keep in mind that your job is not to teach your child to read. Leave that to the teacher. While you can certainly help if your child runs into a specific difficulty, your primary job is to help him enjoy and feel confident about reading.

STIMULATE YOUR CHILD'S LANGUAGE DEVELOPMENT. The ability to use language is critical to reading ability. Toward this end, provide your child with a language-rich environment. Talk with him often. (One survey found that parents talk with their children an average of a few minutes a day.) Encourage him to share his experiences or ideas, ask him thought-provoking questions, and listen attentively. Write down your child's made-up stories and then read them back to him. Teach young children nursery rhymes, rhyming games, and alphabet songs. Trips to places of cultural interest give your child background knowledge and expand his vocabulary, both of which will enhance his reading comprehension.

READ TO YOUR CHILD FROM AN EARLY AGE. This is the single most important thing you can do to promote your child's reading. Nonetheless, according to a recent U.S. Department of Education report, 30 percent of parents do not read to their children regularly. Jim Trelease, author of *The New Read-Aloud Handbook,* believes that parents should begin reading to children at six months and should read daily to children by age two. Read slowly and with expression, stopping to answer your child's questions or ask some of your own. In addition to reading to your child before bedtime, you might read to him while taking trips in the car, waiting for your order in a restaurant, or sitting in a doctor's waiting room. A child who is read to from an early age learns to feel comfortable and confident around books and begins to associate reading with warmth and security. It is also a time to bond with your child, to share something pleasurable. A well-written and illustrated children's book can be a delight to adults as well as children. And don't stop reading to your child once he is able to read. A. A. Milne, the author of *Winnie-the-Pooh,* read to his son Christopher (the model for Christopher Robin) until he was well into his teens. It is also important that fathers as well as mothers read to their child so that reading is not seen as a female activity.

Pick books that both you and your child find interesting. If you find the book dull, your reading will likely be uninspired and uninspiring. You can read books to your child that he is not capable of reading himself. This helps to enrich his vocabulary and broaden his experience. A typical first-grader has a listening vocabulary of almost ten thousand words and should be able to understand many books above his reading level. As you read, ask your child questions about the stories—not yes or no questions, but rather questions designed to provoke thought or conversation ("Why do you think he did that?" "What do you think is going to happen next?" or "What did you like about the story?"). If you find that your child's attention is wandering, stop and come back to the story another day.

HAVE YOUR CHILD READ TO YOU. This gives him a chance to practice and also provides you with a good opportunity to praise your child for his reading. Let the small errors go. For errors which change the meaning of the sentence, supply the right word or help him sound it out so the flow of the story is not lost, but do not turn this into a reading lesson. Keep in mind that understanding, not perfection, is what you are aiming for. You might have your older child read to your younger child.

ENCOURAGE YOUR CHILD TO READ FOR PLEASURE. Studies indicate that many children who are capable readers nonetheless do very little reading. One study found that 90 percent of fifth-graders read four minutes or less a day outside of school. Children who choose not to read are denying themselves a wealth of important information and a rich source of enjoyment. As Mark Twain said, "The man who does not read books has no advantage over the man who cannot read them." The best present you can give to your child is a love of reading. While you should not force your child to read, here are some specific strategies to encourage reading:

1. Provide a comfortable, quiet place to read. Children especially enjoy beanbag chairs. Set aside some shelves in your child's room for his books.

2. Allow your child to stay up fifteen or thirty minutes later at night if the time is spent reading.

3. Give him reading materials keyed to his interests. This may be a book on a sports hero or a vacation destination, a joke book, or a booklet on how to care for a rabbit.

4. For your child's birthday, give him a gift certificate to a favorite bookstore.

5. Have your child join a book club. The prices are usually reasonable and he will be excited when the books arrive.

6. Help your child make a paper chain or mobile listing the books he has read. Have him add to it every time he finishes a book.

7. Help your child get started with a long book by reading the beginning pages or chapter to him. This may whet his appetite enough to get him to continue on his own.

If your child still shows no interest in reading, don't despair. This may change with time. Children go through different phases in terms of pleasure reading. If your child loved to read at an earlier age, chances are he will rediscover the joy of reading later on.

HELP YOUR CHILD FEEL POSITIVE ABOUT READING. Your job is to help your child discover the joys and value of reading—not to teach him how to read. Reading with your child should be something pleasurable rather than a chore. Your child will give you cues if he is not enjoying the activity. Pay attention to them. Persisting with reading tasks that children do not enjoy can engender frustration and anxiety and ultimately resistance to reading. While there is nothing wrong with playing letter or word games with your child, make sure they are fun. But do not feel that you have to drill your child in letters and sounds before he enters kindergarten or give him reading exercises once he is in school. The time is better spent reading to your child.

FAMILIARIZE YOUR CHILD WITH THE PUBLIC LIBRARY. The public library offers a gold mine of riches to the eager and reluctant reader alike. In addition to providing books, tapes, records, and CDs, libraries sponsor programs for different age levels related to reading, including storytelling, films, book readings, and awards programs to encourage reading. Take advantage. You might schedule a specific time each week to visit the library with your child. Also consider obtaining a library card in your child's name. When he turns eight or nine, show him how to use the card catalog or computer to look up books. Allow him plenty of time to browse among the stacks. Librarians can guide you toward books appropriate to your child's reading level. Assume that his independent reading level is somewhat below the level of his reading book in school. A child who is reading at or above the third-grade level can read a wide range of books. While you or the librarian may suggest books, let your child make the final decision (with some rare exceptions). You might also consult books that review and recommend children's literature (see appendix B, "For Further Information"). Be on the lookout for books that have won the prestigious American Library Association Awards: the Caldecott Medal for illustration and the Newbery Medal for writing. Also ask the librarian for the "Children's Choices," an annual list of books recommended by other children in an extensive survey conducted yearly by the International Reading Association and Children's Book

Council. If your child chooses an occasional book above or below his ability, don't make an issue of it. He may like the challenge of a more advanced book and an easy book may still be satisfying. Do not insist that your child finish books he borrows from the library.

MAKE READING PART OF YOUR FAMILY LANDSCAPE. Be sure that your household has a range of reading materials—books, magazines, and newspapers—that are both appropriate and interesting to your child. For your younger child, make tapes of his favorite books so he can follow along as he turns the pages (make sure to signal on the tape when to turn the page). Consider having your child subscribe to a child's magazine. Anticipating its arrival and finding it in the mailbox can be a real treat for a child. Check out sample copies at the public or school library. (Appendix C includes a list of children's magazines with addresses.) Keep in mind that there are a variety of reading materials in and out of the house that your child may enjoy reading or find useful, including recipes, bumper stickers, television listings, newspaper comics, baseball cards, directions for putting together a toy, stamp catalogs, restaurant menus, the backs of cereal boxes, street signs, and even junk mail.

Also recognize that your own reading habits can have an impact on your child's habits. Let your child see you reading and talk to him about what you have read. You might even have a quiet hour in your house when the TV is off and family members are encouraged to read.

USE TELEVISION TO PROMOTE READING. Many children will find it much easier to turn on the TV than to open a book. It's okay for your child to watch some television as long as it falls within reasonable limits (see chapter 7). Some programs may even stimulate your child's interest in reading. *Reading Rainbow* is a notable example. Try to use programs as jumping-off points for reading about subjects of interest to your child. Movies your child has enjoyed may stimulate his interest in reading the book.

WRITING: THE SECOND "R"

Children enter elementary school with a joy of written expression. We need only look at the marked-up walls at home and the pavements scrawled in chalk to know of their enthusiasm for writing. Schools need to tap this enthusiasm by introducing writing soon after children enter elementary school. Kindergarten and first grade are not too early for children to begin expressing themselves in written form, whether it be through words or pictures. At this level the goal is to build on students' natural enjoyment of written communication by having them write in whatever form they can without the critical judgment of the teacher. The focus then at this early stage is more on writing to communicate than on the mechanics of writing.

With time, instruction, and practice, students will refine their writing until it conforms with the proper rules of written English. In this way the process of writing parallels the process of speaking. Three-year-olds who say, "The mouses runned away," will with time learn to say, "The mice ran away." It is the same with writing—as long as a foundation has been laid of comfort and confidence in writing.

At this early stage of writing teachers should not dwell on the mechanics of writing (spelling, grammar, punctuation, and handwriting) lest they discourage children and lessen their joy in writing. Children do not need a full understanding of grammar and syntax to be able to write. Research demonstrates that correcting every error on a child's composition does little for a child's writing ability and can dampen his enthusiasm for writing. Similarly students should not be graded on everything they write. The primary goal during these early elementary years is to help children learn to enjoy and value writing. (Think of the damage that has been done to students' enthusiasm for writing by making them write as a punishment.) The mechanics of writing will come with time and a desire to communicate with others in written form.

This is not to say that students will learn the rules of proper written expression without teacher instruction. Learning the formal rules of grammar, punctuation, and syntax is vital, but these concerns should not dominate the writing program. If they do, children will come to see writing as a tedious, lifeless task. Writing, after all, is more about communicating meaning than it is about figuring out where to place a comma or when to capitalize a word. A child can have a good grasp of grammar but still be a poor writer. The measure of a good writer is his ability to convey ideas with clarity and interest.

Students in the early elementary grades will learn the basics of writing: the formation of letters and words and the construction of sentences. By the end of third grade your child should be able to put his thoughts on paper in well-formed sentences and he should be learning how to develop paragraphs. Students in later elementary grades take these newly learned skills and put them to use in writing reports and stories. While students in upper elementary grades will learn about the technical aspects of writing, they also need to learn to feel comfortable expressing themselves on paper. Many students in these grades are not confident in their writing ability. Some even develop writing blocks. By the time a student completes sixth grade, he should be able to write a well-constructed paragraph with supporting details. He should have also learned the skills necessary to complete a report, including planning what to write, writing a draft, revising it to final form, and proofreading it.

Ideally students should write in school daily. Just as children learn to read better by reading more, so too children learn to write better by writing more. The writing should go beyond handwriting exercises or copying passages verbatim (a practice from years past) and include writing compositions on topics of student interest or teacher suggestion. If a student cannot yet write, he can convey his ideas in picture form. Writing should be incorporated into various subjects such as social studies or science rather than restricted to just one subject. Children also need to learn how to write in different forms and thus they should have exposure to explanatory, persuasive, and creative writing. Through various exercises, they learn how to vary the tone and style of a composition to suit its purpose and audience.

Some teachers foster the ability to write by having their students "publish" books. The student begins by writing a story, learns to edit the draft, and then has it typed. After stapling and binding (a good task for parent volunteers), the student has his first publication, which he can then share with his classmates. Another good practice is to have students keep a journal that is for the teacher's eyes only. The teacher reads the journal and writes back to the student with her reactions. In this way, the student experiences writing as a safe, enjoyable activity where there is no fear of criticism or evaluation.

Promoting Your Child's Writing Skills

Your role is particularly crucial in promoting writing because many schools do not give writing the attention it deserves. Schools that do provide writing instruction often dwell on the more technical aspects.

Standardized test scores may rise with this approach but the quality of the students' writing may not. You should have concerns if your child is doing little writing in school or the primary focus is on mechanics. Let the school know that you would like writing to be a major focus of the curriculum.

The following suggestions may help you foster your child's writing skills:

STIMULATE YOUR CHILD'S LANGUAGE DEVELOPMENT. Just as with reading, writing is enhanced by a child's facility with language. You can stimulate your child's verbal skills by reading to your child from an early age, talking with him about places he has visited and experiences he has had, having him explain what he means without interruption, and playing word or rhyming games. Reading and writing go hand in hand, so encourage your child to read by taking him to the library often and providing a range of reading materials at home. By reading and listening to stories, your child learns how to construct a story and sees how authors use words to convey thoughts and feelings.

WRITE DOWN STORIES YOUR YOUNG CHILD TELLS YOU. Have your child dictate a madeup story or play to you while you type it or write it down. Then read it back to him to see if he wants to make changes. You might also have your child illustrate the story. After he is finished, staple the pages together to create a book, which you might then loan to family or friends. In addition, you might write down your child's descriptions of his pictures or record new endings he has made up to fairy tales. If he needs help getting started, give him the first sentence or ask questions to prompt him. This process of recording your child's thoughts helps impress upon him that ideas can be communicated in writing.

ATTEND MORE TO THE MEANING THAN THE MECHANICS. Because children are often insecure about their writing, your primary job is to bolster your child's confidence and foster his enthusiasm for writing. Be positive and encouraging about his efforts and focus more on what he did well than on technical errors. For example, you might say, "I like the way you described how the people were feeling." Noting all of your child's errors or dwelling on his sloppiness is a sure way of turning your child off to writing. Pay more attention to the contents of your child's composition, asking questions as a sign of interest. If you choose to address some technical problems with your child's writing, stick to the major mistakes but don't sweat the small stuff.

PROVIDE OPPORTUNITIES FOR YOUR CHILD TO WRITE. There are a variety of enjoyable writing activities that your child can do at home. The box below offers many examples. These activities help children appreciate that writing serves a purpose beyond pleasing the teacher or getting a good grade. Many magazines for children publish letters, poems, and stories by children (see appendix C). One magazine, *Stone Soup,* is even written entirely by children. There are few things more thrilling for a child than seeing something he has written published. One other opportunity is worthy of special note: having a pen pal. The pen pal may be somebody in your family (for example, a cousin of the same age in another part of the country) or somebody your child has never met.

WRITE IDEAS

The following is a list of writing activities that your child can do at home. These may not only be rewarding in themselves but may also help him appreciate that writing serves important purposes.
- A letter to a friend, relative, or pen pal
- A letter or story submission to a children's magazine (see appendix C for a list of magazines)
- A letter to a favorite children's book author, care of the publisher (authors often write back)
- A postcard while on vacation
- Thank-you notes
- Invitations
- A family newsletter
- A list of chores of family members
- A sign for a bedroom door
- A journal or diary
- Lyrics from songs

- A letter to a government official expressing a view or complaint (addresses available from your public library)
- A letter to a company asking for a refund, registering a complaint, or offering an idea
- A request for a free sample from a company
- A letter to a celebrity
- A list of things to do
- A list of items (for example, a shopping list, items in a collection, items to bring on a trip, or gift list)
- A child's written rationale for a purchase or new privilege
- Captions on child's artwork
- Captions on family photos
- A script of a play by child
- Telephone messages on an erasable message board
- A letter to a newspaper
- Homemade birthday cards or personalized get well cards
- A letter to a tourist bureau requesting information

DISPLAY YOUR CHILD'S WORK. The best way of showing appreciation for your child's written work is to display it. You might also send something he has written to a relative or friend.

TAKE ADVANTAGE OF TECHNOLOGY. Dust off your manual typewriter and let your child play with it. If you have a computer, install a word processing program designed for children (for example, Bank Street Writer or Kidworks 2) and a sign-making program (for example, The New Print Shop). By fourth or fifth grade, if not before, your child should be able to use these kinds of programs. The benefits of word processing over handwriting will become readily apparent to your child. He will find that it speeds up the process of writing, provides an easy way of correcting his work, and prints a legible copy. For students with handwriting difficulties, word processing is especially welcome because it allows them to focus on their ideas and not get bogged down with the mechanics of handwriting.

SERVE AS A MODEL FOR YOUR CHILD. If your child sees you writing, he will be more inclined to write. And he will appreciate that writing serves important purposes. Let your child witness the process you go through as you write, including writing a rough draft, editing, and proofreading. And then, if appropriate, read what you have written to your child to get his reaction. Your family might even have a "writing hour" in which everyone is encouraged to write.

ENCOURAGE SCHOOL ACTIVITIES REQUIRING WRITING. A number of school activities such as the yearbook, the school newspaper, the literary magazine, and English contests are valuable opportunities for secondary students to hone their writing skills.

SHOW YOUR CHILD EARLIER PAPERS TO INDICATE PROGRESS. Note the date on the papers your child shows you, put them in a file, and bring them out later in the year to show your child how much progress he has made.

GIVE PRESENTS RELATED TO WRITING. You should be able to find something from the following list to give to your child for a gift: magnetic alphabet letters, pens or pencils (pencils with your child's name will be a big hit), pads of paper, pencil sharpener, correction fluid, fancy erasers, personalized stationery, stationery-making kit, label maker, alphabet stamps with pad, typewriter (a used one is fine), desk lamp, dictionary, thesaurus, crossword puzzle book, journal, and diary. And, if it fits within your budget, consider a computer with word processing capability.

Handwriting

While the essence of writing education is to learn to communicate ideas, the mechanics of writing require instruction as well. Yet many schools today devote little attention to handwriting. They may believe that handwriting is of less importance in the age of computers. This is no doubt true but neglecting handwriting instruction can give rise to problems. Most notably, poor handwriting mechanics can interfere with written expression. Students who struggle with handwriting may be so preoccupied with forming letters properly that the content of their work suffers. A student who finds handwriting tedious and writes slowly may not be able to keep up with his thoughts. Again, the content may suffer (as will his ability to take notes in later years). And perhaps most significantly, a child who has difficulty with handwriting may lose his desire to write.

For these reasons, teachers should provide formal instruction to help students develop legible and fluent handwriting. Instructional strategies might include teaching students to grip the pencil and position the paper properly, modeling of the writing of letters, and giving feedback to students' on their efforts. Handwriting instruction should be provided primarily in the context of writing assignments rather than through isolated drills.

While your child is not likely to begin formal handwriting instruction until first grade, he should be able to at least write his name, many letters, and some numbers by the end of kindergarten. Instruction in printing, also called manuscript, will continue through second or third grade. In learning the shape of each letter, your child may have to unlearn ways of forming letters learned earlier. Many children enjoy the repetitive nature of learning how to print, although others with fine-motor weaknesses may find it frustrating and difficult.

Beginning in second or third grade, your child will learn cursive writing. For many children, learning to write with the fluid lines of script is a big step up in the world of school, a sign to them that they are growing up. As a result, many children greet the introduction of cursive writing instruction with enthusiasm. This transition from printing to cursive may take a number of months. By the end of third grade, most students should be fairly comfortable writing in cursive. Some have difficulty making this transition and continue to use print.

Handwriting exasperates many students, especially boys, who are more prone to learning problems in general. Students may have difficulty forming letters, staying on the line, spacing properly between words, writing at an appropriate pace, or copying from the board. They also may reverse letters when they write (for example writing *b* for *d* or *m* for *w*). While these problems can sometimes suggest a learning disability, in other cases children simply need more time to develop these skills. If you see evidence of problems with your child's handwriting, contact the teacher. She may be able to adapt her instruction or use special materials such as a pencil grip or special paper. (If your child is left-handed, he may need special instruction in positioning the paper.) Or she may reassure you that what you are seeing is not uncommon for your child's grade. Reversals, for example, are not unusual with first- and second-graders. They are less common among third-graders and may signal the need for an evaluation to assess the need for special education.

If your child brings home papers from school where the handwriting is sloppy, you may want to give gentle suggestions about handwriting. If so, reinforce the key elements of handwriting: size, shape, slant, and spacing. Keep in perspective, however, that the substance of what he has written is more important than the form and that legible handwriting is more important than beautiful handwriting. Do not give your child handwriting exercises at home unless he wants to do them. Not only do you risk causing him to dread writing but you may confuse him if your approach differs from that of the teacher. A better approach is to encourage him to engage in fine-motor activities, especially those that involve drawing or writing.

SPELLING

Spelling, a basic ingredient of writing, continues to occupy a prominent place in public school education. The advent of the electronic speller and the computer spell-checker, while making life easier for problem spellers, has not lessened the importance of spelling instruction. Poor spelling can create lasting impressions with negative consequences for both children and adults, including poor grades on reports, failure to obtain job interviews, and low ratings on job performance.

Learning to spell in the English language is a formidable challenge for many children. Because it has its roots in French, German, Latin, and other languages, the English language contains many words that are not spelled as they sound. These irregular words, which must be learned through memorization, can be exasperating to students. About 20 percent of the words in the English language are spelled differently from how they sound. Some words are pronounced the same but spelled differently (for example, *their, there,* and *they're*). Some letter combinations can be pronounced a variety of ways (for example, the *ea* in *bead, great, lead, heart,* and *earth*). Some words with foreign origins do not conform to the rules of phonics (for example, *lieutenant*). Is it any wonder then that so many children find spelling a tedious and difficult subject?

Spelling instruction has not changed much over the years. Because of the need to memorize the spelling of many words, notably those which defy the rules of phonics, the teaching of spelling necessarily involves drill and practice. Your child may begin bringing spelling lists home as early as first grade. Students may either be separated into spelling groups or receive spelling instruction as a class. Some teachers use spelling books, while others draw their spelling words from the subjects the students are studying. Many teachers continue to use the following time-honored approaches to teach spelling:

- teaching words that are most frequently written
- presenting spelling words in a list
- teaching phonics and the structure of words (prefixes, suffixes, and roots)
- using a pretest-study-test method
- having students correct their own tests and study misspelled words
- integrating spelling words into writing assignments

To be a good speller, a child must be able to discriminate the sounds of words that are spelled phonetically and visualize the words that are not. Children with poor visual memory skills have difficulty retaining the visual images of words and are prone to poor spelling. Spelling problems may also be caused by difficulty in hearing the differences in sounds, called auditory discrimination. A child who cannot hear the differences between, say, *pin* and *pen,* will have difficulty spelling words phonetically. If you suspect your child has auditory problems, consider obtaining an evaluation of his hearing by an audiologist. Also talk with the teacher if your child is struggling with spelling. Find out whether the spelling list is too difficult or too long for your child and needs adjustment. Ask how you can support your child's spelling skills so as not to conflict with the teacher's approach.

Do not worry about your child's spelling errors in the early elementary grades. They are to be expected. Many educators now believe that young children should be allowed to write using their own spellings of words without being corrected. With most children, their "creative spelling" will eventually be replaced by accurate spelling, especially as their reading improves and they are exposed to words over and over. *Tm* will eventually become *tim* which will eventually become *time.* Placing too much emphasis on spelling mistakes at an early age will inhibit the child's desire to write. Parents as well as teachers should be mindful of this principle. At the same time, if an older elementary child is consistently making the same mistake, correct it to avoid having him practice mistakes.

In working with your child, the following strategies may be helpful:

BE PATIENT AND POSITIVE. Because spelling can be anxiety pro-voking for children, try not to be impatient or short with your child. If he frustrates easily, try working with him in short segments rather than one long stretch. You may have unpleasant memories of spelling from your own school days but try not to pass on your feelings to your child with negative comments about spelling. If your child has problems with spelling, reassure him that good spellers are no smarter than poor spellers.

FIND A METHOD OF STUDY THAT WORKS FOR YOUR CHILD. You may have to experiment to find out which technique works best. Some children learn more effectively by writing down words that are dictated to them, while others do better spelling the words out loud. The National Education Association recommends the following method of study for spelling:

1. Pronounce the word slowly while looking at each part of the word.
2. Spell the word out loud.
3. Spell the word to yourself while visualizing it.
4. Write the word.
5. Repeat if necessary.

A few do's and don't's are in order here regarding helping your child with spelling. Do help your child understand word families (for example, sand, hand, and land). Do encourage him to proof his own papers for spelling errors. Don't make him write spelling words many times. After a few times, the value is lost. Don't bombard your child with spelling rules. He will only retain a few of them so be selective. (The "i before e except after c" rule should be one you reinforce.)

USE A MULTISENSORY APPROACH WITH A YOUNG CHILD. If your child is having difficulty retaining spelling words, reinforce the visual image of the word through sight and touch. Have your child write the word in large print and then trace the letters with his fingers as he pronounces them. He should repeat this until he can do it from memory.

DEVELOP A SPELLING BOX. Write down words that your child misspells on three-by-five-inch cards and place them in a box for occasional review. You can also record them in a notebook. Be selective, including words that are relatively common and your child is expected to know. You and your child might develop sentences to help him remember the correct spelling (for example, "You get re*lie*f when you *lie* down"). You might highlight or color code the troublesome letter combinations and group words together that have similar spelling patterns.

GET YOUR CHILD A DICTIONARY. While a dictionary is an important reference book for your child to have, do not expect him to look up every misspelled word, especially if he is prone to spelling errors, or he will quickly become turned off to writing. Other references are available to help with spelling, including *50,000 Words Divided and Spelled,* by Harry Sharp, *Webster's Instant Word Guide,* which lists words in alphabetical order and helps children find correct spellings quickly, and *How to Spell It: A Dictionary of Commonly Misspelled Words,* by Harriet Wittles and Joan Greisman.

PLAY WORD GAMES. A variety of word games popular with children promote spelling skills, including hangman, word search, Scrabble for Juniors, Speak & Spell, Wheel of Fortune, Spill & Spell, and Boggle. You may want to modify the rules to make the game more rewarding and less pressured.

MAKE USE OF TECHNOLOGY. For many deficient spellers, the way to spell relief is technology. Many computer word processing programs feature spell-checkers, which highlight and even correct spelling errors. The electronic speller solves the dilemma of a child having to look up in the dictionary a word that he cannot spell. To use this device, type in the word the way you think it is spelled and the electronic speller will most likely show you the correct spelling. These are not teaching devices as much as they are tools to check and correct spelling.

MATH: THE NEW AND THE OLD

As with reading and writing, math is a skill that permeates almost every aspect of our lives. We use the math skills we learned in school when we balance our checkbook, measure a room for carpeting, calculate the sales tax on a purchase, or figure out the better buy in the grocery store. Just to make sense of the daily news, we often need a basic understanding of statistics. But the importance of math goes beyond its value to our daily lives. It is also a key to the pursuit of various careers.

Yet if test scores are to be believed, American students are not faring well in math, especially when compared to their counterparts in other countries. According to the International Assessment of Educational Progress, American nine-year-olds scored eleventh on a recent measure of math skills given to same-age students from fourteen countries. American thirteen-year-olds were also disappointing, scoring fifteenth in a survey of students from twenty countries. In 1987, the National Research Council's Mathematical Sciences Education Board concluded, based on three studies, that the math skills of American elementary and secondary students were "among the lowest of any industrialized country." These results should not come as a shock to educators. American students have been performing poorly compared to students from other countries for decades.

These dismal results sent distress signals throughout the educational community. The concern about the quality of American math instruction echoes similar concerns raised during the late 1950s. After the Soviet Union's success with the launching of Sputnik, pressure mounted to improve the math and science skills of American students to keep pace with their Soviet counterparts. This pressure contributed to the advent of what became known as "the new math." Concepts and understanding were at the forefront of this new approach, and computational skills were deemphasized. But the new math was not the success that educators had hoped for. Students were confused by the concepts and had difficulty applying them to solve math problems. Teachers also strayed too far from the teaching of computational skills. With the back-to-basics movement of the 1970s, educators returned to an approach stressing computation as well as drill and practice.

In recent years math educators have again introduced changes in American math instruction in response to the poor test performance of American students. These changes amount to a dramatic shift in direction, with more emphasis placed on understanding and less on rote memorization, more on problem solving and less on computation, more on real-life application and less on isolated math skills, and more on active student participation and less on teacher lectures. Underlying this approach is the notion that the more thoroughly students understand a concept, the better they will retain and apply it. In addition, connecting math skills with real-life experiences helps students appreciate the value of what they are learning. At the same time, this approach recognizes the importance of learning computational skills and memorizing basic math facts.

The overriding goal of this curriculum overhaul is to help students become creative solvers of real-life math problems, not just number crunchers. Students learning with this approach spend less time filling in work sheets and listening to teacher explanation and more time learning how to solve problems, including understanding what steps to take in which sequence and how to sort out relevant from irrelevant information. Rather than completing endless pages of math problems, students are learning to reason mathematically by applying learned skills to real-life problems. Rather than learning to divide fractions by simply using the old adage—"Yours is not to reason why, just invert and multiply"—students today are more likely to learn the rule as well as the reasoning behind it. These changes have not completely taken hold of math classrooms throughout the country but are happening gradually. You can assess whether your child's math program is embracing these changes by reviewing his classwork and homework. The move to a more real-life approach to math should be most evident in the upper elementary and middle school grades.

Whatever approach is used, math teachers must adhere to some basic tenets of instruction. First and foremost, math must be taught sequentially since one lesson builds upon another. A student cannot learn division until he knows multiplication. Algebra requires that a student have mastered the four basic operations of addition, subtraction, multiplication, and division. Schools may differ in when they introduce topics (for example, regrouping may be introduced in first grade in some schools, second grade in others), but the sequence will be essentially the same. Because having a good foundation in math is important to the mastery of more advanced skills, review is an important part of math instruction. At the same time, too much review makes for bored students, so teachers want to aim for a balance between review of previously learned skills and introduction of new skills. Teachers also need to monitor students' work frequently to ensure they are not simply practicing mistakes.

All public school students receive math instruction daily through at least the end of middle or junior high school. Grouping by ability is a common practice in math because of the varying math abilities of students. The teaching of math begins with the introduction of math readiness concepts in kindergarten. Here children will learn such skills as understanding the connection of numbers with their quantity (one-to-one correspondence), recognizing, writing, and counting numbers from one to ten, identifying basic shapes, understanding words of comparison (for example, larger and smaller, higher and lower), learning the meaning of ordinal numbers (first, second, third, etc.), and recognizing and knowing the value of a penny, nickel, dime, and quarter. The aim in the early years is not just skill development, however. Just as important is to help children feel comfortable around numbers so that they approach math with confidence.

Because math concepts can be hard for young children to grasp, math educators often make use of tangible objects—what teachers call manipulatives. These may be blocks, beads, poker chips, Cuisenaire rods, sand, water, indeed anything that can be counted or that conveys quantity or amount. Manipulatives help children visualize the concept in a way that work sheets can't. By counting the number of pennies in a cup, for example, students come to see numbers as quantities rather than abstract concepts. With time and intellectual maturity, students will be able to move from the concrete to the conceptual. Manipulatives are most commonly used in kindergarten and first grade but may be used in higher grades as well (for example, a fraction tile).

Sometimes children do what appears to be advanced math skills when in reality they don't grasp the underlying concept. One kindergartner impressed his teacher by counting from one to fifty. Beaming with pride at his accomplishment, he paused and then asked quizzically, "What's a fifty?"

Rote memorization is of little meaning without understanding what's behind it. Manipulatives help provide that meaning. Teachers need to be careful about moving to workbooks and other pencil-and-paper tasks before students are ready. A kindergarten or first-grade teacher who is teaching math concepts primarily through workbooks or work sheets will not achieve optimal understanding and retention from her students.

Addition and subtraction are introduced in first grade. First-graders typically learn to add and subtract one- and two-digit numbers not requiring regrouping (borrowing and carrying). Among the other skills they are likely to work on are counting by twos, fives, and tens, telling time, learning place value, and solving basic word problems.

In second grade, more complicated addition and subtraction problems are learned, and regrouping is introduced. Multiplication and the concept of parts of a whole are discussed by year's end. Third-graders refine their skill with regrouping in addition and subtraction, continue with multiplication and the memorization of the multiplication tables, begin division, and learn to round off numbers. Fractions and decimals are also touched upon. By the end of third grade, your child should be familiar with the four basic operations (addition, subtraction, multiplication, and division).

Success in math in the upper elementary grades rests on the foundation that was established in the earlier grades. Because students in fourth grade and above are better able to deal with abstract concepts, there is more emphasis on problem solving than computation although review of previously learned skills is ongoing. Fourth-graders tackle more challenging multiplication and division problems, begin to add and subtract fractions as well as decimals, and work on word problems. The basics of geometry are also discussed. In fifth and sixth grade, students delve into more complex multiplication and division problems and refine their skills with fractions, decimals, estimating, word problems, and geometric concepts. Sixth-graders begin working with percents.

The calculator is a valuable tool for students, especially after they have mastered basic computational skills. While some fear that students may grow dependent on the calculator and thus not master basic facts, the evidence is otherwise. Numerous studies indicate that the use of calculators, when combined with traditional math instruction, can enhance students' computational and problem-solving skills. In addition, students using calculators approach math with more enthusiasm. The calculator can relieve students of laborious calculations and allow them to put their time and energy into the understanding and solving of problems. (Students taking the Scholastic Aptitude Test are even allowed to use calculators.) Calculators thus allow students to advance further than they could if they had to do the calculations by hand. At the same time, calculators are no substitute for knowledge of math facts or mastery of the basic operations. As adults, students will need to do quick mental calculations on an everyday basis and will need math facts readily accessible. Moreover, if math facts are not at your fingertips, then you may not know if an answer makes sense.

Computers are also useful for teaching math. Indeed, schools make more use of computers for math instruction than for any other subject. A computer can serve as a personal math tutor for a student, indicating the source of his error and steering him in the right direction. Even if used only for drill and practice, the computer is very effective at motivating children to do math problems.

Promoting Your Child's Math Skills

You can enhance your child's math skills by helping him to see how math is all around us and the ways in which math is of practical value. Show him how math is used in everyday life by encouraging him to engage in activities that incorporate math skills. A lemonade stand, for example, is not only fun but teaches your child about money and math skills as he decides on prices, gives change to customers, and calculates his earnings. Giving your child an allowance also helps him learn about money and fosters financial responsibility. And when your child has saved enough money, have him open up a savings account and introduce him to the concept of interest. The kitchen provides an abundance of opportunities to reinforce math skills.

The following are examples of other activities that may be fun and instructional. Have your child

- count the number of vans on the highway
- read *How Much Is a Million?* by David Schwartz (Lothrop)
- count how much is in his piggy bank
- figure out how many days until his birthday
- pay for an item at a convenience store and count the change
- determine which books he can order from the book fair given a set amount of money
- measure how tall he is with a tape measure
- assume the role of banker while playing Monopoly
- cut a sandwich into halves and then quarters
- figure out the ingredient amounts on a recipe that is doubled
- keep track of how much you have spent at the grocery store by using a calculator
- determine the length of a car trip by using the odometer readings
- weigh fruit at the grocery store and estimate what it will cost
- figure out how many miles your car is getting to the gallon
- calculate interest on a bank account
- figure out batting averages

There are a multitude of games (board games as well as cards) that children can play that promote math skills. In addition, many good math software programs are available for children (see appendix B, "For Further Information"). Remember to keep these activities tension-free. The purpose is not only to hone math skills but to develop confidence and a positive association with math.

If your child is having problems with math, try to diagnose where he is having difficulty. Review his schoolwork and, if necessary, have him talk through his problem-solving process to identify the source of the error. Consider the following possibilities: failure to understand the concept; a problem in computation; poor math facts; difficulty in reading or understanding a word problem; or failure to line up the columns properly.

If you work with your child on math skills, consider using some of the following strategies:

- Where possible, make it fun by playing math games.
- Encourage your child to go slow, check his work, and consider whether his answer makes sense.
- Praise your child often. This is particularly important because children are often insecure about their math skills.
- Begin with easy problems and gradually proceed to more difficult ones when he is ready. Exposing your child to continual frustration will turn him off to math and teach him to avoid it.
- Help your child read word problems carefully. Suggest that he read the problem a couple of times if needed and point out key words.
- Model how to solve the problem by verbalizing the steps as you do it on paper. Have your child do the next one while you watch.
- Be careful about giving your child a different approach for solving a problem than he learned in class. This may add to his confusion.
- Use flash cards to help your child learn math facts. You can buy them at most toy stores or make up your own. On one side, write the problem and on the other, the problem and answer.
- If your child is having difficulty grasping a concept, use concrete materials to help him understand. For example, you might cut an apple into parts to demonstrate the concept of fractions.
- Review your child's work on a difficult assignment after a few problems. You want to avoid having him practice mistakes.

If you find yourself becoming impatient with your child, it is probably best to back off and let him struggle on his own. Your impatience is only going to sour your child on math. If his difficulties and frustrations persist, contact his teacher. The classroom pace may be too fast or the level too difficult. It may be that your child needs bolstering of specific skills, perhaps through extra help from the teacher or remedial help. The teacher may be willing to give him a math diagnostic test to identify his strengths and weaknesses. You might even consider hiring a tutor, although this should be discussed with the teacher. A small percentage of children have a learning disability that impedes development of math skills. They may reverse numbers when reading or writing, fail to recognize numbers, or add columns improperly. Where these or other specific difficulties are causing significant problems in math and other subjects, special education may be warranted.

Family Math is a program of math education for parents and children offered in many school districts across the country. Consisting of six sessions given outside school hours, Family Math aims to demystify math by helping children as well as their parents see the relevance of math to the world around them. By having parents do problems with their children requiring the application of math skills, the program has been found to improve both children's and parents' attitudes towards math. If you want to learn how you can implement this program in your district, contact Family Math, Lawrence Hall of Science, University of California, Berkeley, CA 94720; telephone 510-643-6525.

Math Anxiety

Math is a troublesome subject for many students and often engenders anxiety and avoidance. This may become a self-fulfilling prophesy as students become anxious and insecure about math, resist the subject or put forth minimal effort, and thus fail to develop the necessary skills. Their resulting poor performance in turn lessens their confidence and intensifies their anxiety.

Girls are especially prone to math anxiety. And, if you believe the false messages they receive from various quarters, well they should be. Girls are told in subtle and not so subtle ways that they are not expected to excel in math, that math is for boys. This message may come from parents as well as teachers. Parents may be more likely to do math activities with their sons while teachers may encourage boys more than girls to succeed in math (for example, boys are more likely to be called on in math class). Even if girls have good math skills, they may shy away from succeeding in math because of fear of peer ridicule. This "real girls don't do math" message is pervasive and is communicated at an early age when attitudes are forming. If you are dubious about the societal programming that takes place, consider that a Barbie doll was programmed to say: "Math class is tough." (After many complaints, the manufacturer removed this statement from the doll's repertoire.) Girls thus learn early to avoid math. This may take the form of not pushing themselves as they do in other subjects or not pursuing advanced math courses at the secondary and college level. As a result, they may narrow their career options and be filtered out of scientific and select professional careers. Some public schools have responded to this problem by offering girls-only math classes to promote their participation and foster their confidence.

Parents can play an important role in chipping away at the math blocks of their children. You need to make a special effort to encourage your daughter's performance in math and acknowledge her successes. In addition, provide her with the same math games and toys that you provide your son. You also need to monitor your attitudes and comments about math. You may have unpleasant memories of math when you were in school and may find yourself making negative comments about math or your child's skills ("You've inherited my rotten math genes," "I couldn't stand math either when I was in school," or "Most girls find math hard"). Bite your tongue. These comments may transmit your own anxieties about math to your child. Rather, make comments suggesting why the math skills she is working on are important.

SOCIAL STUDIES

Once students have mastered the basics of reading, writing, and mathematics, they can put these skills to use in understanding the world in which we live. Social studies is a seemingly boundless subject, encompassing the study of history, economics, government, geography, and anthropology. It is through this subject that students learn about past historical events and consider present social issues. The ultimate purpose of social studies instruction is the same as it was when it originally became a part of the public school curriculum: to help students learn constructive social skills and become informed and responsible citizens.

Despite this noble purpose, social studies does not always receive the attention it deserves in elementary school. In some classrooms, it is a regular part of the curriculum; in others, it is taught irregularly, namely, when there is an opening in the schedule. Teachers also differ in their choice of topics and their method of presentation. There is no national consensus about what a social studies program should include.

What most teachers of social studies do share in common is an "expanding" approach to instruction. This means that as a student progresses to the next grade, the topics studied expand in geographic scope and complexity. Social studies instruction begins in the first year of public school by drawing on what students already know. Kindergartners learn how to cooperate in a group while first-graders may talk about families. Second-graders may find out more about their neighborhood, while third-graders may move farther afield to study their town or city. In fourth grade the focus may be on their state as well as on concepts of geography. The scope of study may widen in fifth grade to include specific periods of American history as well as national traditions. And in sixth grade the lens may expand to embrace aspects of world history.

In the lower elementary grades, social studies instruction relies primarily on listening and hands-on activities. Some teachers will use "newspapers" to teach about current events. (Remember *My Weekly Reader*?) Once students are skilled at reading for information, textbooks may be introduced, allowing them to pursue topics in greater depth. Social studies instruction may be enhanced by incorporating art, drama, and music into the teaching process.

The community offers a wealth of resources for learning how government and business work. Students may visit the police or fire department, tour city hall, or take a trip to the post office. They may learn the basics of market economics by visiting a farm one week and then going to the farmer's market the next week to see crops being sold. And later in the year they may visit a bakery to see bread being made and sold to consumers. These visits broaden students' understanding of how people work together.

The teaching of social studies has been the subject of much debate. Some contend that social studies should return to its roots and stress historical events, which they see as basic to developing cultural literacy. Others argue that social studies should emphasize the study of people around the world, examining similarities and differences across cultures. According to this view, more attention should be given to how people have lived in different periods throughout history and how events influenced their lives—what is called social history —and less attention given to wars, treaties, and dictators.

Whatever the focus of instruction, there must be an effort to promote understanding and not just present facts. Historical information is certainly important, but social studies is much more than a grab bag of facts and dates. Unless these facts are taught within a framework of concepts and ideas and students learn to make connections between historical events, then the facts will have little meaning and may be quickly forgotten. Students are more likely to retain facts if they have an interest in knowing them and a meaningful context in which to place them. In short, students need to learn the *why* underlying an historical event, not just the *who, what, when,* and *where.*

If you want to learn about the quality of your child's social studies program, you can observe his class, review the textbook and other teaching materials, go over the work that he brings home, and talk with him to assess his enthusiasm for social studies. The tests and assignments should help you determine whether memorizing of facts is the focus of instruction to the exclusion of concepts and ideas. As students move into higher grades, social studies tests should increasingly include questions requiring understanding and not just true-or-false or fill-in-the-blank items.

How Parents Can Help

Students whose social studies teacher emphasizes rote learning may come to see the subject as dull and lifeless. Parents can help revitalize history by finding ways to relate it to their child's own life and taking advantage of "teachable moments." You may find the following suggestions useful in extending and enriching your child's social studies instruction.

VISIT HISTORICAL PLACES. It is one thing to read about Washington's severe winter at Valley Forge, quite another to actually go there. There are a multitude of historic sites across the country that will help to make history seem more real and relevant. Restoration villages (for example, Colonial Williamsburg in Virginia or Sturbridge Village in Massachusetts) are especially intriguing to children, allowing them to see what life was like in days gone by. And there is no better way of learning about government than visiting your state capital or Washington, DC. As you tour these historic sites, offer observations or ask questions that make your child think about issues that might otherwise elude him.

HELP YOUR CHILD UNDERSTAND HIS FAMILY HISTORY. There is no better way of making history come alive for your child than through his own family. He will be fascinated by family connections with cultural trends and historical events. Leaf through old photo albums with your child and show him family artifacts while pointing out what was going on in the larger society at the time. Do a family tree with your child, noting when and where family members were born and what their occupations were. Also encourage him to talk with his grandparents about their experiences. If you live in an old house, do some research with your child about the house, identifying when it was built, the former owners, and so on. The town historical society is a good starting point.

PROMOTE SENSITIVITY TO ISSUES OF PREJUDICE. Help your child understand at a level appropriate to his age what discrimination is, citing specific examples. Let your child know that discrimination is hurtful and wrong and that expressions of prejudice are unacceptable. Set an example yourself by making sure that your language, jokes, and actions are free of bigotry toward any racial, cultural, or religious group. If your child has been the target of prejudicial comments, help him learn how to respond assertively but not antagonistically. You might role play with your child, giving him some sentences that he can use in response. Also encourage him to talk with the teacher. If he is reluctant and the problem persists, you may need to inform the teacher.

MAKE CURRENT EVENTS A PART OF YOUR FAMILY CONVERSATION. Talk with your spouse and children about events in the news. Watching the television news (preferably the national news, where less attention is paid to violent crime) with your child will further his understanding of current issues and may prompt questions from him. Take his questions seriously and try to answer them to his satisfaction. If your child has a concern or question that you cannot answer, encourage him to write to a government official. He will likely get a response. Encourage discussion of issues. Listen attentively to his views, allowing him to voice his opinions without fear of being criticized or proven wrong. In talking about social issues, help your child see that there are usually two or more sides to an issue so that he comes to appreciate that there is not always a right or wrong answer to a social problem but rather different points of view with different consequences.

FOSTER RESPECT FOR PEOPLE FROM OTHER COUNTRIES AND CULTURES. You can help your child understand the traditions of other countries by taking him to cultural fairs and exhibits as well as ethnic restaurants. These activities can promote a respect for people from other cultures and their diverse customs. Of course, there is no better way of helping children of different backgrounds feel comfortable with each other than by having them socialize together.

MAKE USE OF THE MASS MEDIA. Be on the alert for television shows and movies that are accessible to children and focus on social and historical issues. Also encourage your child to read biographies of famous historical figures. Your library may have a biography shelf in the children's section.

MODEL COMMUNITY INVOLVEMENT. Your involvement in community affairs sets a positive example for your child. There are a myriad of opportunities for community involvement, from participating in the community fair to being on the zoning board to campaigning in an election to coaching a soccer team. Talk with your child about your activities and let him see you in action. Encourage him to become involved in groups appropriate to his age that perform community service (for example, Scouts). When you vote, bring your child with you so that he gets to see democracy in action.

SCIENCE

Children are scientists by nature. They have a seemingly boundless curiosity about the world around them. They are eager to know how things work and why things are as they are. Like other scientists, they observe closely, ask questions, and try to figure out the reasons for what they see. Underlying this quest for knowledge is a basic premise of science: the world can be understood.

The job of a science teacher is not only to promote students' understanding but to nurture their inquisitiveness. While the study of science can be a journey of discovery and excitement, students rarely travel this route in elementary school. The reality is that elementary students receive relatively little science instruction. Indeed, it is the most neglected major subject in elementary school. When science is given, it is typically taught by teachers with minimal science background, little or no guidance from a science supervisor, and a paucity of resources. The teacher will likely rely on a textbook and lectures and expect students to learn largely through rote memorization. When taught in this manner, science may come to be seen as an incoherent patchwork of topics unrelated to real-life experiences. This approach drains science of its excitement and deadens students' curiosity. Some even learn to dread science. Is it any wonder that so many adults are scientifically illiterate and uncomfortable with matters of science?

The content of the science curriculum varies from state to state and even from school district to school district within each state. While there is no typical sequence that elementary schools follow, you can expect that your child will study basic concepts in such areas as human biology, geology, astronomy, life science, energy systems, and physical science. Because your child will delve deeper into some of these topics in middle and high school, it is probably less important at the elementary level that your child receive a good grounding in scientific concepts than it is that he learn to think scientifically and have a positive attitude toward science.

The ideal elementary science program blends hands-on activities and experiments with knowledge imparted by the teacher. Seeing "science in action" helps students grasp how the natural world works, captures their interest, and stimulates their motivation. (A science class conducting an experiment in a Houston school actually uncovered a real problem. In measuring the amount of carbon dioxide in the air, the class found a genuine health hazard.) It also helps them learn to think critically and solve problems. These activities begin as early as kindergarten and should be adapted to the students' thinking ability. Kindergartners, for example, may sort shells according to shape and color to learn to appreciate nature's diversity while sixth-graders may place items of various sizes in a pail of water and observe the results to learn about water displacement. Hands-on activities should be supplemented by teacher explanation, classroom discussion, and related reading assignments, if appropriate.

Hands-on activities need not involve elaborate experiments nor require sophisticated equipment. And the teacher need not have the expertise of Mr. Wizard to conduct the experiments. Indeed, some of the easiest experiments can be some of the most rewarding and educational. For example, classroom experiments with plants can shed light on important concepts of life science. Exposing plants to differing conditions of water, light, and warmth can raise various questions for discussion: Why do plants grow toward the light? Why do some plants droop? What is the purpose of roots? What happens if plants are deprived of water or light? Why do some leaves turn yellow and fall off? These questions can lead to a discussion of what plants need to stay healthy and how plants use sunlight to convert water into food. Teachers may involve students in all aspects of an experiment, including formulating a question to investigate, designing an experiment to answer that question, predicting what will happen, observing and recording the results, perhaps in the form of a graph, and drawing conclusions. This is the essence of the scientific method. When students engage in this process, they are learning to think like real scientists.

How do you know if your child is getting a good science education? You will need to do some research. If your child talks with interest about what he learned in science class and seems eager to learn more, consider this a very encouraging sign. When you visit the school and classroom, look for other signs that science is treated seriously. Do you see exhibits or displays related to science? Are there science-related materials in the classroom—plants, animals, magnets, a magnifying glass, a model of the solar system, a microscope, or collections of objects such as rocks or shells? Is there any equipment for use in conducting science experiments? Are there books or magazines in the classroom on science-related topics?

You might also want to talk with the teacher. Find out what topics are covered, how often science is taught, and whether the lessons incorporate hands-on activities. While the elementary schedule may not allow for a daily class in science, once a week is too little. Science should be a substantial part of your child's elementary curriculum in every grade. Inquire whether classroom teachers attend workshops in science instruction and whether a science supervisor is available to support classroom teachers. You may want to offer some help to the teacher as a way of enhancing the science program, perhaps by arranging a guest speaker, suggesting a field trip, designing a school bulletin board on a science topic, or sponsoring a science club.

You can also stimulate your child's interest in science at home. And you don't need a scientific background or a costly microscope kit to do this. What you need is a healthy respect for your child's curiosity, a willingness to satisfy that curiosity, and a positive attitude about science. Respect the comments your child makes and the questions he asks. Don't dismiss them as silly or foolish or give pat answers. Instead, encourage your child's inquisitiveness by praising the questions and offering a serious response in keeping with his age and degree of interest. If your child shows an interest in a particular area of science, go with it. Take him to the library and find books on the topic. If time allows, you might even find some simple science experiments you can do at home. Your public library will have books on science experiments that you can do with your child (see appendix B, "For Further Information").

Of course, one of the best ways to convey the wonders of science to your child is to take him on trips to such places as a planetarium, science museum (preferably those with hands-on exhibits), zoo, botanical garden, nature center, and aquarium. There are also many opportunities at home to teach your child about science, such as growing a garden, baking a cake, fixing a toaster, making a terrarium, having a pet, observing the changes in the moon, and starting a leaf or rock collection. Stimulate his thinking about the activity by asking questions such as "Why do you suppose a cake rises while it is baking?" Also consider having your child subscribe to a children's science magazine (see appendix C). Many toys are available that have scientific merit, from building blocks to chemistry sets, from magnifying glasses to bug kits. There are also many good child-oriented television programs that can stimulate an interest in science. While there are a myriad of activities you can do with your child if he has a thirst for knowledge about science, do not bombard him with questions, information, and activities if he shows no interest. That will only turn him off to science and stiffen his resistance to future science learning.

Girls can shy away from science just as they do from math. They may be discouraged from pursuing science seriously and may come to view it as a subject more appropriate for boys. These early attitudes have later consequences. Despite the strides women have made in opening up professional doors that were previously closed to them, men continue to dominate the fields of science. While women comprise almost half of the nation's workforce, they make up only about 15 percent of the employed scientists and engineers in this country. These discrepancies reinforce the importance of science teachers being vigilant about not discriminating against their female students. At the same time, parents must monitor the messages they give to their daughters about science, making sure to stress its importance and encourage their interest and effort.

CHAPTER SIX

BEYOND THE BASICS

The educational offerings in most school districts go beyond the core group of subjects discussed in the previous chapter. Elementary schools typically provide students with the following "specials": art, music, physical education, and, in recent years, computers. Middle schools usually offer a somewhat more elaborate array of courses, including foreign language. The amount of instructional time allotted to these special subjects varies from district to district and is a matter of some debate. Some contend that the primary job of public schools is to teach the "basics," namely, reading, writing, and math, relegating special subjects to the status of educational frills—fine to pursue if they fit within the curriculum and budget, but easily discarded if they do not. And this is the course that some school districts are following. Facing the need to reduce their budgets, many boards of education have chosen to cut back or even abolish these programs.

While educators disagree about whether these special subjects are basic components of an educational program, what is beyond debate is that such subjects are fundamental to a well-rounded education. In addition to emphasizing skills that are not learned elsewhere in school, these special subjects enhance children's enjoyment of school and promote their appreciation of the arts. Perhaps most important, children who have difficulty excelling in academic subjects may find an opportunity to achieve success in these nonacademic areas. Abolishing these programs at the elementary level can also have negative consequences in later years. For example, eliminating instrumental music programs in elementary school reduces the prospect of good music programs in middle and high school.

ART

Art comes naturally to children. From the time children are old enough to hold a crayon, they are eager to make their mark as artists. (Unfortunately for many parents, those marks are often on the bedroom wall!) Their eagerness and enthusiasm for art usually continue as they enter school. The job of the art teacher is not simply to teach children about methods and materials of art but also to harness this enthusiasm and liberate their creative instincts.

Art may be taught by your child's regular teacher or by a certified art teacher. A trained art teacher experienced in working with children of different ages is important to the program's success, but so too is the availability of sufficient space, materials, and time for children to do art. Time is often in short supply during the school day and the attention given to art may lessen as students get older and academic subjects are increasingly emphasized. The art instruction they receive will differ from the more academic instruction in that they will be given more freedom to create and express themselves personally. Art classes are typically given once or twice a week and range in length from thirty to fifty minutes. In some states, art is not required in elementary school and thus may not be part of the curriculum in some districts.

While the overriding goal of art education is to lay the foundation for a lifelong enjoyment of art, it accomplishes other objectives as well. In addition to helping children develop artistic skills and the ability to focus their concentration, art instruction aims to foster an appreciation for the creative process. It also provides an opportunity for children to express their feelings. After Hurricane Andrew, art teachers in Florida asked schoolchildren to draw about their experiences as a way of conveying feelings that they could not express verbally.

Art instruction also enhances students' ability to think creatively and independently. When given the freedom to determine which media to work in and what to create, children become more confident in making decisions and tackling problems on their own. An artist, even a young one, is always making decisions and solving problems. Students in art class may grapple with some of the following questions: What colors should I use? Where should I place the objects on the page? What should I emphasize? How much water should I add to the clay? How much glue should I use? How can I attach the handle to my clay mug so it won't fall off? And as they work, they are learning to evaluate their project and revise it to suit their aesthetic preferences. They also learn to work cooperatively with other children. Children doing a group mural on dinosaurs have to decide together on the types of dinosaurs, the background, and the placement.

A goal of any art teacher is to help students feel comfortable expressing themselves through art and confident in their skills and judgments. A student who feels good about her work and develops confidence in her skills will persist and take risks—an important ingredient to creating art. A teacher bolsters confidence by providing a nonthreatening climate where students are encouraged to experiment and explore. She respects their artistic expressions and offers positive expressions of her own about the artwork of all her students. A child who comes away from an art class saying, "I can't draw" or "I stink at painting" may not be getting the support and encouragement she needs and may learn to steer clear of anything connected with art. An important way of reinforcing the students' pride in their work is to have displays of their art around the school. Some schools have art shows featuring the work of the students.

Art is an important part of the kindergarten curriculum. Many believe that art lays the groundwork for learning how to write by developing fine-motor skills. Much of the kindergarten art program involves the creation of art projects. Students often copy the teacher's model, with the result that the projects look very much alike. Art projects can be useful for learning to follow directions as well as specific art tasks such as cutting and pasting or working with clay. This "make-and-take" approach can also be satisfying because it yields an end project that can be brought home. But if this constitutes the bulk of the art program, students may learn to depend on the teacher for direction and inspiration and may come to see art as a process of replication rather than experimentation. Younger students should have a chance to experiment with a variety of materials and minimal guidance. Kindergarten is not the time for specific and detailed art lessons. And the focus should not be on coloring within the lines. This open-ended approach is not only enjoyable for children, it is also instructive. Experimentation leads to discovery, and discovery leads to retention. The child who discovers that mixing blue and yellow paint makes green will never forget her discovery.

As your child moves on to higher grades, she will be exposed to a variety of artistic materials and receive more formal instruction in various skills of art. She may also learn to appreciate art as well as create it. Some art teachers may introduce students to the works of famous artists as well as different styles of art. They may be encouraged to express what they like and dislike about what they see. While the teacher may help students learn to evaluate a work of art and know what to look for, she should also underscore that art appreciation is personal and subjective and that students' artistic preferences are equally valid.

Art teachers are increasingly using art to reinforce concepts and lessons in other subjects and thus deepen understanding. This process of integrating art into the academic curriculum is called discipline-based art education. The art teacher works with the regular classroom teacher to develop projects to complement the themes being studied in the regular class. This approach is used most often with social studies. For example, a second-grade class studying Japan may make flowers out of tissue paper to illustrate the Japanese art of flower arranging. Students studying symmetry in math may gain a firmer grasp of this concept by doing a project in art in which one-half of the project is a mirror image of the other half.

If your child shows an interest in art, you can offer a variety of opportunities to pursue this interest in your home. She will not have the time limitations that she faces in school and may enjoy having a stretch of time to work on a project. Try to set aside an area for art in your home. Consider some of the following materials: paint, crayons, brushes, markers, colored pencils, scissors for children, drawing paper, construction paper, tissue paper, paste, glue, clay, and collage materials (for example, buttons, shells, wallpaper samples, and Styrofoam). Set up the area so your child can work independently and experiment, but also insist that she participate in cleaning up. As she gets older, she may take special pleasure in doing crafts projects (for example, weaving, jewelry, and pottery). Most toy stores offer a wide variety of crafts kits. Show interest in her work and ask her to talk about what she has done but rather than ask "What is it?" say something like, "How did you do this?" or "Tell me about your work."

Praise her efforts but curb your impulse to tell her how to do it better and let her decide when the project is done. Consider framing her best efforts and then find areas of the house to display her art. You might even set aside a wall in your home for her drawings and paintings.

Exposing your child to various kinds of art is the key to enhancing her appreciation. Don't balk at taking your child to an art museum or gallery, but keep the visits short to avoid museum burnout. Elicit her thoughts ("What do you think the title means?") and offer comments of your own, but don't tell her how she should be thinking or feeling. Keep in mind that art is not restricted to museums. It is all around us —on billboards, in commercials, on magazine covers, in the layout of a park, in the design of a building. Point out to your child aspects of art that may have eluded her, perhaps noting how the color, shape, or texture enhances the work. If you are involved in any aspect of art (for example, photography), invite your child to participate or at least observe while you explain what you're doing and what you're trying to achieve.

MUSIC

Music education, like art education, competes for time and resources with academic subjects—and often loses. Many schools view music education as a frill, as an unnecessary part of the curriculum that diverts students from studying basic academic skills. Yet music offers children important and diverse learning experiences. Music education is more than singing songs or playing instruments. It involves learning to enjoy and value music of different kinds. It involves learning about the cultural heritage of different countries from their music. And it involves learning to create and perform music, which can be a source of great pride and esteem to students, especially those who struggle academically.

In the not-so-distant past, many classrooms had pianos, and classroom teachers often made music a part of the everyday routine. Today music instruction is more likely to be provided by a certified music teacher who meets with students once or twice a week. Using such resources as a piano, tape recorder, musical recordings, and basic instruments, the music teacher will pursue goals and activities appropriate to the students' grade level. The overriding goal of music instruction is to help children develop an appreciation for music that will spur them to pursue it in some fashion after they leave the classroom.

Music education begins in kindergarten as students learn to play musical games, move in time with the music, play simple rhythm instruments, and of course sing songs. The teacher may begin to encourage students to react to the music by identifying what they like and dislike. As they move on to higher grades, the teacher will progress to higher-level skills. They may learn about pitch, melody, tempo, harmony, and mood and then try out some of these skills as they are taught to play an instrument such as the recorder. The basics of reading and writing music may be introduced, and they may learn to identify different kinds of music, various types of instruments, and the sounds of those instruments. In short, students will learn to develop musical intelligence.

Around third or fourth grade, your child may be given the opportunity to sign up for instrumental music lessons in school. Encourage your child but don't insist. If she is interested in taking an instrument but is unsure of which one, talk with the music teacher about the different instruments. Also take note of which sounds your child seems to find appealing. Do not rush out to buy an instrument. Rent one, at least initially. You can commit to buying the instrument when you are confident your child is staying with it. Many children switch instruments or give them up altogether during the first year.

Whether or not your child takes lessons in school, you may want to pursue lessons outside school. If so, choose a music teacher with care. A good music teacher can make the difference between an enjoyable experience and an unpleasant one, between your child staying with an instrument and giving it up. Consult with other parents and interview one or more teachers before making a decision. There are different schools of thought about the proper age to begin taking lessons. Be skeptical about rigid age rules. In making a decision, factor in your child's age, maturity, motivation, attention span, and schedule of other activities as well as the demands of the instrument. Some children may be ready at age five or six, others not until age eight or nine. Even if your child starts a year or so later than her peers, she will most likely catch up with time.

You also need to consider your child's willingness to practice. To improve on most instruments, she will need to practice on a regular basis. Treat her practicing much as you do homework by scheduling a regular practice time. If your child strongly resists practicing at all, consider dropping the lessons. She may go back to the instrument at a later time. If she practices only occasionally but still enjoys playing, stay with it in the hopes that she will practice more as she becomes more proficient. Consult with her teacher if you are unsure what to do. What you want to avoid is a daily battle with your child over practicing. You also take on some responsibilities when your child takes lessons: listening to her practice on occasion, praising her efforts, and attending her recitals.

You can nurture your child's interest in music in other ways as well. Very young children love to march to music while playing instruments. A set of instruments, including a triangle, cymbals, bells, drum, and woodblock, can be found in most toy stores, or you can make your own from items in your home. Make music a part of your family experience, whether through singing together, attending concerts, or listening to or watching musical programs. Your child may protest your choice of music, but her early exposure to different kinds of music may eventually lead to her later appreciation and enjoyment. Encourage her to join the school chorus, which is typically open to all who want to join, and the school band or orchestra.

PHYSICAL EDUCATION

Physical education, better known as gym or p.e., generally receives rave reviews from elementary students. For some, it is a chance to release energy they have been storing up during the day. For others, it is a chance to succeed in a way they cannot in the classroom. For still others, it is a chance to simply have fun. And for their teachers, it is a chance to promote their students' physical development, teach them the rules of various games, help them learn to play fairly, and foster their enjoyment of physical activity.

Physical education is generally given once or twice a week in elementary school. While physical education is a vital part of the school program, it is unrealistic to expect that a school will allot more than two periods a week to gym, given the demands on students' time. The class will usually be taught by a certified physical education teacher who may work at more than one elementary school and may also teach related subjects such as fitness, health, and nutrition.

Like other subjects, physical education has changed course in recent years. Gym class has become increasingly democratic, with the focus more on promoting the physical competence, health, and fitness of all students and less on fostering the athletic excellence of the few. The goal is to help students enjoy physical activities and feel confident in their abilities, a particularly important goal to pursue at the elementary level when attitudes are being formed. Toward this end, cooperative activities are often stressed at the expense of competitive activities. Students who shy away from team sports may be offered alternative activities rather than risk the humiliation of failing before their peers. Students who have difficulty climbing rope may be given the option of jumping rope. Even the range of activities has widened. Students in gym may now take nature hikes, do aerobics, or choreograph a dance. This more egalitarian approach is not without its critics, who maintain that the pursuit of excellence in athletics has been relegated to second place.

The physical education program should have a curriculum with specific goals and objectives as well as activities designed with the students' physical and emotional development in mind. Most students in the early elementary grades are not ready for competitive games. They are not old enough to understand the rules of complex games, and the pressures of winning and losing may prove overwhelming to them. The focus at this level should be on developing large-muscle skills (throwing, catching, kicking, jumping, tumbling, etc.), as well as on playing simple noncompetitive games. Some gym teachers may rush young children into competitive games prematurely, causing some to be distressed. If you see signs of this with your child, talk with the teacher. There will be time in later grades to deal with the pressures of competition. At this level, the goals are to help students develop coordination and gain confidence in their physical abilities.

Students in the upper elementary grades, many of whom play competitive team sports, are better able to understand the rules of complex games and withstand the ups and downs of competition. Reflecting these changes, gym will now involve more game playing, although physical skill development still remains a priority. Fitness may get more attention, and the students may learn to do calisthenics.

Physical education should emphasize skill development at every grade level. A gym teacher who has his students playing the same game week in and week out while doing little teaching is doing an injustice to his students. In addition to needing exposure to a variety of games, children require instruction and activities designed to improve their body awareness, eye-hand coordination, agility, stamina, balance, strength, and flexibility. Physical education should also educate beyond the physical. Gym teachers need to help students learn how to be part of a team, cooperate in a group, play fairly, and win and lose gracefully. This is as much a part of physical education as the activity itself.

Children who are clumsy, slow, or overweight often feel self-conscious during gym class. This is especially the case when their performance is on public display or when they are playing a team sport. Being picked last for a team, not being able to do any chin-ups as others watch, or being taunted by classmates for their awkwardness can be real blows to their self-esteem. These experiences can cast a shadow over their school day and dampen their enthusiasm for school. Some children are so upset at the prospect of having their inadequacies showcased before their peers that they resist going to school on gym days. Gym teachers must be especially sensitive to these children, intervening when they learn of ridicule and minimizing the attention drawn to children's physical failings. As discussed above, teachers may balance team activities with individual activities, where there is no risk of disappointing teammates.

Students with coordination problems may be eligible for what is called adaptive physical education. This is individualized physical education for children whose physical deficiencies make it difficult for them to participate in regular gym class. In some school districts, adaptive physical education is only available to students eligible for special education.

Girls are of course just as capable of participating in physical education as boys and should have the same opportunities. While the athletic opportunities available to girls in school have risen dramatically in the past twenty-five years, discrimination against girls still happens in gym or on the athletic field. Yet it is not just unfair to discriminate against girls, it is also illegal. Title IX, a federal law passed in 1972, forbids sex discrimination in school courses or programs. As a result of this law, boys and girls generally take physical education together.

Physical achievements can be a source of great pride and esteem to girls as well as boys, so parents who feel that their daughter is being denied opportunities because of unequal expectations or treatment should contact the school and voice their concerns.

Parents can promote their child's physical development by providing her with resources and opportunities to develop physical skills. The equipment need not be elaborate, but it should be appropriate for the child's age and physical development (for example, a basketball hoop that can be raised and lowered). Encourage your child to play team sports but do not insist. Children who are intimidated by the prospect of playing team sports may be open to more individual physical activities (for example, biking, swimming, and hiking). You may want to suggest activities to your child, but let her make the final decision. Respect her choices and provide encouragement and support. Also keep in mind that you are an important role model for your child: she will be more inclined to engage in physical activity if she sees you doing the same.

COMPUTERS IN THE SCHOOLS

In 1983 *Time* magazine made an unusual choice for its "man" of the year—the computer. Many believe that this announcement sparked the proliferation of computers in public schools in the early 1980s. This was not to be another educational fad that fizzled. Rather, computers have gained a solid foothold on the educational mainland, and it is clear they are here to stay. Today about 95 percent of our public schools have at least one computer. Experts estimate that schools have on average one computer for every twenty students.

This focus on computers is well placed. While computers are not a panacea for the ills of public education, they are powerful teaching tools and vital learning resources. In addition, computers will play a prominent role in the future lives of most children, so it behooves schools to make sure that their students are computer literate. Students who are not conversant with computers may be at a marked disadvantage when pursuing careers or further education.

The computer can enhance academic and cognitive skills through what is called computer-assisted instruction. While the computer cannot supplant a teacher (computers still cannot convey compassion, warmth, or enthusiasm), it features many of the characteristics of individualized instruction: it gives students undivided attention; it can tailor instruction to their skill level, work pace, and learning style; it can teach a skill in sequential steps; it has infinite patience and can repeat a task as often as needed; it is nonthreatening and nonjudgmental; it provides continuous and immediate feedback; it minimizes failure and frustration; it lessens the need for class grouping, which can be stigmatizing to students; and it can measure students' progress.

The computer can be used to help a wide range of students, including the slow learner and the gifted student. Its potential for helping students with learning and physical disabilities is especially promising. Computers can also serve a variety of purposes with schoolchildren. The most common usage is drill and practice, which computers can do very effectively. But if its only use is as an electronic workbook, then the potential of the computer is barely being tapped. Students may also use computers to master a body of information, develop critical thinking skills, perform computer simulations, do research, and learn word processing. Learning how to use the computer as a tool is more important to most students than knowing how to program the computer or understanding its inner workings.

The computer is part of a technology explosion that promises to revitalize public school education. Powerful multimedia technologies have been developed that make earlier computer hardware and software seem primitive by comparison. These technologies, already being used by some school districts, have the potential to give students access to a world of people, ideas, and information in ways that will captivate their attention and increase their breadth and depth of understanding.

The following three technologies provide a glimpse of what may be in store for students in the very near future, if not in the present. The videodisc player is a device that plays two-sided discs that can hold enormous amounts of text, graphics, audio, still images, and video. Teachers can play specific segments of the disc that are suited to their lesson in a sequence of their own choosing. They can even use videodiscs to make their own documentaries by connecting them to a computer and editing them. The CD-ROM drive is a small unit that is attached to a computer and can play discs that store extraordinary amounts of information, including text, graphics, audio, video, and animation. CD-ROM drives, which are relatively inexpensive, can thus merge the power of computers with the potential of multimedia. The modem enables students to communicate with other computer users via the telephone line. As one example, students in rural Tennessee used a computer with a modem to communicate with a student in Bosnia, who gave them firsthand reports on the experiences of war. Even parents and teachers may benefit from technological advances. In some school districts, teachers bring home laptop computers and plug into the district's computer network. In several southeastern states, Bellsouth, the telephone company, offers voice-messaging services that help parents stay in touch with their children's schools.

The key to realizing the promise of computers and related technologies in education is to make sure that teachers are adequately trained and continually updated. If they are not competent in and comfortable with the use of computers, then students' exposure to computers may be limited to drill and practice programs and computer games. The unfortunate reality is that most teachers have had little if any training in the use of computers. A recent study indicated that only about one-third of public school teachers have had ten hours or more of computer training. The implication of this study is that most teachers have little idea how to integrate computers into their curriculum. This must change if the potential of computers is to be fully realized.

Precisely because schools have been slow to take full advantage of the educational benefits of computers, parents can play an important role in prodding schools in this direction. The school district may have a committee on technology. If so, request that a parent, preferably one with technical expertise, be a member. If not, contact the person in the district responsible for computer technology and let him know of your interest in learning how the district is using computers. You will want to know much more than simply the ratio of computers to students, although this information is important. (A desirable ratio, according to some experts, is one computer for every seven students.) You will also want to ask the following:

- Is there a school official or committee responsible for computer technology? Is this person or committee informed about new developments in computers and related technologies?
- What is the school technology budget?

- What training do teachers receive in using computers to enhance instruction? Are teachers updated about new developments?
- Are all students given an opportunity to use computers?
- Are the school's computers sophisticated enough to use with other technologies (for example, the CD-ROM)? Do they have sufficient memory for using advanced educational software?
- For what purposes are the computers used?
- Are there computers in regular classrooms that can be used to enhance skills and understanding in those subjects?
- Is the use of computers lessening the district's commitment to the teaching of writing mechanics, spelling, and math facts?
- Do students have the opportunity to learn keyboarding and word processing?
- Does the school have a variety of educationally beneficial software and not just drill and practice programs or computer games? Is the software compatible with the curriculum?
- Is the school district adequately preparing students for the technological requirements of the workplace?

Having a computer at home is not essential for your child to succeed in school. But it can certainly help. Even if your child does not use it for educational purposes (and many do not), she will benefit by becoming more comfortable and confident in using a computer, in short by becoming computer literate. If you decide to buy a computer for your child, consider one identical to or compatible with the one she uses in school. Your child will adapt more quickly to the home computer if she has used a similar model in school. As an added benefit, she may be able to give you some computer lessons. You may hesitate to buy a computer because you fear that it will quickly become outdated. In these times of rapid-fire technological change, this is always a possibility but remember that outdated does not mean obsolete.

If you buy a computer, make sure that your child eventually learns word processing. Children as young as seven may learn to use a basic word processing program; Bank Street Writer is especially good for young children. As they get older, they may begin to do school assignments and papers on the computer. (Make sure your child checks with her teacher, who may prefer that assignments be handwritten.) Word processing is an increasingly important skill for students to learn and offers many advantages: students find it less tedious than writing by hand and are better able to focus on content; they are not frustrated by problems of handwriting; they can edit their papers easily without the need for retyping; and they have a neat, legible document at the end. Many word processing programs have spelling and grammar checks built into them.

TEACHING CHILDREN TO THINK

The back-to-basics movement of the 1970s focused on mastery of the three "R's" but in recent years teachers have expanded their coverage to include a fourth "R": reasoning. The attention given to higher-order thinking skills has been spurred by test scores and other evidence suggesting that the reasoning skills of American students have declined. Explanations for this decline vary, but most point to the movement to emphasize basic academic skills. Schools adopting this approach stressed the teaching of skills that were measured by standardized tests and gave little attention to teaching students to think critically about what they were learning. Others have looked to children's preoccupation with television and the reduction of reading for pleasure to help explain this decline in reasoning abilities. Whatever the reasons, this embrace of higher-order thinking skills has had a wide-ranging impact on education—from curriculum content to teaching approaches to testing methods. Even the Scholastic Achievement Test has been redesigned to include more reasoning-based tasks.

To think critically is to look beneath the surface of an issue and to go beyond the information given. A child who thinks critically does not passively receive information but rather actively assesses its merits and implications. Critical thinking includes the following skills:
- evaluating validity
- identifying basic assumptions
- distinguishing relevant from irrelevant information
- understanding cause and effect
- detecting fallacies or inconsistencies
- drawing conclusions
- anticipating consequences
- generalizing to other situations
- developing novel ideas supported by logic or evidence

Critical thinking is an essential tool not only for academic success but for everyday living. Children who can think critically have the ability to analyze problems, generate possible solutions, evaluate their merits, and anticipate consequences. They can employ these skills in school, on the playing field, in social situations, and on the job. Indeed, these problem-solving skills are the key to dealing with the variety of temptations and perils facing children today. The goal then of teaching children to think critically is to help them become better decision makers and problem solvers.

Fortunately critical thinking skills can be taught. Indeed, experts tell us that these skills will not develop to their fullest without instruction, coaching, and practice. This does not mean, however, that your child should be given a course in reasoning. For learning to think is not so much a separate subject as a way of approaching the learning of all subjects. Critical thinking is thus best taught not as an isolated skill but rather in the context of traditional subjects and real-life problems. Thinking skills should be integrated—infused is the educational term—into the curriculum of various subjects. Knowledge and skill building remain important, but students need to develop a deeper understanding of the subject matter, making connections between what they learn and their own lives, between the past and the present, between principles and their applications.

Many commercial programs to teach critical thinking skills are in use across the country. But a teacher need not use a formal program to teach these skills. Indeed, many teachers promote these skills quite naturally through their teaching methods. A teacher fosters critical thinking skills when she poses questions designed to provoke thought and discussion, when she lets the class grapple with these questions rather than providing an answer immediately, when she gives assignments that demand drawing conclusions and making inferences, and when she gives tests that require more than short answers. While these teaching methods come naturally to some teachers, they do not to others. Many teachers require training to learn how to integrate higher-order thinking skills into their classroom instruction.

Teachers also promote thinking skills when they require students to write. The act of writing forces students to wrestle with ideas and clarify their thinking about a topic. As George Orwell said in his book

1984: "If people cannot write well, they cannot think well, and if they cannot think well, others will do their thinking for them."

Critical thinking skills are also learned effectively in the context of real-life, everyday problems. A teacher may present actual problems for students to grapple with or work with problems brought to her by the students. She may give students responsibility for solving a problem while guiding them through the problem-solving process. For example, if some students are upset because they are being picked on by older students on the playground, the teacher may help the students analyze the situation, generate possible solutions, choose the best solution, and implement it.

Parents can evaluate whether critical thinking skills are a part of the teacher's instructional approach by taking a look at their child's schoolwork. Look for evidence of assignments and tests that require thought and application of information. If your child uses textbooks, leaf through them to see if attention is paid to underlying issues and concepts and not just facts and figures. And if your schedule allows, consider going into the classroom to observe a lesson. When you meet with the teacher to review your child's overall progress, make sure to ask about critical thinking skills. You might ask the following about your child: Does she understand underlying concepts easily? How well does she make inferences from what she has read or heard? Is she able to apply what she has learned?

Parents can hone their children's thinking and problem-solving skills in their normal interactions with them. How you talk with your child and what you say convey important concepts. For example, your use of proper tenses teaches your child about sequence, your use of "if . . . then" statements provides a lesson in cause and effect, and your use of questions helps your child learn what is important and relevant. Encourage your child to be intellectually curious and to think on her own. Be respectful of her ideas, opinions, and questions. Rather than telling her that she is too young to understand something, try to explain it at an appropriate level for her. When she makes a statement that is not well thought out, you might gently challenge the statement by asking how she knows that to be true. Occasionally pose questions to your child designed to make her consider things she may not have thought about. Rather than asking yes or no questions or questions that begin with "who," "when," or "where," ask questions that begin with "Why do you suppose . . . ?" At the same time, don't bombard your child with questions or she will feel as if she is being grilled. As she gets older, discuss current events with her and help her to see differing perspectives on issues.

Use your child's experiences to further develop her problem-solving skills. For example, your child may not be sure whether to pursue dancing or play soccer, or she may be uncertain about how to deal with a child who is teasing her. Allow her to struggle with these and other problems and show confidence in her ability to solve them by not intervening too readily. If she gets stuck or seeks your assistance, help her think through the problem by analyzing the situation, evaluating the possible solutions, and then having her choose the solution that she believes will work best. Of course, there may be some matters, principally those related to safety, where you will want to assume responsibility for resolving the problem.

Parents and teachers can receive training from the Great Books Foundation to promote higher-order thinking skills. This organization teaches adults to lead discussion groups about literary classics with children from second grade through high school. They learn to stimulate students' thinking by asking probing questions and challenging them to support their opinions with evidence from the books. You can receive more information about how to start a Great Books program in your district and receive training by writing to the Great Books Foundation, 35 E. Wacker Drive, Suite 2300, Chicago, IL 60611-2298.

THE TEACHING OF VALUES

The process of instilling values in children begins at an early age. By the time children enter kindergarten, they have already taken a course in values, one taught by their parents. This is only appropriate, for parents should assume primary responsibility for shaping the values of their children. They should be their moral anchors.

Yet parents are not the only adults who influence children's values. A coach may convey to children the value of determination and teamwork. A Scout leader may teach about self-reliance and honesty. And a minister or rabbi may help children learn about spiritual values. But for many children the most important influence on their emerging value system other than their parents is their teacher. This is not surprising when you consider that a child may spend as much time during the school year with her elementary teacher as she does with her parents.

Some parents want teachers to check their values at the door when they enter the classroom. In reality, there is no such thing as value-free education. Teachers are communicating values to their students almost all the time. And values are embedded in more than just the teacher's lessons or the teaching materials. The teacher's appearance, speech, manner of relating with students, sense of humor—all teach lessons to students about ways of acting, thinking, and feeling. A teacher who shows an interest in the culture of a child from another country is teaching her students to respect children from different backgrounds. A teacher who encourages a child to handle a problem on her own is promoting the value of independent thinking. The values the teacher communicates to her students constitute the hidden curriculum in the classroom. These lessons may not be evident in the course descriptions or the curriculum guides but they are nonetheless an important part of your child's education.

That teachers convey values to their students is not necessarily cause for concern, unless the values being taught are objectionable or being taught poorly. Indeed, many believe that values education is an appropriate role for teachers. Martin Luther King, Jr., had this in mind when he said, "Intelligence plus character—that is the goal of true education." The Association for Supervision and Curriculum, an educational organization, contends that "schools have an obligation to teach values to students." Given that teachers are communicating values almost all the time, the question of whether schools should teach values is beyond debate. The more important question is: What values should be taught and how should they be communicated?

These are not new questions in education. Just as teachers through the centuries have wrestled with the question of what academic topics to teach, so too they have struggled with whether to teach values and, if so, which ones. John Dewey, a prominent educational philosopher who greatly influenced American education, argued that schools have an obligation to instill values in their students. Various efforts at values education have been tried. For example, the McGuffey Readers, which you may have used as a child, had stories with direct moral messages.

In the late 1960s and early 1970s, values education took the form of what was called values clarification. Programs were developed to help students clarify their own values and beliefs and learn to make choices. Students were given exercises in ethical thinking and asked to reflect on the values they deemed important. But this approach drew criticism for suggesting that all value judgments were of equal importance and that right and wrong was a matter of personal preference. Many felt that these programs undermined parental authority. Moreover, the exercises that students were asked to do were often simplistic and detached from everyday experiences.

Values clarification programs are less in vogue today, but values education is still an important part of the school landscape. Indeed, with the large number of children living in families stressed by social problems and fragmentation, many have looked to the schools to provide children with a value-based frame of reference to guide them in leading their lives. Values education begins as early as kindergarten when children are taught, among other lessons, to wait patiently in line, to raise their hand rather than yell out, to be considerate of their classmates, and to be accepting of children who are different. These values and others continue to be reinforced as children move through school. Different teachers accent different values. Some emphasize being courteous and kind to classmates; others stress being obedient and respectful of authority; others place a priority on being dependable and responsible; and still others convey the importance of thinking for yourself and standing up for your beliefs. Some school districts employ formal programs to teach peaceful methods of resolving conflicts.

Just as with teaching children to think, teaching values to children is often done in the context of traditional subjects and real-life issues. At the elementary level, teachers use the class and school as the basis for teaching children about such matters as courtesy, respect for property, compassion, fairness, sportsmanship, resistance to group pressures, and acceptance of children who are different. As students move into higher grades, these same issues may be discussed but in the context of the larger community and at a more conceptual level. Social studies provides a natural opportunity for examining these issues. Students gain valuable insights by reading about great figures in history and learning how they coped with moral issues.

It is one thing to teach core values relating to standards of behavior —matters about which most parents agree. It is quite another to teach about deeper moral values. Teaching about morality is a delicate task because moral issues do not lend themselves to consensus. Parents will have differing views about virtually any moral issue, so that teaching about morality risks offending some parents. This does not mean, however, that schools should sidestep issues of morality or steer clear of controversial subjects. Students should not learn in a moral vacuum. Sensitive issues such as the Holocaust or AIDS and controversial topics such as gun control or homelessness should be discussed, although schools must weigh the students' age and maturity level in deciding when and how to raise these issues. When discussing controversial issues, the teacher's role is to provide information, raise questions, and stimulate discussion while making sure not to project her personal views. The goal is to expose students to differing points of view rather than to indoctrinate them in one point of view.

What public schools cannot do is promote religion in any way. To do so is a clear violation of the constitutional principle of the separation of church and state, as decided by the United States Supreme Court in 1963. The Supreme Court ruled that schools may not read excerpts from the Bible or conduct prayers even if the prayers are nondenominational and participation is voluntary. While efforts to legalize official prayers in the public schools have been unsuccessful, some states have enacted a minute of silence during which students are allowed to pray or meditate. These laws have been upheld as legal as long as they are not found to have a religious purpose. While schools are thus barred from promoting religion, they are permitted to teach about religion. Parents who wish their children to receive education in the tenets of a particular religion can either have their children attend parochial school or religious classes outside of public school.

If there is one area that calls out for parents to assume the role of primary teacher, it is sex education. Yet many parents shirk this responsibility and schools have been called upon to fill this void by teaching about such topics as sexual reproduction, pregnancy, contraception, sexually transmitted diseases including AIDS, dating, emotional commitment, and personal responsibility. Schools have not always responded to this call. They too have shied away from educating children in matters of sexuality, perhaps because of fears of dealing with parent reactions. Only a minority of states mandate sex education in schools, and as a result many children do not receive sex education either in school or at home. Yet, as the alarming rate of teenage pregnancy and the AIDS epidemic make poignantly clear, sex education is more needed today than it has ever been. And sex education seems to work. Studies indicate that adolescent girls who are given candid information about human sexuality are far less likely to become pregnant accidentally.

School districts that provide sex education often make it part of the health program. It is typically called family life education or family living. The quality of these programs varies dramatically. A good sex education teacher is well-informed and comfortable teaching the subject, covers a variety of topics including both the physical and emotional aspects of sexuality, and gears the method and content of instruction to the age and maturity level of the students. You should be able to find out the content of the sex education program in your district, grade by grade, by contacting the school principal or the teacher. Many states give parents the right to remove their child from the sex education program if they are opposed to its contents. If you are considering removing your child from the program, also consider her possible awkwardness if she is the only student not participating. Whether your child receives sexual education in school or not, take your role seriously in teaching your child about sexual matters. Listen to her concerns and respond candidly. Research shows that children who have discussed sexual matters with their parents are less likely to engage in sexual activity at an early age.

The values education your child receives in school will help to shape the kind of person she becomes, so pay careful attention to the kinds of messages your child is receiving. Review the work your child brings home—textbooks, work sheets, homework assignments—but also talk with her to find out what is being discussed in class. If you have reason for concern, consider going into school to observe a lesson or set up a meeting with the teacher.

Of course, the surest way of instilling desirable values in your child is to teach them to her at home. Yet many parents feel as if their own efforts at values education are stymied by the competing forces of television, peers, and the mass media. While it is undeniable that children are affected by these factors, parents can nonetheless have a profound impact on their child's values and moral reasoning. To maximize your influence on your child, reflect on the kinds of values you cherish and want to communicate to her. Consider what you are doing to communicate these values to your child, but be aware that what will influence her most is not what you say but what you do. It is the everyday actions of parents that speak most loudly to children. And children are expert at noting inconsistencies between a parent's actions and words—the parent who is often rude to people but lectures her child about treating others with respect, the parent who stresses honesty but keeps excess change given to her by a salesperson, or the parent who preaches the virtues of forgiveness but holds a long-term grudge against a family member.

CHAPTER SEVEN

THE HOME FRONT

The foundation for your child's attitude toward school is laid at home. It is here, guided by your words and deeds, that your child's values start to take shape and his sense of what is important begins to evolve. If your child is like most, he has a keen eye for what you do and a sharp ear for what you say. With time, he will absorb your views about school and your standards regarding education. He will eventually internalize these values, carrying them with him when he goes to school, when he tackles a challenging assignment, and when he chooses how to spend his leisure time.

You can convey to your child your commitment to education in a myriad of ways. You speak loud and clear about what you deem important when you insist that homework take priority over television, when you emphasize good school attendance, when you diligently attend parent-teacher conferences, and when you monitor homework. You nurture his interest in learning when you show an interest in his schoolwork, when you help him see the relevance of the teacher's instruction, when you take advantage of "teachable moments," and when you expose him to a variety of learning opportunities outside of school. And you help him become a confident learner when you praise and highlight his accomplishments, find opportunities for him to demonstrate his competence, listen attentively to what he says, and avoid dwelling on and criticizing him for his academic failings. This chapter helps parents build a solid educational foundation by focusing on the home front. We begin with that most troublesome of issues: homework.

THE HOMEWORK WARS

"It's not my fault," grumbled nine-year-old Peter. "My teacher didn't write the assignment on the board." His mother wasn't buying it. After all, she had heard that excuse before—and many others from her son's vast repertoire. So had Peter's teacher, who had called earlier in the day to say that Peter wasn't turning in homework. His mother assured the teacher that she and her husband would talk with Peter. The evening scene was painfully familiar. Peter's parents lectured and pleaded, he responded with a litany of excuses, and a screaming match ensued.

Homework is an emotional battleground in many households. Indeed, homework is among the most frequent sources of tension between parents and children. Peter is like many other children for whom homework is something to be avoided, forgotten, or raced through. His parents share much in common with other parents who recognize the value of homework but are uncertain of their role in ensuring its completion. This ambivalence mirrors a central issue of parenting: maintaining a balance between providing supervision and encouraging independence.

Homework brings this issue into sharp focus. Parents are eager for their children to succeed in school and know the importance of homework to academic success. At the same time, they are advised by educators that homework is the child's job. Stay out of it, they are told. As parents of first-graders quickly discover, it is not that simple. Parents soon find themselves caught up in a delicate balancing act. If they are too involved in homework, they may foster dependency with a younger child or elicit rebellion from an older child. If they are uninvolved with homework, they may not become aware of academic problems with their child or his failure to complete homework until the parent-teacher conference. This section will help parents walk this fine line, overseeing their child's schoolwork while at the same time encouraging independence and responsibility.

The Value of Homework

Homework practices reflect societal trends. In the 1960s, following the flight of Sputnik, homework requirements increased as Americans felt pressure to keep pace with the Russians. Teachers eased homework demands during the 1970s due to concern by educators and parents about the impact of homework on children's mental health and recreational activities.

Then the pendulum swung back during the more conservative 1980s. National commissions were established out of concern for the quality of public school education. The National Task Force on Education for Economic Growth concluded in its 1983 publication, *Action for Excellence,* that "states and local school districts should establish firm, explicit, and demanding requirements concerning homework." The National Commission on Excellence in Education went one step further in its 1983 report, *A Nation at Risk,* by recommending more homework for high school students. A recent Gallup poll indicated that many parents agree: nearly 50 percent want more homework for their children.

As educators and parents look to *increasing* homework as one remedy for the perceived ills of public education, the question "What is the value of homework?" takes on special importance. Homework, when properly designed, reinforces academic skills and expands students' understanding by encouraging creative use of what they have learned in school. In addition, homework teaches children to be independent learners who can budget their time and study effectively on their own. In effect, homework is a no-cost way of extending the school day beyond six hours. Adults also benefit from homework: teachers find out if their lessons are effective and which students need further help while parents learn what their child is studying and how he is doing. Homework thus serves as an important connecting link between home and school.

Research supports the value of homework. The US Department of Education reviewed studies on homework effectiveness and concluded in its 1986 publication *What Works* that "student achievement rises significantly when teachers regularly assign homework and students conscientiously do it." The research indicated that homework benefited students of all levels of ability. For example, one study found that students of low ability who did one to three hours of homework per week received comparable grades to students of average ability who did no homework. Similarly, average-ability students who did three to five hours of homework per week attained grades comparable to those of high-ability students who did no homework.

In short, spending more time on homework usually leads to better grades.

More homework does not always lead to more learning, however. The content of the assignment and teacher response are crucial. Studies suggest that students benefit most when homework is carefully tailored to their level of understanding, when its purpose is clear and directions are carefully explained, and when it is reviewed promptly and feedback is given by the teacher. Also, students who perform poorly on homework should have the chance to review the assignment with the teacher.

Homework without feedback is of little value. Feedback is most helpful when it goes beyond the recording of right and wrong answers by providing personalized comments designed to help students understand specifically where they made mistakes and how they can remedy them. These comments should also highlight what the student has done well. Large classes, of course, make it more difficult to individualize assignments and provide personalized feedback.

Students learn little from busywork—dull, repetetive exercises that bore more than they benefit. This is especially true in math. Completing page after page of the same type of multiplication problem teaches little to the able student. The less able student, who needs the review most, may give up in frustration or spend time practicing mistakes. Practice exercises work best when they are carefully matched to the level of the student and gradually increase in complexity. A few carefully selected problems can be as instructive as many pages' worth.

How Much Homework Is Appropriate?

The amount of homework your child receives will depend on his age, the philosophy of the school, and the policy of the teacher. Schools may have explicit guidelines about the amount of homework to be assigned. Some schools, usually those with many low achievers, may set a minimum amount of homework time while other schools, typically those with considerable academic pressures, may set a maximum amount of homework time.

A commonly used rule of thumb is that elementary students should receive about ten minutes of homework for each grade. For example, children in first grade should receive ten minutes of homework, second-graders twenty minutes, and so on. While this guideline is a rough estimate of what children should receive, it may not apply to your child. Children, like adults, have different work rates, and some may need more time to complete an assignment.

If you have concerns about the amount of time your child is spending on homework, observe his work habits, noting whether he organizes his time well and is on task most of the time. If not, offer some tips to help him organize himself better. Also, check with other parents to see if your child's classmates are running into the same problem. Then confer with the teacher. The teacher can estimate how long assignments should take (but keep in mind that studies show that teachers often underestimate). If the level of work is appropriate but your child is a very slow worker, the teacher may agree to shorten assignments—for example, allowing him to do every other problem. If the work is well above or below the level of your child, the teacher may be willing to give him an assignment more suitable to his ability.

Back-to-school night, when parents visit with their child's teacher, is a good time to find out about the teacher's homework policy, including the homework schedule, how long typical assignments should take, how you will know if your child is not turning in homework, what to do about homework if your child is ill, and parent responsibilities. When you return home, review with your child the teacher's homework rules and let him know you expect him to follow them.

Parents can help chart a school's homework policies as part of a school committee. They may tackle some of the following issues: How much homework should be assigned in each grade? Should there be a minimum or maximum amount? Should it be given on weekends? Should homework be graded? What role should parents play? What action should the school or teacher take with students who consistently fail to turn in homework?

The Parent as Coach

After the third reminder, Jessica finally sits down at the kitchen table to answer chapter-end questions from her social studies text. Fifteen minutes later, the only marks on her paper are doodles. "I don't understand this," she whines. Her father is quick to the rescue. Eager to relieve her distress, he dictates the answers to Jessica.

The temptation to rescue a frustrated child from a difficult assignment can be hard for parents to resist. But parents need to fight off this impulse. If you consistently give your child answers or complete his assignment, he may learn less from the homework than from your response. The lesson learned by your child is that he lacks competence to complete assignments on his own. He learns to distrust his own abilities and rely on others. Self-confidence wanes and dependency grows. In addition, overly helpful parents may give the teacher a false picture of their child's strengths and weaknesses. As a result, the teacher may not provide the appropriate help.

Does this mean that you are to be uninvolved in your child's homework? Not at all. Supervising his homework is an important way of promoting his school success. But supervising does not mean working side by side with your child. First and foremost, impress upon him the importance of homework. Let him know that school assignments take priority over other activities and that their completion is nonnegotiable. If an unavoidable obligation prevents completion of an assignment, let your child know that it must be completed the next night.

Think of yourself as a consultant or resource person to your child. Be available to help if he asks, but do not impose your help or your way of doing something (especially in math, where alternate methods can cause confusion). You might say the following to your child in explaining your homework policy: "Doing homework is your job. I'm available to help if you run into a problem or if you need me to check something, but you need to do as much as you can on your own."

Helping your child does not always require an understanding of the assignment or the subject. You can provide assistance by helping him get organized, clarifying directions, reviewing with him for a test, suggesting where information can be found, drilling math facts, or checking completed work. Look for opportunities to praise his performance and bolster his confidence. If your child rejects your offer of help, leave him alone. Do not insist, do not badger, do not bombard your child with questions about homework.

When it comes to long-term assignments, parents often exchange their consultant's hat for that of project manager. A walk through a typical school science fair will provide convincing evidence of parental overinvolvement. Sophisticated projects beyond the ability of children to execute or understand stand side by side with much less sophisticated projects obviously done by children. The intense involvement of parents in their child's project may win their child a ribbon but may rob his confidence. Children gain a sense of mastery when they complete a project on their own. They gain a greater feeling of accomplishment from an imperfect project that bears their signature than a flawless project that bears the imprint of their parents. The role of parents is to help translate their child's ideas into a doable project by making suggestions and asking questions designed to make them think. The execution, namely the research, the gathering of materials, the assembly, and the written work should be done mostly by the child. If your child is like most, he is prone to procrastination and may only begin the project with a few days remaining. You can help your child avoid "project panic" by encouraging him early on to set up a realistic schedule for the project and then tackle it in stages.

Handling Homework Resistance

Jason is very motivated when it comes to schoolwork—motivated to avoid it, that is. He will do almost anything to escape doing what he calls the "h" word. His favorite ploy was to "forget" to bring home his books—until his parents solved that with a "no books, no television" rule. But the problem persists. He dawdles until it's almost bedtime and then gets out his books. Sometimes he finishes; mostly he succumbs to frustration and fatigue and completes only part of the work.

Jason, like Peter, is a homework resister. They are by no means alone; many students join the resistance yearly. Some join because they find homework tedious and unchallenging; others find it difficult and discouraging. Some are lured by more enjoyable activities (the television and telephone are the two leading culprits). Still others derive adult attention from their resistant posture or express anger indirectly at their parents or teacher through their failure to do homework. Usually it's a combination of reasons.

While parenting a homework resister is often exasperating, it is by no means hopeless. First, address the basics (see "Homework Helpers for Parents," below). Make sure you have impressed upon your child the importance of homework and communicated a "homework comes first" policy. Avoid lecturing, screaming, or threatening your child. He may react to this approach by digging in his heels and not budging. Rather brainstorm with him to try to find the cause of the problem: Does he understand what to do? Does he have the materials he needs? Is the work too difficult? Is he distressed about something and unable to concentrate? Does he have problems studying and organizing himself?

If your child is having consistent difficulty in understanding the homework, schedule a conference with the teacher. Find out whether the teacher is also observing problems and whether she believes tutoring or an evaluation for special education is warranted. If the teacher is unwilling to recommend an evaluation despite your concerns about a possible learning disability, you can make a written request for an evaluation to the principal (see chapter 9).

If you conclude that your homework-resisting child understands the assignments, let him experience the consequences of shirking at school, be they detention, loss of recess, or poor grades. At the same time, consider developing a monitoring system. Talk with the teacher and arrange for your child to bring home an assignment sheet daily noting new assignments—both short- and long-term. Your child's job is to record the assignments and then get the sheet signed at the end of the day by his teacher, who verifies its accuracy. Your child then brings the sheet home for you to review and sign, and then returns it to school the following day to begin anew. Your job is to insist that your child complete this form daily and bring it home. You and the teacher can also use the form to write notes to each other. This system—or a similar plan of your own design—lets you monitor your child's assignments, lets the teacher know you are involved, and lets your child know that you will be checking to make sure that all homework is done.

You may want to use this assignment sheet to keep track of your child's progress and to provide incentives for improved performance. Stars and stickers are especially appealing to young children. You might reward your child for attaining a specified number of stars or stickers with a special privilege or family activity (for example, a visit to your child's favorite restaurant). With time and steady progress, you can gradually phase out the incentives.

School problems, whether with homework or academic performance, sometimes give rise to an intense parent-child battle. If you find that you are unable to unlock from this power struggle and school nights are marked by frequent confrontation and conflict, consult a family counselor.

Homework Helpers for Parents

There is no magic formula for ensuring responsible homework completion. What works for one child may not work for another. If you find an approach is not effective with your child, try another. But keep in mind that homework is your child's job, not yours. After all, you have already passed second grade. Some of the following suggestions may be helpful.

ADAPT YOUR APPROACH TO YOUR CHILD'S AGE. As a general rule, parents should be more involved with homework with younger children. For example, during first, second, and third grades, you may want to help your child start the assignment and review the completed work. By fourth grade, however, a little prodding to get going and an occasional offer of assistance should be all that's necessary. As your child gets older, expect him to handle most of the homework-related issues, such as arranging his homework schedule, discussing instructions with the teacher, or calling friends for assignments.

PROVIDE A HOME SETTING CONDUCIVE TO STUDY. Most children work better in a quiet, well-lit setting free of distraction and family traffic, although some study effectively with background music. This may be at a desk in your child's bedroom but it may also be at the kitchen table or while your child is sprawled on the living room floor. Where he does his homework is less important than how he does it. If he is completing homework conscientiously and correctly, don't make an issue of the location—or his method of study. Provide your child with sufficient writing area and storage space as well as needed materials, including pencils, paper, a scissors, a ruler, a dictionary, and an assignment pad. A thesaurus, atlas, and encyclopedia may also be helpful for older students. Keep a supply of index cards handy for projects.

DEVELOP A HOMEWORK ROUTINE EARLY IN THE YEAR. Talk with your child and agree upon a set homework time. Try to stick to the schedule. Some children can complete homework right after school, others need time to unwind. Some are better off doing homework in two or three blocks of time. Avoid scheduling homework right before bedtime; homework often takes more time than children expect, and children will not be so alert. Encourage your child to do his toughest subjects during his prime time. Get in the habit of marking long-term assignments on a calendar—or better yet, have your child do it.

ENFORCE A "HOMEWORK BEFORE TELEVISION" POLICY. While your child may insist he can do homework with the television on, permitting this sends a message to your child about how much you value homework. Establish a rule that homework be finished before the TV is switched on. Allowing a child to watch television as soon as the homework is completed, however, may tempt some children to race through homework to get to their favorite program. If you run into this problem, designate a quiet time each evening when the television is off and your child is to do homework or, if homework is completed, engage in other quiet activities. This should apply to parents as well. Children will find it difficult to give their full attention to homework if parents or siblings are watching television or playing a game nearby.

HELP IF ASKED, BUT DON'T DO IT FOR HIM. Do not force your child to work with you; parent insistence usually leads to child resistance. Let your child know that you consider homework his responsibility but that you are willing to help if asked. Be available to help during homework time and check in with your child every so often. When working with him, try to provide clues or pose leading questions rather than simply supplying the answers. Or demonstrate how to solve one problem and then have your child do the next one while you watch.

BE POSITIVE AND SUCCESS-ORIENTED. The job description of a homework-helping parent should place a premium on boosting the child's confidence so that he is more willing to tackle assignments independently. Begin with relatively easy problems to generate confidence and understanding and gradually move to harder problems that are still within his ability. Compliment your child on his efforts and successes and avoid negative or disparaging comments. Criticism is usually harder for your child to accept from you than from his teacher. Monitor your own reactions: if you find yourself feeling frustrated, impatient, or irritable—as all homework-helping parents occasionally do—you are probably conveying this to your child and it is time for you to stop. Encourage him to continue on his own. In general, you will be more successful if you work with your child at a time when neither of you is too tired or pressured. And be careful about overloading your child.

REINFORCE YOUR CHILD'S HOMEWORK THROUGH FAMILY DISCUSSIONS AND ACTIVITIES. Showing your child how an academic skill relates to real-life activities (for example, having your child use his division skills to help you figure out your car's miles per gallon) will enhance understanding and retention as well as stimulate interest in classroom learning. Also, consider scheduling trips to places of interest to coincide with topics being studied.

CONTACT THE TEACHER IF NECESSARY. As a rough guide, if your child is getting more than 25 percent of the problems or items wrong, the assignment may be too hard to be of optimal educational value. If your child is having persistent problems in understanding homework, is taking much longer than you think is necessary, or claims he never has any homework, confer with the teacher. You cannot always count on teachers, especially at the secondary level, to contact you if your child is not turning in homework. This discussion with the teacher may prompt some changes in teaching style, educational program, or homework assignments for your child. If your child's teacher assigns no homework, you may want to request some. Whatever the outcome, always avoid criticizing the teacher in your child's presence.

WORK AROUND YOUR CHILD'S LEARNING STYLE. Take note of your child's homework habits and be creative in problem solving. If he is easily distracted and inattentive, build study breaks into his homework routine. Consider using a timer so that he works for twenty minutes, takes a break (also timed), and then returns to work. Some students who are easily distracted are able to block out noise by wearing earplugs or headphones. Students who struggle in understanding directions may benefit from reading directions aloud or having them read or restated to them. If your child frustrates easily, help him take the assignment step by step by breaking it up into smaller, more doable parts. Or you might suggest your child switch from a difficult subject to an easier one and then return to the difficult subject later. Budgeting time is another potential pitfall. Some children need help in estimating how long assignments will take and allocating sufficient time.

DEVELOP WAYS TO MONITOR HOMEWORK EVEN IF YOU CAN'T BE THERE. Children with evening activities may need to do homework after school. If you are not available after school to ensure that homework is done, you might phone home at the beginning of the prearranged homework period or set an alarm to go off at the time your child should begin. Schedule a time to go over what your child completed earlier.

IN A JOINT CUSTODY ARRANGEMENT, DEVELOP SIMILAR HOMEWORK PROCEDURES IN BOTH HOUSEHOLDS. While it is not essential that the routine be the same, it will lessen your child's confusion and help foster consistent work habits. It is also important that the two parents inform each other of key school information. Ideally, they should share information directly. If this is not viable, they might communicate via a notebook that goes between both households as well as between home and school.

LOOK INTO STARTING A HOMEWORK HOTLINE. Some school districts or parent groups offer telephone assistance from teachers for students having trouble with their homework (and for frustrated parents). The teachers will not provide your child with the answer as much as help him work through the problem. Some districts provide homework assistance programs in the public library while others are experimenting with television to help students with homework problems. Propose a homework hotline (sometimes called a Dial-A-Teacher program) to your board of education if one does not currently exist. Local companies may be willing to help with funding.

REPORT CARDS

If homework is the number one culprit in generating parent-child conflict, the report card runs a close second. Its arrival is often anticipated with anxiety by children and greeted with disappointment by parents. While your child's report card is no doubt important in helping to shape his academic experience and future, the value of learning can sometimes be lost in this preoccupation with grades.

Yet schools must evaluate their students to determine whether they are learning what is being taught. For most schools, the report card is the primary method for communicating academic performance to students and their parents. It is intended to help answer the following questions: Are students mastering the course objectives? Are they progressing as expected? Can they move on to the next grade? Are they keeping pace with their classmates? Are any students in need of extra help? Grades may also be used to help schools decide whether a student should be retained or skipped ahead, or placed in high- or low-level classes.

The report card is also a motivational tool. Almost all children want to get a good report card. They know their parents are more likely to be pleased with A's and B's than C's and D's. They feel better about themselves when they get good grades. And they come to realize (although sometimes too late) that high school grades affect career and college opportunities. (Some car insurance companies even provide discounts for insured students who are on the honor roll.) The good things that good grades bring are usually sufficient to spur students to work hard. Poor grades may even serve as a wake-up call for apathetic students.

Schools use a wide variety of formats for reporting students' progress. Many districts continue to use the traditional system of giving letter grades from A to F or numerical grades from 0 to 100. Elementary schools, especially in kindergarten through third grade, may employ grading systems that soften the impact of the grades such as V (Very Good), S (Satisfactory), and N (Needs Improvement). Elementary students are often evaluated on specific skills (for example, "knows basic math facts") rather than on subjects. Some districts do not give grades in the early elementary years but rather rely on written reports and parent conferences. Report cards may also have codes that allow teachers to convey to parents in a simplified manner comments regarding homework completion, participation in class, and classroom behavior. Teachers, especially at the elementary level, often supplement the grades and codes with written comments. Districts may send interim reports in the middle of the marking period to alert parents that their child is in danger of failing and to give him a chance to improve before the marking period ends.

Teachers typically have different ways of figuring grades. Some grade strictly on achievement. Others consider such factors as the student's effort, level of improvement, and classroom participation. While some teachers will be influenced by the student's classroom behavior, grades should not be a way of punishing students for poor behavior or rewarding them for good behavior. The grade should be determined primarily by the student's mastery of the subject and compliance with academic requirements.

Report cards can sometimes be hard for parents to interpret. It is often difficult to tell how your child is performing from a letter grade or even a verbal description. With one teacher, a C might signify average performance compared with others in the class; with another teacher, a C might be given to a student who is struggling with the subject but is working conscientiously. A teacher may give a B to a hardworking student with limited ability but give a C+ to an apathetic student with superior ability, even though their classroom average is the same. A grade of B in reading given to a diligent student may mask the fact that he is in the lowest reading group.

Even written comments can be vague and misleading. Does "excellent progress" mean that your child is performing above his grade level in the subject or does it mean only that he is doing better than he did previously? What does the grade of N for "Needs Improvement" mean? After all, all students can stand to improve. Secondary school teachers are typically more explicit about their grading criteria and often communicate them to students. Most have formulas for determining grades in which tests, quizzes, reports, and homework are all assigned a certain weight. Students are within their rights to ask the teacher how she arrives at the grade.

The perfect report card has yet to be devised. But that should not stop you from trying. If you are dissatisfied with your district's report card, consider joining with other parents to request that the school district review this issue. Many districts have revised their report cards in reponse to parent concerns.

A report card is not a definitive assessment of your child's abilities but rather a snapshot of his performance at a particular point in time with a particular teacher. At best, it is a rough estimate of how a student performed in a subject and what he learned. But it does not let the parent know what entered into that grade. If the grade is low, it provides the parent with no idea of why he did poorly or what should be done. These limitations highlight the importance of looking beyond the report card to understand your child's school performance. Comparing your child's papers over the course of the year allows you to note his growth in specific areas. Of course, you will also want to review your child's standardized test scores and attend parent-teacher conferences. These meetings allow for a dialogue with the teacher that the report card does not. Also talk with your child about school to assess his enthusiasm for learning. You might even have your child teach you something he has learned in school.

Responding to your child's report card in a constructive manner that does not result in a battle can be a challenge. You need to walk a fine line between not dwelling excessively on the grades and not dismissing them as unimportant. Grades are certainly important. They can affect a child's self-image and influence post-graduate opportunities, but good grades are not the ultimate pursuit. The report card is neither a measure of your child's worth nor of your parenting skills.

When the report card arrives, sit down with your child and calmly review the grades, giving praise where warranted. If your child received some B's, avoid the temptation to say, "I'd like you to bring those up to A's." The message to your child is that he cannot do anything to please you. Identify areas in need of attention and offer help if needed. If necessary, remind your child what you expect from him in terms of studying, homework, and class behavior. This is more effective than specifying what grades you expect him to achieve.

Many parents try to spur their children to good grades with a carrot-and-stick approach. The carrot is often a tangible reward for each good grade (for example, five dollars for each A). The stick may be the removal of certain privileges for receiving poor grades. This approach is often to no avail. Research has shown that tangible incentives and punishments that are tied to grades do not raise grades and may even lower academic performance. If a child has a skill deficiency, promising the child money is not going to correct the problem. Moreover, this approach conveys a wrong message: namely, that learning is valued for the tangible benefits it produces rather than for its own sake.

This does not mean that you should not praise your child for a good report card or even celebrate on occasion with perhaps a trip to your child's favorite restaurant. But contracting with your child to pay him for good grades places too much emphasis on grades and too little on learning. It is more effective to respond to children in a way that promotes the intrinsic value of learning and fosters his internal drive.

How should you respond to a bad report card? First, take note of what you should not do. Angry outbursts or harsh criticism are likely to be ineffective and may even contribute to a worsening of your child's grades. A low-key, calm but serious approach in which you express concern about his performance and then problem-solve with your child about how to improve is likely to be more productive. Keep in mind that poor grades can be very demoralizing for a child and can sap his confidence. He may come to see himself as "dumb" and may stop working or lower his own expectations of what is satisfactory. Thus, part of your job may be to help bolster his confidence so that he feels better about himself and doesn't give up in school.

Try to find something positive in the report card. It may be that your child did well in a particular subject, or that he participated in class, or that he was conscientious in returning homework. Then turn to the subjects he had difficulty with and ask questions to try to identify the source of the problem. Is the work too difficult? Is he so bored that he is not putting forth effort? Is the teacher hard to follow? Is homework being handed in consistently? Are tests his downfall? Is your child distracted by a family or peer problem? Reviewing past report cards may suggest a trend (for example, he may do better as the year goes along or show consistent difficulty in a specific subject).

Once you understand the source of the difficulties, work with your child to develop a plan of action. Focus on what he needs to do differently and whether extra help is needed. Is tutoring called for? Should homework be monitored more carefully? Does he need help in studying for tests or in organizing himself? Should his outside activities be curtailed? If your child's poor grades coincide with low test scores, it may be that he is a candidate for testing by the district's evaluation team to determine whether he has a learning disability. You may need to confer with the teacher to get answers to some of these questions. If so, call or write her and schedule a meeting rather than waiting for the regularly scheduled parent-teacher conference.

For some children poor grades stem from a casual and half-hearted approach to schoolwork. You may need to help your child reorder his priorities. If his television watching is interfering with his studying, don't hesitate to set some limits. The same is true of outside activities. If your child's busy schedule is getting in the way of schoolwork, something will have to give. Make sure it is not schoolwork! The point here is to convey to your child in no uncertain terms that schoolwork is your child's primary job and it comes before other activities.

TAMING THE TELEVISION MONSTER

Consider the following statistics:
- The television is on for about seven hours a day in a typical American household.
- Children watch an average of three to four hours a day of television.
- By the time a student graduates from high school he will most likely have watched about 15,000 hours of television and attended school for about 13,000 hours.
- A child will see on average 20,000 television commercials every year.
- By the age of fourteen, a child will probably have seen about 11,000 murders on television.
- The average cartoon has twenty-six violent incidents.

The picture that emerges from these statistics is sharp and clear: television is a powerful influence on children. Through its vivid images, it can captivate children and command their attention in a way few teachers can. Indeed, television rivals teachers and parents for its educational influence on children. Newton N. Minow, former chairman of the Federal Communications Commission, has called television "the most important educational institution in America." The problem is that television's "curriculum" is not always beneficial for children and is sometimes even harmful.

Television, when watched to excess, can numb the mind and dull the spirit. It is often a passive activity requiring minimal thinking and leaving little to the imagination. At the same time, it can shape children's thoughts and mold their values—often in ways that run counter to parents' preferences. Television can also mislead children with its unrealistic portrayals and its easy solutions to complex problems. Also, TV programs frequently reinforce stereotypes by depicting minorities, women, and the elderly inaccurately and unfairly.

While these concerns should give parents pause, it is television violence that presents the greatest peril to children. Studies indicate that children who see violence frequently on television may become less sensitive to the pain and suffering of others and more fearful and mistrustful of people in general. In addition, children who watch violence on television may view aggression as an acceptable way of solving problems and may be more likely to be aggressive in dealing with others. This too is borne out by research. The National Institute of Mental Health concluded in an extensive study that children who watch violent TV shows are more likely to act violently. (Some attorneys have even used this as a defense for their clients' criminal behavior, claiming they were influenced by the violence they watched on TV and thus are not responsible for their actions.) Responding to pressure from advocacy groups, commercial networks agreed in 1993 to place a warning to parents on television shows containing violence. A better step would be for broadcasters to simply decrease the amount of violence shown during children's prime viewing time.

Television can also impede children's academic development and school performance. Studies indicate that children who are heavy television viewers (four hours or more per day) typically put forth less effort on schoolwork, receive lower grades, and have poorer reading skills than light viewers (one hour or less). They also have fewer outside interests and less developed social skills. While it is not clear that heavy TV viewing causes poor academic performance, nonetheless children who spend so much time in front of the TV have little time left over for other worthwhile activities.

Television is not inherently harmful. Indeed, it can be a force for good. *Sesame Street* is just one example of television's rich educational potential. Many schools are trying to capitalize on television as a teaching tool by bringing educational television into the classroom. Even noneducational television can have positive results. For example, when Fonzie, the character in the 1970s show *Happy Days,* took out a library card, library card applications shot up fivefold across the country. Similarly, when Fonzie put on a seat belt in a car, the use of seat belts by children rose dramatically.

Parents are unlikely to be able to ban TV from their child's lives— nor should they. Television is an integral part of our society and culture. The task then for parents and educators is to harness the good that television has to offer while minimizing its negative effects. Toward this end, parents should consider the following strategies:

SET GROUND RULES REGARDING TELEVISION VIEWING. As a first step to establishing some rules, you might keep a log of your family's viewing patterns for one week. Once you have a picture of how much TV your family watches, you can begin to develop some realistic rules. Parents have different standards for what they feel is reasonable. Some limit their child to two hours of television a day or one hour on school nights and two on other nights. Some prohibit television viewing altogether on school nights. The Federal Commission on Reading recommended that school-age children be allowed to watch no more than ten hours of TV per week. You may want to place your child on a TV diet and designate certain times of the day when the television is turned off—for example, during meals, homework, and family quiet time. If you have a video cassette recorder, offer to record your child's favorite shows for viewing at another time. And if you are serious about limiting your child's TV watching, keep a TV out of his bedroom.

TEACH YOUR CHILD TO BE A WISE VIEWER. Some children have bad television habits. They may turn the TV on and watch whatever comes on. Or they may keep it on throughout the day or evening to serve as background noise. Help your child become selective in what he watches by having him go through the television listings at the beginning of the week or in the early evening to choose those shows he wants to watch and that fit within the time constraints you have set. This not only keeps his TV watching within reasonable limits but also helps him learn to make choices and compromise with other family members. It's okay to make some shows off-limits to your child. Encourage programs that the whole family can watch as well as those with minimal violence, with characters who care for each other, and with fair portrayals of people. Some parents assign a point value to programs and then allow their child to watch shows totaling a specified number of points over the course of a week. Less desirable programs can be assigned a higher number of points.

SET A GOOD EXAMPLE FOR YOUR CHILDREN. Research has shown that children often adopt the television habits of their parents. If your first act upon entering the house is to flick on the TV, children are likely to do the same. Teach your child to be a discriminating viewer by being discriminating yourself. Watch a program or two and then turn the television off.

SUGGEST ALTERNATIVE ACTIVITIES. It is often easier for children to turn on the TV than to figure out what else to do. The first comment you are likely to hear after the TV is turned off is "I'm bored." Help your child out by offering some attractive alternatives —reading a book or magazine, having a catch, playing a game, doing a puzzle, baking a cake, building with blocks, or doing an art project. If your child shows no interest in any of your suggestions, back off but resist his pleas to turn the TV back on. Your child will eventually find something else to do.

EDUCATE YOUR CHILD ABOUT ADVERTISEMENTS. Advertisers target many of their food and toy commercials at children because they know how impressionable they are. This exploitation expanded during the past decade with the advent of some seventy television programs with characters based on toys. Help your child understand that the purpose of an advertisement is to sell a product and that a commercial will sometimes exaggerate or mislead. Encourage him to evaluate the claims of commercials. You may also want to give him a lesson in nutrition to help counter enticing ads for unhealthful foods.

TALK WITH YOUR CHILD ABOUT THE SHOWS HE SEES. This is an important way of inoculating him against the values put forth on TV that are counter to yours. Occasionally watch some programs with your child. This enables you to not only monitor what he is watching but also allows you to talk with him about the show. Help your child distinguish between what is real and what is pretend. Young children often believe that characters on shows actually exist and that the events are real. Also, talk about how in real life people are actually injured by the violent acts of others. Ask your child questions about the shows to make him think about what he is watching. The following are examples of questions you might ask:

- Do you think it would have happened that way in real life?
- How else might the show have ended?
- If a person actually did that, what do you think would happen to him?
- Do you think that was the right way of dealing with the problem?
- How else might the character have solved the problem without being violent?
- How do you think the person felt about what happened?
- What would you have done if you were in his situation?
- Do you think that's the way most older people act?

TUTORING

The first response of parents to their child's academic problems is often to hire a tutor. While tutoring can be helpful to students lagging behind their classmates, in-school alternatives should also be considered. The teacher may be able to modify your child's classroom instruction by, for example, changing his reading group or adapting the homework assignments. Your child may be eligible to receive extra help in a remedial program. Or he may be showing signs of a learning disability and may be a candidate for testing by the school's evaluation team.

After talking with your child's teacher and considering these or other alternatives, you may decide to stick with your first impulse and hire a tutor. If so, give thought to what you would like to accomplish. Tutoring can serve a variety of purposes, including helping your child perform better in a specific subject, improving his test-taking and study skills, and promoting his confidence. In recent years, many parents have been using tutoring as a way of giving their already high-achieving child an extra edge. When used in this way, tutoring may give rise to avoidable stress and pressure. The key here is your child's responsiveness: if he is eager to pursue a particular subject, enjoys working with the tutor, and does not feel increased pressure, this kind of enrichment can be beneficial.

There are various ways of finding a tutor. The school or community may provide tutoring services. Some schools have established peer tutoring programs in which high-achieving students help students having difficulty. Local colleges or universities, especially those with education programs, may have learning or reading clinics that provide testing and remediation. If you are looking for a private tutor, ask teachers or other parents for recommendations. The school district may keep a list of certified teachers interested in tutoring. Another alternative for parents is a private tutoring center, discussed below.

If you decide to hire a tutor, go about it in the same way you would hire an employee: interview the tutor and obtain references. The following are some questions to consider in deciding which tutor is best for your child:

WHAT ARE HER ACADEMIC QUALIFICATIONS? It is important that she be a certified teacher, preferably in the area in which your child needs help. (At the elementary level, teachers are typically certified in regular or special education; at the secondary level, teachers are typically certified by subject.) If your child has a reading problem, try to find a teacher with a background in reading instruction.

WHAT IS HER TEACHING AND TUTORING EXPERIENCE? Has she taught the subject before? For how long? Has she taught children the same age as your child?

WHAT IS HER APPROACH TO TUTORING? Will she use a separate curriculum and new materials or will she work on the same curriculum and with the same materials that your child is using in school? Will she help your child with homework? Will she teach study skills? With elementary students, it is often important to work on specific skill deficiencies and organizational skills; with secondary students, tutoring is more effective when it focuses on your child's schoolwork, unless the work is well above his ability level.

IS YOUR CHILD LIKELY TO WORK WELL WITH HER? The better the chemistry between the tutor and your child, the more effective the tutoring is likely to be. You might want to have your child meet the tutor to see how he relates to her, and she to him.

WILL THE TUTOR CONTACT YOUR CHILD'S TEACHER? She should be willing to talk directly with the teacher and if necessary maintain ongoing contact to ensure coordination.

WHERE WILL THE TUTORING TAKE PLACE? Will it be at a center, at the tutor's home, or at your home?

WHAT DOES THE TUTORING COST? Private tutoring can be expensive. The tutor will probably charge by the hour. Check whether there are any extra charges (for example, for testing or materials). Find out if she offers small-group tutoring as a way of reducing the cost. Tutoring centers may have a sliding scale or even offer scholarships. An inexpensive tutoring alternative is to hire a capable high school student.

If you choose to hire a tutor, do it with the knowledge of the teacher. Some parents prefer to have their child tutored secretly (sometimes called "underground tutoring") to convey the impression that he is improving on his own. This not only gives an inappropriate message to your child but denies the tutor the ability to coordinate her instruction with that of the teacher. Tutoring is most effective when the tutor is supporting and reinforcing the classroom instruction. It may add to your child's confusion if he is taught with two different instructional approaches or sets of materials. In addition, the tutor should not increase your child's workload by giving homework since he is probably feeling overwhelmed by homework already.

Tutoring should aim to relieve the pressure on your child rather than add to it. While most children will balk at the idea of being tutored, some may be genuinely overwhelmed by having to go to another teacher after school is out. If after a few sessions your child is still strongly resisting the tutoring and the stress hasn't lessened, you may want to reconsider whether to continue. He is not likely to retain much when feeling frustrated and overwhelmed.

Tutoring centers such as the Sylvan Learning Center, Britannica Learning Center, Reading Game Center, Huntington Learning Center, and Humanex Systems International are private companies offering tutoring in academic subjects as well as study skills. Some also offer enrichment instruction. These centers typically provide diagnostic testing, small-group or one-to-one instruction, material rewards to motivate the students, and a variety of learning materials and approaches. The centers may also make use of computers. Sylvan, the largest of the tutoring franchises, guarantees that students will gain a full grade level in the subject being tutored, based on standardized testing, or receive twelve hours of instruction free.

While some maintain that these learning centers are more economical and effective than private tutors, others assert that their claims of success are exaggerated and that the centers often focus on a narrow range of academic skills (for example, reading decoding at the expense of comprehension). Don't feel that you are shortchanging your child if you don't take him to a tutoring center offering an elaborate array of media. Your child may learn just as much from an experienced, warm teacher working with him at the dining room table.

The ultimate goal of tutoring should be to reach the point where it is no longer necessary and your child can perform adequately on his own. Be skeptical of any tutor who sets a time limit or promises specific gains in a set amount of time. If tutoring is prolonged, however, you run the risk of having your child become dependent on the tutor. The best evidence that tutoring is working is improved classroom performance, so check periodically with your child's teacher.

SCHOOL BUS SAFETY

The yellow school bus is a familiar sight across the landscape of America. Every school day 22 million children board 369,000 buses to go to school. While these trips may cause parents of young children some initial anxiety, their nervousness usually abates as they learn that the school bus is a safe means of transportation. Indeed, school buses are said to be six times safer than family cars. But accidents can and do happen. Every year approximately 9000 children are injured and 35 children killed in school bus accidents. While the risk of a school bus accident is minimal, schools and parents must be vigilant about school bus safety.

First and foremost, school districts must ensure that the bus drivers are responsible and well trained. Bus drivers should receive training in applicable laws, safety precautions, first aid, and behavior management. Training may be mandated by the state. School districts should also instruct the students in appropriate bus behavior and conduct safety drills periodically. Adult monitors on school buses are helpful in maintaining order, but Rhode Island is the only state that requires them on elementary school buses. Some schools have arranged for parents to ride on school buses. Video monitors have also been used effectively to alert the driver to potential problems.

Safety experts claim that buses can be made safer by installing seats with high backs and thick padding and eliminating the metal seats and bars. They are less certain about the desirability of seat belts on school buses. Some contend that young children may not be able to unhook the belts in an emergency while others cite studies to show that children can be trained to remove them quickly. There is also concern that belts that go around the waist may cause children to hit their heads on the bars of older buses. Some states require seat belts on new buses.

Parents can also promote school bus safety by reviewing the following rules with their children periodically:
- Stand back as the bus approaches and do not move to the bus until it stops.
- Go directly to your seat and remain seated until the bus stops and you are ready to get off.
- Do not put your hands or head out of the window.

- Do not distract the bus driver by yelling or talking loudly.
- Move away from the bus right after you get off, making sure to stay away from the front or side of the bus.
- Wait for the bus driver to direct you to cross the street and make sure to always cross in front of the bus, allowing about ten feet between you and the bus.
- Do not go back to pick up dropped items until the bus driver has directed you to or the bus has left.
- Avoid carrying glass items on the bus.

Most school bus accidents happen when children are outside the bus and are hit by a passing vehicle or the school bus itself. Children who dart in front of the bus to retrieve an item they have dropped are especially vulnerable. The bus driver has a blind spot of about ten feet around the bus and cannot always see children who are in front of the bus or close to its side. Caution your child about this danger zone. Also make sure that he has a book bag or backpack so that loose papers do not fly away.

Depending on the age and experience of your child, you may want to take other precautions, including the following: driving the bus route with your child from school to home so that he is confident where to get off; memorizing the number of the school bus; and introducing him to the bus driver. It is also a good idea for you to get to know the bus driver in case there are future problems or concerns.

LIFE AFTER SCHOOL

A quick glance at a typical family calendar tells a revealing story. The schedule is frantic and the lives of the children are jam-packed. Monday's soccer practice is followed by Tuesday's gymnastics class. Wednesday is ballet and Thursday is piano. On Friday, it's back to the soccer field. While some children thrive with an abundance of after-school activities, others suffer the effects of overscheduling. Their circuits become overloaded and they are prime candidates for shutting down and burning out. And sometimes schoolwork takes a backseat to these activities. A day jammed with activities may leave the child with little time or energy to do homework or too tired to concentrate in school the next day.

If children's after-school hours are booked up, it is often the parents who are overbooking them. And with good intentions. They may want to give their child an extra edge to prepare him for years ahead. But in arranging a diverse menu of activities, they do not always see that their child's plate may already be full.

This pattern of overscheduling is part of a wider contemporary problem: children are being pushed to grow up too fast. Dr. David Elkind has written persuasively about this trend in his book *The Hurried Child*. He and many others are troubled that children are being rushed through childhood in an effort to fulfill their parents' desire to create "superkids." He fears the consequences for children of the loss of childhood.

While child development experts acknowledge the importance of parents in providing a stimulating, enriching, and nurturing environment, they also agree that parents can do too much for their child. What can parents do who are interested in providing their child with enriching experiences without creating the problems that can plague an overprogrammed child?

Moderation should be your watchword as you help your child set up his schedule. Bear in mind your child's age in your effort to arrange activities that are rewarding but not overwhelming. Limit your three- to five-year-old to one or two activities per school semester, your six- to eight-year-old to two or three activities, and your nine- to twelve-year-old to three or four activities. Keep your child's interests and talents uppermost as you suggest activities, and be careful about imposing your agenda on him. Look for programs that are compatible with his physical and mental abilities and encourage him to sample both athletic and cultural activities. Competitive activities should be avoided prior to second grade. And keep a close watch on the coach to make sure he is more interested in building confidence than building winners.

After you have gathered all the details on the programs your child might pursue, sit down with him a month or two before the programs begin to make the final decisions. Consider what he wants as well as what you think is practical. Reluctant children may need some gentle nudging or encouragement to pursue organized activities. Children who are initially skittish about trying an activity often end up enjoying it and even pursuing it further. Insist that your child stick with the agreed-upon activity for a reasonable time before he can call it quits, but don't make him stay with an activity for six months or a year that he clearly dislikes.

Part of your job is to help your child find a balance between structured and unstructured time. Make sure there is time when his calendar is clear, some down time that belongs to him—and no one else. This is the time when he can try out a new computer game, climb a tree in the backyard, jump rope in the driveway, and yes, even watch a favorite TV program. Down time not only provides a respite from the tension of structured activities and the pressure of competition, it also gives children a chance to learn how to entertain themselves. They may discover some enjoyable solitary activities that will help them cope with the inevitable periods of boredom experienced by children.

You may wish to establish some ground rules on how your child spends unstructured time. Set some limits on how long he can watch TV or play video games. Once he has reached his limit, switch the TV off and tell him to find something else to do. Expect complaints from your child that he is bored. You might suggest some activities but don't be lured into being his social director. He needs to learn how to deal with boredom. Eventually he will find something to do.

SUMMER

The close of school does not mean the end of learning. Indeed, the summer provides an opportunity for children to learn about new subjects, pursue familiar subjects in greater depth, or brush up on academic skills. The challenge for parents is to arrange summer activities that strike a balance between the enjoyable and the educational. With careful planning and some luck, your child may even discover that summer activities can be both.

For children with academic deficiencies, the summer can be used profitably to hone basic skills. As a general rule, children lose some of the skills they have gained during the school year. This is why much of September is spent reviewing the skills of the previous grade. Those with academic weaknesses, who can least afford to have their skills erode, are particularly prone to this regression. Summer tutoring can reinforce the skills learned in school and thus stem this loss of skill. In gauging whether your child is a candidate for summer tutoring, obtain his teacher's opinion and also talk with your child to assess his receptiveness. You may conclude that notwithstanding his deficiencies he needs a reprieve from academic instruction.

If you decide in favor of summer tutoring, you may hire a tutor or you may opt to work with your child on your own. Working with your child is fine as long as you allow him plenty of opportunities to have fun during the summer and the tutoring does not become a battleground. Try to avoid the same kinds of routines you followed during the school year. Rather than do work sheets, which children find tedious and boring, find activities with academic content that are fun and practical.

You or the tutor might check with your child's teacher before the close of school to learn what skills he needs help with and what methods and materials she recommends. Or you might contact a teacher in the next grade to find out what skills your child will be learning in the coming year, which he can then work on during the summer. In this way your child can get a head start on the next year and enter school in September with enhanced confidence. Some districts provide a reading list for middle school students, suggesting books they might read over the summer.

The summer is also an ideal time for academic and cultural enrichment. Summer school has a different connotation today than in the past, when it referred to a program for students needing remedial help or making up a failed course. While summer school programs may continue to provide remedial help, they may also offer students the opportunity to pursue academic subjects in depth as well as leisure-oriented activities. Typically sponsored by school districts, communities, or colleges, these summer programs may offer choices in such areas as science, music, art, drama, dance, photography, foreign language, and athletics. In addition to promoting new skills and talents, these programs give children a chance to meet others with similar interests. Children generally respond well to these programs. While the content may be academic, the format is not. The pressure to perform is minimal, the instruction is informal, there are no tests and likely no homework, and there are few if any discipline problems. In choosing a program, consider the training of the staff, the adequacy of the facilities and equipment, and the appropriateness of the materials.

Another summer option is to send your child to day or overnight camp. While most camps offer an array of activities, an increasing number are specializing. You can find camps where the focus is on art, music, drama, sports, science, or computers. Camps are also available for learning disabled and mentally retarded children (see appendix B, "For Further Information"). In choosing one of these camps, make sure the area of specialty is appealing to your child—and not just you. Giving your child an intense dose of an activity in which he has little interest is a sure way to turn him off.

Children do not necessarily need the structure of a formal program to have a productive and satisfying summer. The summer can also be a time for children to experiment and explore on their own. Encourage your child to try new activities or develop fresh interests. The following are some examples:

- learning a computer word processing program
- developing a neighborhood newspaper
- starting a neighborhood club
- learning how to ride a horse
- reading books on a particular theme
- volunteering in the community (for example, assisting at a township recreation program for younger children)
- getting a job (for example, baby-sitting or mowing lawns)
- pursuing a hobby (for example, photography)
- growing a vegetable garden and selling the products
- participating in a summer drama program

Parents need to weigh a range of factors in deciding on their child's summer program, not the least of which is what fits in with their work schedule. Make sure to obtain the views of your child. Let his interests guide you although you may want to gently encourage a reluctant child to pursue a skill or subject that you think he will like. In arranging your child's summer schedule, make sure to build in some free time. He is entitled to some time when he is not part of any formal program and can pursue his own interests and whims.

HOME SCHOOLING

Home schooling is just what its name implies: children are educated at home rather than in school. Some parents may do this because they are not satisfied with the instruction in their public school and feel they can do better. Others are dismayed with the climate in the school and want to provide an education more attuned to their cultural, religious, or social values. Some parents believe that schools are too regimented while others think that schools are too lax. Whatever the reason for home schooling, this trend is on the increase. According to the Federal Department of Education, more than 500,000 children are now being educated at home, compared with 10,000 to 15,000 children who were schooled at home in the mid 1970s.

Home schooling is actually an old-fashioned concept. Most children in the United States were educated at home until the middle of the nineteenth century by either their parents or another adult. Many prominent Americans were taught at home, including George Washington, Abraham Lincoln, Woodrow Wilson, Margaret Mead, Thomas Edison, and Albert Einstein. When compulsory school attendance was finally instituted, it was resisted by parents who felt their rights were being usurped.

While all states now require children to attend school until a specific age, most allow parents to teach their child at home if certain requirements are met. The purpose of these requirements is to ensure that home-schooled children receive a sound and well-rounded education. Numerous states have tightened these rules in recent years, giving rise to litigation between parents and school districts.

These requirements vary with each state. All states require instruction in basic academic skills throughout the public school year. In addition, states typically require that parents provide the school district with an acceptable education plan and that the child take standardized achievement tests annually. Some states mandate that the home teacher have a college degree or a state teaching certificate. Others require that a school official visit the home and observe the child during instruction. State and local education officials have become more conscientious about ensuring compliance with these requirements as more parents have opted for this approach. (This is partially due to economic concerns: federal and state aid usually depend on local enrollment.)

Opponents of home schooling contend that children taught at home may receive a narrow or inadequate education and lose out on the opportunity to be around other children and develop social skills.

They argue that children learn best in the company of other children. For many parents who are educating their children at home, it is just this social climate as well as the peer pressures that they are trying to avoid. Parents may also be attracted to home schooling because it allows their children to pursue their own interests and learn at their own pace. Parents may supplement their children's education with frequent field trips and real-life experiences and often involve them in peer activities after school or on weekends. Judging by some studies, many parents have been successful. A recent study at Andrews University in Michigan indicated that most children taught at home scored above average on a standardized measure of self-esteem. Other studies show that home-schooled children generally perform above the level of their peers on tests of academic skills.

Parents who are considering educating their child at home should give this plenty of thought. This is a demanding job requiring dedication, organization, skill, and time. To start, examine your motivation. Make sure that you are pursuing this because you believe it is right for your child and not because you are angry with the school district. The next step is to contact your state department of education to find out what conditions you must meet to qualify for home schooling. If you can meet these criteria, ask yourself some additional questions:

HAVE YOU CONSIDERED PRIVATE SCHOOL? If this option is not beyond your means (home schooling can be costly as well), you may be able to find a private school that is compatible with your own standards and values.

HOW COOPERATIVE IS YOUR SCHOOL DISTRICT WITH PARENTS WHO ARE EDUCATING THEIR CHILDREN AT HOME? Find out if other parents in your district have done this, and inquire what their experience has been. Some districts are supportive and will provide you with textbooks and curriculum guidance. Others will provide help grudgingly or even place what parents feel are unreasonable obstacles in their way.

ARE BOTH YOU AND YOUR SPOUSE IN SUPPORT OF HOME SCHOOLING? This program is not likely to be successful if both parents aren't fully behind the idea. It places unusual demands on both parents. Moreover, if one parent is not supportive of home schooling, this practice is likely to become a source of tension.

ARE THERE OPPORTUNITIES FOR YOUR CHILD TO INTERACT WITH OTHER CHILDREN? Because your child may be isolated from other children during the school day, it is all the more important that he be involved with peers in some fashion. Your community likely has a range of activities offered after school, on weekends, or during the summer, including sports teams, Boy Scouts or Girl Scouts, theater, and art and music programs. You may also join forces with other parents of home-schooled children and arrange joint activities during the day.

DO YOU HAVE THE TEMPERAMENT, TIME, AND SKILL TO TEACH YOUR CHILD? Many parents lack the patience and objectivity to help their children with homework, let alone be their exclusive teacher. The parent and child will need to have an unusual chemistry if this arrangement is going to be successful. Also, be prepared to devote most of your day to your child's schooling, either in teaching or in planning the lessons. In terms of skill, many parents find that they have the ability to teach their children during their elementary years but lack the expertise when the child enters the teenage years. As a result, many home-schooled children return to public school when they reach secondary school age.

WHAT IS YOUR CHILD'S REACTION TO HOME SCHOOLING? Your child's views are important in gauging his likely reaction to home schooling. If he is strongly opposed and prefers to attend school, he is likely to be unreceptive to your instruction and you may find yourself locked in an unproductive power struggle.

An extensive support network has developed in recent years for parents teaching their children at home. In addition to local and state support groups, the National Homeschool Association (see appendix A) provides information to parents. Through these groups, you can learn about companies that design home-school programs based on the child's interests and abilities. Books on home schooling are listed in appendix B.

CHILD ABUSE: THE SCHOOL'S ROLE

It is estimated that about half of all children who are abused are of school age. Teachers and other school staff bear a special responsibility in dealing with this serious problem. They spend much time with students and are often in a position to observe physical or behavioral changes suggesting a possible problem. In recognition of the important role of public schools in identifying child abuse, all states require public school staff to contact the appropriate state agency if a student is suspected of being physically or emotionally abused. In some states educators are subject to penalties if they do not notify the state of a suspected case of child abuse. Typically, the person making the report is immune from civil liability or criminal prosecution.

The role of the school is limited to identifying children who may have been abused. A caseworker from the state agency will take responsibility for following up with the child and the family, including trying to determine whether abuse occurred, protecting the child, if necessary, and providing help to the family. These state agencies have specific procedures that caseworkers must follow. They likely have the right to interview a child in school, talk with school personnel, and review his records without parental consent.

While educators have the responsibility to report children suspected of being abused, parents have the right to expect that school staff will use good judgment in deciding whether to make a report, will exercise discretion by only giving information to the people who need it, and will deal with the child in a sensitive manner.

CHAPTER EIGHT

MAKING SENSE OF STANDARDIZED TESTS

"Open your booklets. You may now begin."

Millions of students across the country hear these words every fall or spring as public schools go through the annual rite of testing.

This process is nothing new. Standardized tests have been a part of the public school scene since the 1920s and continue to be widely used today. If anything, testing has become an even more prominent feature of the educational landscape. When the question arises about how public schools are doing, the answer almost always involves student testing. When educational reforms are proposed, testing is often held out as a key to remedying the ills of public education. The ongoing concern with the quality of public school education and the demand for accountability ensure that testing will remain a fact of life for students.

Schools may be more obsessed with tests than ever before. According to Archie E. Lapointe, executive director of the National Assessment of Educational Progress, "the amount of testing of American schoolchildren at the present time is greater than at any time in our history." The National Center for Fair & Open Testing, a consumer group, recently estimated based on a state-by-state survey that elementary and secondary school students take more than 100 million standardized tests a year.

Standardized tests engender both apprehension and confusion in parents. Their apprehension is understandable: the test results provide objective evidence of how their child compares academically with other children. Low scores may arouse anxiety in parents and cause them to question their own parenting skills. The results can also color teachers' perceptions and may be used to make important educational decisions about any child. Their confusion is predictable: parents may be presented with a dazzling array of numbers and terms to describe their child's test performance. Fortunately, parents do not need a Ph.D. in statistics to make sense of the test results.

Because of the potential impact of test results on a child's education, it is vital that parents understand how to interpret the results. This chapter provides an overview of the testing process, describes what the results mean, and suggests how parents can ensure the results are used properly in educating their child. The focus here is on the group standardized tests given to all or most of the students in a school district. Tests given individually to children to determine if they need special education are discussed in chapter 9 while kindergarten screening tests are examined in chapter 4.

WHAT ARE STANDARDIZED TESTS?

Standardized tests are objective tests administered in the same manner and with the same instructions to all children receiving the test. They are designed to give teachers information about their students, parents information about their children, and school districts information about the effectiveness of their programs. The tests are typically field tested or normed on a large population of students reflecting the racial and socioeconomic makeup of the population at large. This is called the norm group. Because of the way a standardized test is developed and administered, a student's test scores can be compared with those of other students in the same grade on whom the test was normed. In this way, we can learn whether a child is above, at, or below her grade level in various academic skills.

Most school districts test all students from kindergarten or first grade through eleventh or twelfth grade. These testing programs are often mandated by the state, although the specific tests, the purposes for which they are used, and the time of administration are often left up to the local district. The test content changes with the grade so that the test taken by a kindergartner differs from that taken by a third-grader. Standardized tests are predominantly multiple choice but increasingly are requiring written samples. Some districts prefer to administer the tests in the fall so they have the benefit of the results for the remainder of the year. Other districts opt for a spring administration so they can assess how much the child has progressed during the year and use the results in planning for the following year.

Tests that yield numerical scores, allowing comparison with other children, are called norm-referenced tests. The results from these tests are helpful in gauging whether students are keeping pace with their classmates. Criterion-referenced tests, which provide a profile of specific skills mastered and not mastered, are gaining increasing popularity. The information yielded by these tests can assist teachers in tailoring instruction to students' specific needs.

School districts usually administer two kinds of standardized tests: achievement tests and aptitude tests. An achievement test (for example, a reading test) measures how much a child has already learned; an aptitude test (for example, an intelligence test) measures how much a child is capable of learning. The distinction between these two tests is not always clear. It is difficult to measure what a child is capable of learning without also measuring to some degree what she has already learned. Nonetheless, comparing a student's results on the two tests is useful in judging whether a child is achieving below her academic potential.

School achievement tests always evaluate reading and math but may also assess spelling, language, science, social studies, and library skills. In recent years schools have added higher-order thinking skills to the assessment program. Reading is usually broken down into vocabulary and comprehension, math into computation and application; these scores are then combined to yield total reading and math scores. Language skills may be assessed with multiple-choice questions on some tests and essay questions on others.

An aptitude test is intended to measure a child's capacity to learn. A wide variety of aptitude tests can be used with students. Some gauge the ability to learn a specific skill or subject (for example, a test of mechanical aptitude or foreign language aptitude) while others measure overall ability to learn (for example, an intelligence test). The Scholastic Aptitude Test attempts to assess a student's capacity to learn and succeed at the college level.

Schools often administer group intelligence tests to determine whether students are performing in school on a par with their ability. In reaching conclusions about your child from intelligence test results, bear in mind that intelligence is not a single trait as much as a composite of diverse mental abilities. Moreover, intelligence test scores can change from year to year, especially with young children. Some states such as California have banned the use of group intelligence tests in public schools because of their questionable reliability and their potential to discriminate against minority students.

Many test publishers offer both achievement and intelligence tests. Through statistical analysis, the test publisher is able to use the intelligence test results to predict a student's expected performance on the achievement test; this is sometimes called the anticipated achievement score. Parents and teachers can then compare this anticipated score with the actual score and reach some tentative conclusions about whether the student is performing at, above, or below academic potential.

The standardized tests administered by school districts are typically published by well-known companies. These companies invest considerable time and research developing the test and selecting test items. The California Achievement Test, the Stanford Achievement Test, the Metropolitan Achievement Test, and the Iowa Test of Basic Skills are examples of commonly used tests. After the tests are administered, companies typically machine-score the tests, prepare computer printouts on each student, and perform analyses of the school's performance as a whole. Because these tests are standardized nationally, a student's scores can be compared to those of other students in the same grade across the country.

Twenty or thirty years ago, few school districts informed parents of how their child did. Today many districts provide parents with computer printouts of their child's test scores. If your district does not send test results to parents, you are still entitled to see your child's results. Federal law (the Family Educational Rights and Privacy Act) ensures that all school records on your child, including test scores, are available to you. You should not hesitate to ask to review these scores by calling the principal of your child's school.

You are also entitled to information about your district's testing program. Indeed, some states have passed "sunshine" legislation, requiring the state or school district to make available to the public information about the tests, including sample questions. Parents who wish to learn about their district's testing program should contact the principal or the district's test coordinator. While you cannot review the actual test, you should be able to obtain information about the academic areas assessed, the validity and reliability of the tests, and the ways in which the results are used.

HOW ARE THE RESULTS USED?

Standardized tests were developed to enable school districts to make better educational decisions about children. Teachers, it was believed, made decisions in a subjective and biased manner. Tests were viewed as a way to help school administrators make these decisions more objectively. The use of standardized tests has expanded in recent years as many states have mandated the administration of tests to answer a variety of questions. As you will see, standardized tests can play an important role in the kind of education your child receives.

School districts may use standardized tests for one or more of the following purposes:

TO DETERMINE PROGRAM ELIGIBILITY. Test scores may be used to assign students to such programs as remedial education, advanced classes, gifted and talented education, or even summer school. Schools may also rely on test scores for decisions about having students stay back a grade or skip ahead to the next grade. Some districts depend exclusively on test scores for these decisions; other districts use a combination of factors.

TO INFORM THE TEACHER ABOUT THEIR STUDENTS' SKILLS. Test scores can help teachers identify their students' strengths and weaknesses, which they can use to individualize instruction. Some teachers use the results to group children for academic instruction.

TO SUGGEST THE PRESENCE OF A LEARNING DISABILITY. Test scores may alert the school to students with potential learning problems who need further evaluation. The more indicators pointing to a learning problem, the greater the need for an in-depth evaluation. Schools are legally bound to conduct a comprehensive individualized evaluation of students suspected of needing special education. The results of group standardized testing should not be used to place a child in special education; indeed, such a practice violates federal law (see chapter 9).

TO INFORM PARENTS ABOUT THEIR CHILD'S PROGRESS. The test results give parents a profile of their child's current academic skills. They can use these results to evaluate their child's improvement from year to year and determine whether she is keeping pace with her classmates. It also helps parents to develop appropriate expectations for their child's academic performance.

TO GAUGE THE EFFECTIVENESS OF PROGRAMS. Test results permit a district to measure the impact of its programs and point to ways the curriculum can be revised to better educate its students.

Many states require that students pass a state-developed test of academic skills to receive a high school diploma. These minimum competency tests help to ensure that students attain at least a minimum level of skills in reading, writing, and math before graduating from high school. Increasingly, these tests are requiring students to provide a writing sample. While some students have failed to graduate with their class because of this test, others have been motivated to work harder to pass the test and thereby attain a diploma. States that employ this kind of test may allow school districts to grant exceptions to students who fail the test but otherwise demonstrate mastery of basic skills.

MAKING SENSE OF THE TEST RESULTS

If you become perplexed as you try to unravel the meaning of your child's test scores, you are in good company. The maze of numbers, graphs, and terms confounds the most sophisticated of parents. Let's begin with a brief lesson in terminology.

Typically parents receive a computer printout of their child's test scores one to two months after the administration of the test. (Keep these printouts so that you can compare results from year to year.) This printout may be accompanied by a computer-generated narrative and definitions of the terms. The following is an example of a portion of a computer printout from the California Achievement Test, one of the more commonly used group tests:

	NP	LP
Reading Vocabulary	27	15
Reading Comprehension	48	37
Total Reading	34	20
Spelling	30	21
Language Mechanics	28	17
Language Expression	51	43
Total Language	39	29
Math Computation	75	55
Math Concepts & Application	63	46
Total Math	71	50
Total Battery	46	31
Reference Skills	43	30

(NP = national percentile, LP = local percentile)

Reports of test scores often use the following terms:

Raw Score: This tells you how many questions your child answered correctly. By itself, this score is virtually meaningless and should not be used to make judgments about your child's performance.

Percentile: Ranging from 1 to 99, this number indicates how well your child performed compared with other children in her grade. More precisely, it tells you what percent of children in your child's grade scored below her. Take the example above. The student scored at the 46th national percentile on the entire test ("Total Battery"). This means that 45 percent of the students in the same grade across the country received a lower score than the student and 53 percent received a higher score. Note that percentile is not the same as percentage. Percentile conveys your child's standing compared to others in the same grade; percentage indicates the number of correct items divided by the total number of items. Thus, a 46th percentile score does *not* mean that your child had the correct answers on 46 percent of the items. Use the following guidelines in making sense of percentile scores:

80—99	well above average
60—79	mildly above average
40—59	average
20—39	mildly below average
1—19	well below average

In comparing scores from year to year, a difference of a few points is not considered significant; a difference of 15 points or more suggests a substantial change.

Local and National Percentile: Local percentile refers to how well your child did compared with same-grade children in her school district. National percentile refers to how well your child did compared with same-grade children across the nation. If she received a national percentile score of 74 in reading comprehension, this means that 73 percent of the children in her grade across the nation received lower scores. A significant discrepancy between your child's national and local percentile scores usually suggests that the academic standards of your community differ from those of the nation at large. This is true in the California Achievement Test scores displayed on the previous page, in which the national percentile test scores are consistently higher than the local percentile scores. This tells us that the academic performance of students in this community is higher than in the nation as a whole.

Stanine: Stanines are more general scores ranging from 1 (lowest) to 9 (highest). Scores of 1, 2, and 3 are below average; 4, 5, and 6 are average; and 7, 8, and 9 are above average. These scores correspond to the following percentile scores:

Stanine	Percentile
9	97—100
8	90— 96
7	78— 89
6	61— 77
5	41— 60
4	24— 40
3	12— 23
2	5— 11
1	1— 4

National Curve Equivalent (NCE): This score ranges from 1 to 99 and allows comparison of scores from different tests since an NCE score has the same meaning for all tests. The average NCE score is 50. Half of the students taking the test obtain scores from 36 to 64.

Grade Equivalent: This indicates the grade level at which your child performed. The number to the left of the decimal point refers to the grade level, the number to the right refers to the month. Thus, a second-grade child who receives a 3.8 grade-equivalent score in math is performing comparable to an average child in the eighth month (April) of third grade. A third-grader who has a grade-equivalent score of 5.4 in reading comprehension is of course reading well above average, but this does not mean that the child should be placed in a fifth-grade reading class. Grade-equivalent scores are notably imprecise when they are significantly above or below the child's current grade placement. Because of the misleading nature of grade-equivalent scores, you may prefer to use percentiles to interpret your child's scores.

Intelligence Quotient (IQ): This is the score received on an intelligence test. Possible scores range from 40 to 160, with 100 as the norm. Scores below 90 are considered below average; scores of 110 or above are considered above average. It is important that you understand the limitations of intelligence test results. An IQ score is an estimate, not a precise calculation, of learning aptitude. Moreover, IQ tests do not measure innate ability because the results are affected by educational opportunities and other environmental factors. Perhaps most important, intelligence test results can change with time, especially with young children, and thus an IQ score should not be seen as a permanent attribute of the child. While intelligence tests attain high marks in predicting school success, they receive failing grades in predicting life success. This is because intelligence tests measure a narrow band of abilities and do not factor into the scores other abilities that are critical to success outside of school, including curiosity, determination, creativity, and social skills.

ACTING ON THE RESULTS

Once you have figured out what your child's test scores mean, you're ready to tackle the next question: Are the results an accurate measure of what your child knows? If educational decisions are going to be based on your child's test performance, you want to be sure the results are reliable and trustworthy. Inaccurate scores can lead to inappropriate educational decisions. The following rules can help you assess the reliability and validity of the scores and judge how much confidence to place in the results (a reliable test yields similar scores when the test is readministered to the same child, and a valid test accurately represents the skills being measured):

- the older the student, the more reliable the scores
- the less extreme the scores, the more reliable they are
- the more comprehensive the test, the more valid the scores
- the more the scores are consistent with other measures of school performance, the more valid they are

Your child's poor performance on group standardized tests may reflect weak academic skills or result from other factors. If your child received low scores, rule out as best you can other explanations before you conclude she is academically deficient. The following are some of the other possible causes of low test scores:

- low motivation
- poor test-taking skills
- reading difficulty
- test anxiety
- inability to concentrate
- failure to understand the directions
- emotional distress
- illness or fatigue
- incorrect marking of the test booklet
- distracting test conditions (for example, too much noise or poor heating, lighting, or ventilation)

Young children, who are just learning how to take tests, are particularly vulnerable to these problems. The greater the gap between your child's test scores and other measures of academic performance (for example, class performance, previous test scores, grades, and teacher observations), the more likely that her test performance was impeded by factors other than poor academic skills.

If you conclude that your child's test scores misrepresent her academic skills, contact her teacher. If the teacher is of the same opinion, request that the school hand-score the test. (Your school may be reluctant to grant this request, but it's worth a try.) If your child's test booklet is part of her permanent school file, you are permitted by law to see it. More likely, the test booklet is in the possession of the test publisher and consequently unavailable for your review.

You may also request that your child retake the test. Test companies typically publish alternate forms of the same test. Before making this request, however, weigh the potential benefit of improved scores against the possible stress to your child of retaking the test. Still another option is to place a statement in your child's file disputing the accuracy of the test results.

More often than not, standardized test scores will provide a good barometer of your child's academic skills. Indeed, most of the tests typically used by school districts are carefully developed measures of academic achievement and aptitude. In reviewing the results, begin by looking at the overall pattern of scores, and don't just focus on one area of weakness. Get out last year's test scores and note whether there has been an improvement or decline in any area. Pay particular attention to reading, given its critical importance to success in and out of school. Once you have the big picture, look for specific skills that are weak. Some computer profiles will provide a skill breakdown by analyzing responses to each item.

If the test results point to academic deficiencies in your child, arrange a meeting with the teacher. This conference should be a two-way dialogue. You may have information for the teacher that is useful in working with your child. Don't hesitate to share your ideas. Also consider asking the following questions:

- Are the results consistent with my child's classroom performance?
- What are her strengths and weaknesses? How does she compare academically with her classmates?
- Do the results suggest the need for changes in the way she is taught (for example, changes in instructional methods, teaching materials, class groupings, or homework assignments)?
- Is my child in need of remedial education?
- Is she in need of a more in-depth evaluation to determine whether she has a learning disability?
- Will tutoring help my child?
- How can I help my child at home?

You may also wish to talk with the teacher if your child receives exceptionally high scores, to determine whether she is being sufficiently challenged. Inquire whether any changes in the teacher's classroom approach or in the child's program are warranted. If your child's classroom performance is well below the level of her test performance, talk with the teacher to try to identify what obstacles are interfering with her success in class.

Parents also need to examine their own approach with their child. Give thought to whether your academic expectations and responses to your child are appropriate in light of the results. Are you pushing her to do work that is beyond her capability? Conversely, do the results suggest that you should revise your expectations upward? Do the results indicate a particular skill or talent that should be further developed? Are there specific areas that you should be helping to strengthen? Also consider the implications of the results for future educational and career opportunities.

PREPARING YOUR CHILD

Many districts prepare children for standardized tests by giving them practice tests. Some districts have even modified their curriculum so that what is taught dovetails with what is tested. What should you do to get your child ready? Very little. Children will not gain much other than anxiety and apprehension from studying for these tests. Parents can, however, help to make the testing process more comfortable and less anxiety-provoking by doing the following:

- Talk with your child about the test a day or two before it is given. (Your school district should inform you of the test dates well in advance; make a note on your calendar.) Keep it brief (perhaps five minutes), low-key, and pressure free. Explain that the tests are used by the school to help children learn better but that the results have no effect on grades. Encourage your child to do her best while not giving the test undue importance. Discussing the test at length and with intense concern will send a message to your child that her worth hinges on her test performance or that her future rides on the results. Parent anxiety, which is readily transparent to children, engenders child anxiety.
- Suggest some of the following test-taking skills to an older child:
  - complete sample exercises
  - pay close attention to the directions
  - ask for help if confused

- pace yourself so you do not spend too much or too little time with one item
- mark the scoring sheet carefully and avoid stray marks
- look for key words to aid in understanding (for example, "not," "but," "except," and "only")
- check your work if you finish early
- work until told to stop
- Have your child get a good night's sleep. Awaken your child a few minutes earlier than usual to avoid a frenzied morning.
- Make a special effort to give your child a nutritious breakfast the day of the testing, but don't make an issue of the matter if she refuses to eat.
- Avoid arguments or discussion of upsetting topics the morning of the testing. Try to keep the morning routine the same.

REVIEWING THE RESULTS WITH YOUR CHILD

Children in kindergarten and first grade are typically too young to review test results with you except in general terms. Older children may benefit from a discussion of their strengths and weaknesses. Give thought to your manner of presentation, and encourage your child to ask questions or raise concerns. Explain the results in a nonjudgmental, relatively matter-of-fact way, using words and concepts appropriate to your child's age. Do not disparage her performance or express disappointment with the results, and avoid making comparisons with the performance of siblings or friends. Special sensitivity is required if your child has performed poorly. Let her know that everybody has areas of strength and weakness, but do not dwell on her difficulties. Try to find some strengths to highlight, even if they are only strengths for your child, and let her know that test scores can change with time.

A PEEK INTO THE FUTURE

Standardized testing has had more than its share of detractors. It has been criticized for trivializing education, for wasting students' and educators' time, for causing districts to teach to the tests, for assessing a narrow range of abilities, for discriminating against minority students, and for favoring speedy responses over thoughtful ones. In an effort to address some of these concerns, test developers have been experimenting with new kinds of tests and different approaches to evaluation. Most notably, tests are increasingly requiring students to write essays and focusing on higher-order thinking skills. This is part of an effort to assess students' ability to reason and not just retain information, to evaluate their ability to think profoundly not just quickly. It will not be too long before students will be taking standardized tests on computers, with the questions tailored to the test-taker's ability level and the results pointing to what the student needs to study. This will help to change the focus of testing from what the student scores to what she knows and does not know.

Another trend on the educational horizon is the development of national standards. These standards would represent benchmarks of what students should know and be able to do at each grade level. Students would then take national tests to determine whether they are attaining the skills expected for their grade level. Critics of this approach contend that school districts should retain control of the academic curriculum.

A NOTE OF CAUTION

We live in a society that endows tests with almost magical properties. Yet tests are undeserving of such confidence. When it comes to children, standardized tests do not tell the whole story. They tell us little about a child's creativity, curiosity, or artistic expression. They shed almost no light on a child's emotional maturity or social insight. They convey little about a child's appetite for learning, her determination, or her patience. And many tests still have built-in cultural biases, which work to the disadvantage of minority students. Tests can be particularly misleading with young children. Their test scores can change dramatically, as can their classroom performance. Some children start off slowly in school and then gradually blossom; others do well in the early grades and then struggle in later years.

The lesson is clear: Parents and educators must make cautious use of test results. They provide a picture of a child's skills at a specific point in time, in effect a snapshot of a moving target. Test results should never be the sole basis for educational decisions. Educational decisions must also consider (1) the judgments of those who know the child's abilities best, namely teachers and parents, and (2) other sources of information about the child, including grades, classroom tests, work samples, homework, and classroom participation.

Because standardized test scores are often used as a barometer of the school's performance, they occupy a place of importance in the school district. While we have certainly progressed from the days of the nineteenth century when teachers were sometimes paid according to how well their students performed, educators today continue to feel pressure to increase test scores. This pressure may give rise to instruction designed to do just that, raise the scores. This is called "teaching to the test." In adapting what they teach to what is tested, teachers may neglect important educational areas not being assessed by the tests. For example, teachers may focus more on teaching their students to remember information than on teaching them how to reason and problem-solve. Some schools have been so concerned about the consequences of low scores that they have kept some academically deficient students from taking the test. Districts have even been known to hold pep rallies to urge students to do well on the tests or to offer money to the highest scorers.

This pressure will persist as long as the public maintains its scoreboard mentality, in which test scores are the gauge of school quality and the primary means of ensuring school accountability. Parents can play an important role in making sure that the pressure for higher test scores is not the primary basis for educational decisions.

CHAPTER NINE

CHILDREN WITH SPECIAL NEEDS

The overriding goal of a school district should be to meet the educational needs of all its students. Given the widely varying ability levels and differing social and emotional needs of students today, this is a daunting challenge for any school district. In a perfect world, regular teachers would be able to adapt their instruction to the needs of their students without outside assistance. But individualized instruction is not possible for all students in today's classrooms, especially with class sizes of twenty-five or thirty students, demands on teachers to adhere to the curriculum, and pressure on schools to raise test scores.

Recognizing that regular teachers cannot be all things to all students, public schools offer programs to students with special needs. The types of programs vary with each district. At a minimum, a school district will offer special education, which is required by federal law. This chapter discusses the most common school programs, paying particular attention to special education and gifted and talented programs. The focus is on helping parents learn how these programs work, whether their child is a suitable candidate, and what they can do at home to meet his special needs.

SPECIAL EDUCATION PROGRAMS

If your child is having significant academic or behavioral difficulties and you have exhausted other school options to resolve the problem, special education may be warranted. Special education is individualized instruction for students with educational disabilities. Underlying special education is the belief that all disabled children, regardless of the nature or severity of their disability, can learn.

Special education is defined more by its method than its location. It can take place in various school settings, including the regular classroom, but the instruction should be carefully matched to the student's educational needs and adapted to his learning style. Because of these individualized approaches, special education programs often have fewer students than regular education programs and special education teachers typically have specialized certification. Special education differs from remedial education, which is instruction in basic academic skills for children who have mild weaknesses but are not educationally disabled.

Parents of children with school problems often ride an emotional roller coaster. They are usually perplexed, often exasperated, and sometimes hopeful. For many, the mere mention of special education elicits anxiety, even panic. If your child is being considered for special education, it may help to relieve your anxiety to know that you do not lose influence over your child's education if he enters a special education program. In fact, you gain rights and protections that are not available to parents of regular education students. Parents of special education students must be involved every step of the way. This is not just sound educational practice. It is the law!

This was not always the law. It was not too long ago that disabled children were segregated in separate wings of the school or in separate schools. They typically attended for a shorter day and year than other students. This all changed in 1975 with congressional passage of Public Law 94–142, the *Education for All Handicapped Children Act* (since renamed the *Individuals with Disabilities Education Act*). This law, hailed by many as an educational bill of rights for disabled children, requires all school districts to provide a "free appropriate public education" for all educationally disabled children from three to twenty-one, regardless of the nature or severity of their disability. Many states have chosen to go beyond federal law by providing educational programs for disabled children under the age of three. Some states provide educational services to disabled persons older than twenty-one. Over four million children nationwide now receive special education.

Public Law 94–142 sets out a number of rights for children receiving or being considered for special education, as well as for their parents. All public schools across the country must comply with these regulations. To begin with, your child cannot be evaluated for special education without your written agreement. Nor can he be placed in a special education program for the first time without your consent. Moreover, you are expected to participate in the development of your child's special education program. If you disagree with any aspect of the school district's decision regarding special education, you have the right to appeal to a third party for an impartial hearing (as can the school district if it disagrees with your decision). More on your rights and those of your child later. First, let's take a look at how children become eligible for special education.

Who Qualifies for Special Education?

Students with educational disabilities present a wide range of learning and behavioral characteristics. Matthew has cerebral palsy but is a gifted creative writer. Sarah has a reading problem that has engendered feelings of frustration and low self-esteem. Yolanda is blind but is able to read and write through the use of braille. Richard has a history of emotional problems and disruptive classroom behavior but has superior intelligence.

The common denominator to these and other special education students is that a specific problem is interfering with their ability to learn in a regular class setting. They have educational needs significantly different from their classmates' and require specialized instruction to learn effectively. Special education is not for children with physical disabilities unless those disabilities interfere with their ability to learn. Nor is it for children who are performing poorly because they are unmotivated or alienated from school. The key question is: Can the student learn effectively in a regular class setting using regular education approaches and materials? If the answer is no, special education is probably warranted.

What Is a Learning Disability?

The most frequent problem for which children receive special education is a learning disability. More common with boys, learning disabilities are found in approximately 10 percent of children nationwide. A learning disability is characterized by specific difficulties in acquiring information, usually causing deficiencies in academic skills. Additionally, a learning disability is not due to mental retardation, an emotional problem, a physical disability, lack of motivation, or environmental disadvantages. Distinguishing a learning disability from these problems can be tricky, and misdiagnosis is not uncommon. Students from minority groups are particularly vulnerable to misdiagnosis.

Finding out that your child has a learning disability (which goes by various names such as dyslexia, minimal brain dysfunction, specific language difficulty, and perceptual impairment) tells you little more than that he is having difficulty learning at the same pace or in the same way as most other children. You need more detailed information to fully understand the problem. That is because learning disabilities come in many shapes and sizes.

Some learning disabled children have difficulty learning to read, a problem that may be restricted to a deficiency in decoding or comprehension. Others may be skilled readers but have problems with written or oral language. They may have difficulty putting their thoughts on paper, so that what they write rarely reflects what they know. Or they may have problems processing what they hear even though their hearing is intact. Some learning disabled children grasp ideas quickly but have great difficulty remembering information. Others are clumsy and have poor eye-hand coordination. And still others may have an attention deficit: they have great difficulty concentrating in class and staying on task. Most learning disabled children do not have just one specific problem but rather a combination of problems.

While learning disabled children rarely have the same profile of strengths and weaknesses, they typically share two characteristics in common: they are not lazy and they are not slow. They are often puzzles to their teachers and parents—and almost always to themselves—because they typically do some things well and others poorly. Many grow frustrated and discouraged by their failure to keep pace with their classmates and may respond in class by misbehaving, withdrawing, or even becoming the class clown.

Children with learning disabilities sometimes outgrow the problem. Recent research indicates that children diagnosed with a reading disability in first grade often are not reading disabled when tested again as third- or sixth-graders. Other learning disabled children, however, do continue to have problems throughout school and sometimes even into adulthood. For these children, the hope is that through specialized teaching techniques and a positive, supportive approach both in school and at home, they will learn to develop some coping mechanisms and adjust to the disability. As a rule, the earlier learning problems are identified, the better the adjustment.

Referral for Special Education

In an effort to identify students with educational disabilities, school districts seek information from a variety of sources, including standardized tests, teachers' judgments, classroom performance, and parents' observations. School staff review this information on a continuing basis and determine which students should be evaluated by the school for a potential disability.

If your child is referred for evaluation, a school official, usually the principal, will contact you to set up a meeting to explain the reason for the referral, the evaluation procedures, and your due process rights. The school district is obligated to give you this information in writing (in your native language). If you do not receive this information, request it. The principal will then ask for your written consent to conduct the evaluation. The evaluation cannot proceed without your signature (unless a judge so orders, a rare occurrence). Your consent at this point only permits the school district to evaluate your child. Placement in a special education program is a separate step requiring further written consent.

You can request an evaluation of your child through a letter to the principal. While the school is not obligated to honor every parent request for an evaluation, it must at least review your child's educational status and determine whether he appears to have an educational disability. If so, the district must conduct the evaluation. If not, the district may refuse your request although it must tell you why in writing. If the district does not evaluate your child, you of course have the option of having your child evaluated privately and then having the results considered by the school district.

At what point should you request an evaluation of your child? This decision should be based on your observations and those of the teacher. Give weight to the views of an experienced teacher. Based on her understanding of appropriate age- and grade-level norms and her review of your child's classroom performance and standardized test scores, she may conclude that your child is performing well below expectations. She may point to reversals in your child's reading or writing (although these are not uncommon in kindergarten through second grade). She may observe that in reading your child is not breaking the code as his classmates have already done. She may note that your child has problems copying from the board and cannot stay on a line when he writes. Or she may tell you that your child doesn't retain information such as letter sounds or math facts.

But don't discount your own observations. You may be getting signals that are not apparent to the teacher that your child is struggling in school. He may resist going to school in the morning or take an inordinate amount of time to complete his homework or have mood changes that coincide with school attendance or exhibit sleeping or eating problems. Of course, before you go the route of evaluation for special education, you will want to work with the teacher first to try to resolve the problem.

The Evaluation Process

The purpose of the evaluation is to determine whether your child has an educational disability and, if so, to provide a suitable school program. The testing itself will not help your child, but it can help you understand why your child is having difficulty and how he can progress. The evaluation will be conducted by a group of professionals—a multidisciplinary team. The name and composition of this evaluation team vary from state to state, but the evaluation usually assesses the same areas. A school psychologist will evaluate the student's reasoning abilities through an individual intelligence test and assess his social and emotional status through observation in the classroom, testing, and talking with him. The evaluation team may also include a learning specialist who will evaluate the student's academic skills and learning style and look for evidence of a learning disability. A school social worker may meet with the parents to elicit their perspective and gain an understanding of the child's developmental history, family background, and social adjustment. The school nurse may test vision and hearing. A medical examination will also be conducted although parents have the option of having this done by their child's physician. The evaluation team may determine that other evaluations, for example, a psychiatric or neurological evaluation, are needed to further understand the student's difficulties.

After completing its evaluations, the evaluation team will review the results and determine whether the child is eligible for special education. The team will arrange a meeting with the parents and the teacher to share the evaluation results. If the student is found to qualify for special education, the evaluation team may assign a specific name to his problem. In many states, a student must be formally classified as having a specific disability to receive special education. Think of this classification as a passport to getting needed help for a student. While states vary in their classification systems, the following is a typical list of disabilities that might be used by a state:

- communication impaired
- emotionally disabled
- hearing impaired
- learning disabled
- mentally retarded
- multiply disabled
- physically disabled
- visually impaired

To be classified as having a specific disability, a student must meet the criteria specified in the state regulations. If you have concerns about the appropriateness of the recommended classification for your child, review these regulations carefully and make your views known to the school.

Parents often fear that the label will stigmatize their child. School districts are sensitive to this concern and most make efforts to minimize the negative effects of the label by keeping it confidential and not drawing attention to the student's special education status. In deciding whether to agree to the classification, parents need to balance the potential influence-shaping impact of the label against the benefits of special education made possible by the classification. If the student clearly needs individualized instruction, the advantages of special education usually outweigh the risks of bias from the classification. The student's special education status may even qualify him for advantages later on, including waiving of certain high school graduation requirements, taking the Scholastic Achievement Test untimed, or receiving special consideration when applying for college admission.

Federal law requires that school districts reevaluate all special education students every three years to determine whether they still require special education. If the answer is yes, the special education program is either continued as is or revised in accordance with the student's current educational needs. If the answer is no, the student is "declassified," meaning he is no longer considered to have an educational disability and no longer eligible for special education.

Developing Your Child's Special Education Program

If your child is evaluated and you agree with the school's recommendation for special education eligibility and classification, you are ready to participate in the development of his special education program, what is commonly called the Individualized Education Program, or IEP. An IEP must be designed for every student who receives special education and serves as a road map to guide the special education teacher. The program cannot begin until the IEP is completed. It must be developed by a team that includes a school official (usually an evaluation team member or a special education supervisor), a teacher, and the parents. Your child may even participate in this meeting, if appropriate.

An IEP is a written document that describes in detail a program of individualized instruction designed to help eliminate or compensate for the student's disability. The school district must implement the IEP as written and without cost to the parents. By law the IEP must contain the following elements:

- the student's current academic skills and behavioral characteristics
- the type of special education program
- related services (for example, speech therapy, occupational therapy, transportation, or counseling) to help with other school-related concerns
- annual goals and short-term objectives of the special education program
- the extent to which the student will participate in regular education classes or programs
- the date for beginning the program and its expected duration
- procedures for reviewing the student's progress

Once the IEP has been developed, the school will ask for your written consent to begin the program described in the IEP. It cannot begin without your signature. Do not succumb to pressure to sign immediately. You may want to ponder the recommendations and talk with others before deciding. You are also within your rights to observe the placement being considered for your child before deciding whether to consent. If you disagree with the recommended program and choose not to consent, the school may try to work out a plan that satisfies both you and the school or it may appeal your decision to an impartial third party.

If you agree with the IEP, the school district must implement the program as soon as possible. School districts are not allowed to place a special education student on a waiting list for a program. Once implemented, the IEP must be reviewed by law every year in a meeting attended by school staff and parents. You may also request a program review before its scheduled time. At this meeting, you will want to consider whether your child has made progress in his areas of weakness and met the goals set out for him. If not, you need to find out why. This review may result in a continuation of the special education program or in its revision.

The IEP controls what educational services your child receives. It gives you power at the same time as it provides your child protection. The school district is obligated by law to do what is in the IEP—and is not obligated to do what is not in the IEP—so make sure that the IEP reflects what you believe your child needs. And be specific. Rather than putting in an IEP that your child will receive occupational therapy once a week, state that your child will receive occupational therapy every Monday morning from 10:00 to 10:45.

Special Education Program Alternatives

Each school district must provide a range of special education programs to meet the varying needs of students with disabilities. The basic special education programs are described below, listed from least to most restrictive. The amount of time a student is in a program and its focus of instruction should be specified in the IEP. State law may limit the number of students allowed in a special education program and the length of time a student may spend in the program each day.

REGULAR CLASS: A student with an educational disability may be able to succeed in a regular class if the teacher makes adjustments in her expectations, her teaching approach, her standards of evaluation, or the teaching materials. The teacher may require the guidance of a special educator or a school psychologist for this placement to work effectively.

REGULAR CLASS WITH IN-CLASS SUPPORT: A student may attend a regular class but receive help in that setting from a special education teacher or aide. This allows the student to remain in a class that would otherwise be confusing or difficult. The success of this arrangement depends on how well the regular teacher and special teacher or aide work together.

RESOURCE ROOM: A student may leave the regular classroom for part of the day to attend a special education program in what is often called a resource room. The special education teacher will provide intensive instruction to the student on an individual or small-group basis. She will either help the student with work from the regular class or teach a specific subject (in which case the special education teacher will give the grade for that subject).

SPECIAL EDUCATION CLASS: A student with a significant disability may attend a special education class for most of the school day. Students in special education classes are usually grouped with others with similar educational problems. Most school districts have special education classes in regular schools, enabling students in these classes to be mainstreamed in regular classes. Depending on the needs of the student and the available programs in the district, a student may be recommended for a special education class in a school other than the neighborhood school. This class might be in another public school in the district, or a public school in a nearby district, or a county school exclusively for special education students, or a private school for special education students. This placement, if agreed to by the school district, is without cost to parents.

Mainstreaming

Federal law requires that students with educational disabilities attend regular education programs if their needs can be met in that setting. This is called mainstreaming. The goal of mainstreaming is to help disabled students learn to adjust academically and socially to regular education classes. A secondary but still important goal is to help nondisabled students learn to accept children who are different in some way. Mainstreaming thus promotes the self-image, confidence, and social skills of disabled students while fostering acceptance and understanding by nondisabled students.

If your child is recommended for special education, then he must be mainstreamed as much as possible consistent with his educational abilities and needs. In special education jargon, a disabled student must be placed in the least restrictive environment. The least restrictive setting depends on the particular student's skills and abilities. What is restrictive for one student may not be for another. Some disabled students attend a special education program for the entire day. Others are in a regular class for the entire day. Most fall somewhere in between, attending some special education and some regular education classes.

In recent years, more and more parents of special education students have been pushing for their children, even those with severe disabilities, to be taught in regular classes. This inclusive education trend has aroused considerable debate. Supporters argue that disabled children benefit from being in a setting with nondisabled children, even if they cannot perform all of the classroom tasks or completely grasp the lesson. Critics contend that severely disabled children lose out academically by being in a regular class and that teachers are not prepared to cope with the demands of children with significant disabilities. Inclusive education is most successful when the regular teacher is adequately prepared and a special education teacher or aide is present in the regular classroom to work with the disabled student.

If you and the school conclude that your child is not yet ready for mainstreaming in academic classes, you should be able to find some nonacademic classes (for example, art, music, or gym) that he can attend successfully. Remember that your child may not follow the entire lesson but may still benefit socially from being among nondisabled students. Placing a disabled student in a regular class or program requires careful planning by both the school and parents, from choosing a flexible, understanding teacher to providing the teacher with information and strategies specifically geared to the student's needs. Also, make an effort to involve your child in after-school activities. Your child cannot be denied opportunities to participate in extracurricular activities such as a club, musical group, or student committee because of his disability. For students with physical disabilities, the school may need to adapt the building to provide access to educational programs.

Your Due Process Rights

Federal and state laws describe a variety of procedures to ensure that the views of parents are considered and rights of children are protected. The federal law (Public Law 94–142) and the accompanying regulations must be followed by all school districts across the country. All states have enacted additional regulations that school districts in that state must follow, so you will want to consult your state's special education code. A basic summary of your rights and the school district's obligations follows.

PARENTS HAVE THE RIGHT TO . . .

- request an evaluation by the school if you believe your child is educationally disabled. If the school decides not to do the evaluation, it must inform you in writing of its reasons.
- have your child evaluated privately and have the results considered by the school district.
- request an evaluation of your child at school expense by professionals not connected with the school (an "independent evaluation") if you disagree with the school evaluation.
- refuse the school district's request to evaluate your child.
- review the results of the school's evaluation of your child, including the reports of the various evaluations.
- examine all school records pertaining to your child, have the results explained to you, obtain copies of those records, and request that records you believe are inaccurate be changed.
- have a person of your choice accompany you to school meetings about your child.
- participate in the development of the special education program for your child (called the Individualized Education Program, or IEP).
- withdraw your consent at any time to the evaluation or placement of your child.
- observe the special education placement being considered for your child.
- participate in the annual review of your child's special education program.
- request a reevaluation of your child's special education status and program before the end of the three-year eligibility period.
- initiate a due process hearing to challenge the school's decision regarding the special education of your child.

THE SCHOOL DISTRICT IS REQUIRED TO . . .

- provide a free appropriate public education to all students with educational disabilities from the ages of three to twenty-one. (Some states provide programs to persons younger than three and older than twenty-one.)
- obtain your written consent before it can evaluate your child for possible special education placement.
- obtain your written consent before it can place your child in a special education placement for the first time.
- obtain your written consent before it can release your child's records to any person or organization outside the school district (with a few rare exceptions).
- conduct the evaluation in your child's native language.
- base its decision on special education eligibility and placement on multiple evaluations from different perspectives.
- develop and implement an Individualized Education Program (IEP) for your child if he is determined eligible for special education.
- provide your child with related services needed to benefit from special education.
- provide your child with an educational program in the least restrictive setting. This means that the program must allow your child to be with nondisabled children as much as possible while still meeting his educational needs.
- inform you in writing before it changes your child's special education program.
- inform you in writing of its reasons for not granting your request to change your child's special education program.
- conduct an annual review of your child's special education program at a meeting at which you participate.
- reevaluate your child's special education eligibility at least once every three years. (Some states require this every two years.)
- inform you of meetings early enough to give you a chance to attend.
- communicate with parents of children receiving or being considered for special education in their native language. Parents who are hearing impaired have the right to an interpreter.

Your Role in the IEP Meeting

If your child is recommended for special education, the most important meeting you will attend is the IEP meeting. You will find the strategies discussed in chapter 3 in the section entitled "Parent-Teacher Conferences" useful as you prepare for and participate in this meeting. In addition, you may want to take some of the following steps to help you become a full and equal member of the IEP team.

GET TO KNOW YOUR CHILD'S STRENGTHS AND WEAKNESSES. Observe your child in different situations at home and review samples of his schoolwork. You might even want to observe your child in school before the meeting, but make sure to call the school in advance.

TALK WITH YOUR CHILD before the meeting to find out about school subjects and activities he likes and dislikes, his own assessment of his strengths and weaknesses, classroom conditions that help him learn, and suggestions for program change.

DO YOUR HOMEWORK. Talk with parents who have gone through a similar process. They can guide you in what will be discussed and decided at the meeting, inform you about how to participate effectively, and tell you what you need to know about school policies and procedures. Special education parent organizations can be helpful as well. Also, familiarize yourself with key provisions of your state's special education code. The school should give you a copy of this code at the time of referral or at the IEP meeting. If not, make sure to request one. If you need help deciphering the rules, contact the special education division of the state department of education.

CONSIDER WHAT YOU WANT IN THE IEP. Review the components of the IEP and note which services you would like your child to receive and which goals you think are appropriate.

MAKE A LIST OF YOUR QUESTIONS. Bring them to the meeting and be sure to get answers to your most important concerns.

CONSIDER BRINGING ANOTHER PERSON WITH YOU TO THE MEETING. This person—a relative, a friend, another parent experienced in the IEP process, a therapist, or an advocate—may have special education expertise or knowledge of your child and may help you to raise important issues. If someone is accompanying you, let the school know in advance as a courtesy.

THINK ABOUT HAVING YOUR CHILD ATTEND ALL OR PART OF THE MEETING. The perceptions of your child may be valuable in designing aspects of the educational program. Moreover, he may be more receptive to an educational program that he has helped to develop. The older the child, the more likely it is that he will be able to participate meaningfully.

OFFER YOUR VIEWS. You probably know your child better than you think you do. In addition to letting school staff know what he likes and dislikes and any areas of special sensitivity, you may be able to offer some hints to the teacher about what will work with your child and what will not. For example, you may have learned from working with him that he works well in segments of fifteen minutes followed by a break. Or that he learns best when the lesson is supplemented by concrete activities. Or that he needs an example or two before proceeding on his own.

CONSIDER TAKING NOTES. This not only provides a record of what was discussed but may help focus your concentration.

REQUEST CLARIFICATION. Ask for an explanation whenever you do not understand terms, acronyms, concepts, or procedural issues. Request examples, if necessary. Special educators often use initials and assume you understand. But there is no reason for a parent to know what EMR, WISC-III, ADD, LD, IEP, or LRE stand for. Don't hesitate to ask for a translation. You might also restate what another person has said to make sure you are on the same wavelength.

ASK ABOUT THE VARIOUS PROGRAM OPTIONS AND REQUEST TO OBSERVE THEM. Observing the special education programs under consideration can help you make an informed decision about your child's program. Consider having your child accompany you so you can gauge his reactions.

ASK SCHOOL STAFF FOR SUGGESTIONS ABOUT HOME ACTIVITIES. Find out what you can do to support your child's school program without overburdening him or causing unnecessary pressure.

Helping Your Child Adjust to Special Education

Your job doesn't end once you have helped to develop an IEP and given the school the go-ahead for the program to begin. In some respects, it is only beginning. You will want to monitor the program closely to make sure your child is receiving the services described in the IEP. Pay careful attention to his schedule to make sure that he is clear about where to go and not overwhelmed by the various teachers or programs. You will also want to keep tabs on your child's progress and step in if he is not making gains. The IEP is not etched in stone. It is a living document that can be changed at any time as long as the school and parents agree.

You will be most successful in keeping track of your child's program and progress if you develop a good working relationship with his teacher and keep in regular contact with her. This might be in the form of a weekly telephone call or a notebook for teacher and parent comments that goes between home and school daily. You also may want to meet with the teacher soon after the school year begins to lay the groundwork for a productive relationship and provide key information regarding your child.

In addition to working with the teacher to reinforce school skills at home, pay attention to your child's self-esteem. Students with disabilities have a history of failure and often are down on themselves. Many become discouraged. Others even feel defective. In the words of one disabled child, "I feel like I'm broken." Be sympathetic to their difficulty and let them know you understand their frustration. Focus more on their strengths than their shortcomings. Look for opportunities to praise and encourage them and highlight their accomplishments.

Because of the obstacles educationally disabled children face, your role is vital in advocating for your child. After all, nobody knows as much about your child as you do and nobody will fight as hard as you will to protect his interests and obtain needed services. Many districts have begun groups for parents of special education students, often called SEPTA, for Special Education PTA. Through these and other groups (see appendix A), parents have addressed special education concerns with the board of education, established recreational and social programs for children with special needs, and provided a forum for parents to share concerns with each other. Other parents can offer a wealth of information about raising a disabled child and negotiating the special education maze. They can also provide the understanding and emotional support that can only come from those who have gone through a similar process.

GIFTED AND TALENTED PROGRAMS

Experts estimate that 3 to 5 percent of the nation's schoolchildren are academically gifted. In addition, many other children demonstrate talents in nonacademic areas. These students merit special attention just as students with disabilities do. Their abilities need to be nurtured and cultivated if they are to attain their full potential. Yet schools do not always recognize the gifts and talents of their students or provide instruction suited to their abilities.

This is partially due to the lack of a strong federal commitment to gifted children. Federal law does not mandate educational programs for gifted students as it does for disabled students, although about half of the states require local school districts to provide gifted education. And many of the nonmandated programs have been the first to go where there have been budget cutbacks. Moreover, many educators cling to the belief that gifted students can make it on their own. They contend that the gifted have the ability and drive to reach their potential without special attention.

This may be true for some gifted children but for many it is a myth. Gifted students often become bored and frustrated with the slow pace of regular class instruction and the tediousness of the assignments. Their boredom may take the form of inattentiveness, withdrawal, incomplete assignments, or even fooling around, and is sometimes mistaken for inability or laziness. Even Einstein was pegged as a slow learner at the age of twelve. For these children, their gifts may go undetected and their intellects unchallenged. Some become so discouraged that they drop out of school before attaining a high school diploma. It is estimated that up to 10 percent of the students who drop out are gifted. This problem was highlighted in a 1993 federal report that concluded that American schools are not challenging their brightest students and are spending little money for suitable educational programs.

Some gifted students feel out of step socially as well. They may have different interests from their classmates and values that depart from the norm. Peers may view them as weird and esteem them only for their brains. As described by David Cooke, a gifted fifteen-year-old, in a 1985 article in *The New York Times:* "I look like a normal ninth-grader but I am not treated like one. I am instead treated like something other than human, as if I had just beamed down from Mars." In an effort to fit in, gifted students may downplay their abilities by intentionally giving wrong answers or not speaking up when they know the right answers. (This is particularly true in middle school when conforming often takes precedence over performing.)

Even school staff may fail to appreciate gifted students. Teachers may see them as rebellious or disrespectful because they challenge rules they perceive as illogical or ask endless and difficult questions. Their maverick thinking may be disparaged rather than applauded. The end result is that many gifted students feel isolated from their peers and misunderstood by their teachers.

A caution is in order here. While gifted students frequently feel out of place with their classmates, many others are well-rounded youngsters with good social skills. Moreover, long-term studies indicate that gifted children often become accomplished and satisfied adults.

The school experience of many gifted students makes it clear that they cannot be left to fend for themselves educationally. Public schools have a responsibility to affirm their special abilities and challenge them to be their best. Unfortunately, this is not happening in many schools across the country. Because there is no federal requirement for gifted education, the programs provided to gifted students depend on the mandates of states and the initiatives of local school districts. As a result, the services for gifted students vary dramatically from state to state and district to district.

Despite the absence of a federal mandate for gifted education, Congress does understand its importance. In 1988, it passed the Jacob Javits Gifted and Talented Students Education Act. This legislation recognized that gifted and talented students are a "national resource vital to the future of the nation" and established a national center of gifted education to gather information and fund model programs.

Identifying Gifted Students

When people think of gifted students, they usually think of very bright youngsters who excel academically. This is a narrow view of giftedness but one that is embraced by many school districts. Children can of course show exceptional ability in other than academic areas. Some have great promise in art or music. Others are gifted in dance, drama, or writing. And still others demonstrate superior leadership ability or keen social insight. This broader view of giftedness, spurred by the work of Harvard psychologist Howard Gardner, recognizes that there is not just one kind of intelligence but rather many different kinds.

The educational ideal is to identify children with academic as well as nonacademic gifts and then provide programs that cultivate all these talents. Most schools fall well short of this goal. This is reflected in the process by which schools identify gifted students.

Most school districts continue to use the intelligence or IQ test as the primary yardstick for judging eligibility for gifted programs. Some districts use group-administered intelligence tests while others use individually administered tests. Individual tests are preferred because the results are more reliable and trustworthy. The two most common individual intelligence tests are the Stanford-Binet Intelligence Scale and the Wechsler Intelligence Scale for Children. Districts that use the intelligence test to determine eligibility often require that students score at or above 130, which is comparable to the ninety-eighth percentile rank (see chapter 8 for a discussion of testing). Because school districts often use numerical cutoffs to qualify students for gifted programs, the same student may be considered gifted in one district but not gifted in another.

While the intelligence test is less biased toward minority students than in the past as a result of revisions, it remains controversial. It is a good measure of reasoning ability but not of other qualities that define giftedness such as creativity and persistence. It predicts academic success well but falls short in predicting life success. In addition, reliance on the intelligence test may cause late bloomers, poor test-takers, minority students, or disabled children to be overlooked for gifted programs. At a minimum, programs to identify gifted children should supplement the intelligence test with other measures such as an achievement test, a test of creativity, samples of the child's work, and teacher and parent assessments.

Gifted programs that use intelligence or achievement test results to determine eligibility often miss excellent candidates. Research shows that most adults who are accomplished in their fields scored below the ninety-fifth percentile on standardized tests as children. An approach to selecting gifted students that attempts to correct this problem provides enrichment activities to all children and then offers further enrichment to students who demonstrate exceptional ability, creativity, and commitment during the initial activities. This approach recognizes that the talents of some children only emerge while they are engaging in stimulating and challenging activities.

Programs for the Gifted

Programs for gifted students attempt to provide educational activities that challenge their intellect and allow them to pursue areas of special interest or skill. Gifted education does not mean giving a gifted student the same kind of work as other students in a larger dose or at a faster pace. This will turn off most students. Rather it means providing activities that arouse their curiosity and stretch their imagination. These may include group discussions, in-depth explorations of topics of student interest, projects involving real-life problems (for example, alternative energy sources), and trips to places of cultural interest. The hope is that through gifted education children will develop leadership skills, hone their higher-level thinking skills, and learn to approach problems from a variety of perspectives. The role of the teacher of gifted students is not just to dispense information but also to nurture their talents through guided exploration and self-discovery.

Programs for the gifted are not without controversy. Many feel that these programs are elitist because they single out children for special treatment and convey a message of mediocrity to those not selected. Declaring some students gifted also means declaring others ungifted. Segregating gifted students from ungifted students undermines an important mission of education: to help children of diverse characteristics learn to get along with each other.

Sensitive to these concerns, many school districts have opted for a more inclusionary approach in which gifted students spend the majority of their day in regular education programs but are pulled out of class to participate in an enrichment program. This approach to gifted education as well as others are described below:

PULLOUT PROGRAM: A child may be pulled out of his regular class for one or more hours a week to work in a small group with a teacher who provides enrichment activities. Children of different ages or grades may work together. This approach is most appropriate at the elementary level. Parents should make sure that their child does not miss crucial regular class instruction and should be alert to signs of stress from the additional workload. They should also ensure that their child is being challenged in his regular class and has an opportunity to move at his own pace.

SPECIAL CLASS: Full-day special classes for the gifted are more likely in large than small school systems. Some urban school systems even have special schools for the gifted. New York City, for example, has developed high schools for students showing promise in the sciences, the creative arts, and community leadership. Full-time programs for the gifted have the disadvantage of removing positive role models from regular classes and may promote elitist attitudes among the gifted.

ADVANCED COURSES: Exceptionally able high school students may be enrolled in honors or advanced placement courses or even college courses. Some school districts may arrange a community mentorship (for example, working with an artist in his studio) in the student's area of talent.

ACCELERATION: In elementary school, gifted students may be placed in a higher grade for a specific subject or even skipped to the next grade for all subjects. Gifted secondary school students may skip courses in which they can demonstrate mastery. Some may even graduate early from high school. The school and the parents need to consider the "whole child" in making the decision to accelerate a student, including the impact on his social development and confidence (see "Skipping a Grade" in chapter 10).

A comprehensive approach to gifted education developed by Joseph Renzulli of the University of Connecticut is being employed by school districts in all fifty states. The hallmark of this approach is that all children have unique gifts that need to be cultivated. Children in regular classes are given projects and exercises that stimulate creative thinking. The students who qualify for special attention beyond the regular class enrichment are those who not only have above-average ability but also demonstrate unusual creativity and a high level of task commitment in their regular class.

Parents should also look into programs outside school to challenge their child. Summer programs offering in-depth study of a range of topics are available in many communities, community colleges, and universities. After-school and weekend programs also offer opportunities for gifted students to take on intellectual challenges and pursue their interests. The Center for Talented Youth (see appendix A) sponsors programs for gifted students. If suitable programs are not available in your community and you are feeling particularly ambitious, join with other parents to organize activities for children with similar interests and talents.

Advocating for Your Child

Students are typically nominated for gifted programs by their teachers, but parents may also request consideration for their child. You may want to make this request if your child has above-average academic skills and in addition demonstrates many of the following characteristics:

- grasps concepts easily and quickly
- has an excellent understanding of cause/effect relationships
- has creative approaches to problems
- is an independent thinker
- persists with challenging tasks
- can concentrate for a long period
- has a love of learning and a thirst for knowledge
- has a wealth of information about a range of subjects
- has a large vocabulary and uses complex sentences
- is unusually sensitive to social and moral issues

Your child's teacher will likely have a good sense of age-appropriate norms and can help you determine whether your child's skills and abilities differ markedly from those of his classmates. The principal or guidance counselor can give you information about the district's programs and the procedures for qualifying. If your child is found eligible, work with the school to find the right educational fit between the school's program and your child's strengths.

If the school district is unwilling to consider your child for the gifted program, you may want to have your child tested privately by a psychologist. (Your child's physician or the state's psychological association can recommend someone.) The results of an individual intelligence test, even if administered privately, can go a long way toward convincing the school district that your child qualifies for the gifted program. Bear in mind that in your eagerness to obtain special help for your child, you may be placing subtle pressures on him to qualify for the gifted program. If he does not qualify, he may feel as if he has let you down. Make sure that you do not convey to your child that his participation in the gifted program is critical to you or vital to his educational future.

If your child does not qualify for the program, you may still want to talk with the teacher to ensure that your child is learning at his own pace. Chapter 10 (under "Skipping a Grade") discusses ways that your child may be challenged while attending a regular class. If your school district does not have a gifted program, you may want to take on the challenge of persuading the board of education that it should. Visit other schools to find out what they are doing for gifted students and talk with professionals in the state department of education about state mandates as well as funding issues. Rally other parents in support of this cause before you approach the board of education.

Raising a Gifted Child

Raising gifted children poses special challenges for parents. These children have the same needs for love and acceptance as other children but in addition they may have a strong streak of independence and a ready willingness to challenge your rules and limits. Most parents of gifted children are aware of the importance of such activities as reading to their children from an early age, familiarizing them with the library, talking with them about a range of topics, and taking them to places of cultural interest. The following are some less obvious principles to keep in mind as you help your child develop his talents in a way that preserves self-esteem.

PROMOTE YOUR CHILD'S INTERESTS AND SKILLS. While you may have interests that you would like your child to pursue, let him discover for himself what he has an interest in and then provide the time, materials, and opportunities to allow him to pursue that. Once he gets involved in an activity, restrain yourself from taking over or being overly intrusive.

SET REASONABLE LIMITS AND STICK TO THEM. Bright children can often be difficult to discipline. They want to debate every point and often do so with the skill of a Clarence Darrow. Choose your battles carefully. Once you have determined which issues are important to you and what restrictions are age appropriate, stand your ground. If you give in frequently to your child's pleas, you will be teaching him to manipulate and showing him that rules are not to be respected.

ENCOURAGE YOUR CHILD TO EXPRESS HIMSELF. Show interest in your child's thoughts and feelings and be respectful of his views, even those which are different or novel.

DON'T NEGLECT YOUR CHILD'S EMOTIONAL AND SOCIAL NEEDS. It is easy to forget that an eight-year-old who thinks like a ten-year-old is still emotionally an eight-year-old. Allow your child to act his chronological age. He may be light-years ahead of his peers in his ability to read or write a story but he likely has the same needs for emotional support and nurturing as well as peer acceptance. He needs to know that your love is unconditional and not related to his special talents. Promote your child's social development by giving him opportunities to play with children his own age and expand his interests beyond his special abilities.

BE SENSITIVE TO THE PRESSURES YOUR CHILD MAY BE FEELING. As the great philosopher Linus said to Charlie Brown: "There's no heavier burden than great potential." Gifted children often feel the weight of their giftedness, especially if their parents have dwelled on their need to live up to their potential or have showcased their talents for friends or family. Pressure to perform is something that comes quite naturally to gifted children. Additional pressures from parents can be counterproductive and may even engender rebelliousness. Praise him for his accomplishments and avoid dwelling on his failures.

ENCOURAGE YOUR CHILD TO TAKE CHANCES. Some gifted children are reluctant to take risks for fear of failing. In so doing, they may deny themselves worthwhile opportunities for growth and enjoyment. If they try and fail, they will have the chance to learn to deal with defeat, which may be a novel experience for them. Avoid discussion of their gifted status or they may avoid challenges for fear of discovering that they are really not gifted.

CONSIDER THE NEEDS OF YOUR OTHER CHILDREN. The brother or sister of a gifted child can develop feelings of low self-esteem and jealousy if the family is always placing the gifted child in the spotlight. While it is not necessary or desirable for parents to have the same standards of performance for all their children, it is important that they try to find areas in which siblings can shine.

AVOID STEREOTYPING YOUR GIFTED DAUGHTER. Even the most enlightened of parents can fall prey to sexual stereotypes. Monitor your own biases in talking with your daughter. Don't steer her toward certain subjects or careers or away from others because of her gender. If she shows an interest in science or math, for example, support and encourage her.

OTHER SCHOOL PROGRAMS

Schools will typically offer a range of other programs to help students with special needs. Some of these programs are required by law. Others may be offered at the initiative of the local school district. The most common of these programs at the elementary and middle school levels are described below. Vocational education, while a high school program, is discussed because parents may need to plan for this program during middle or junior high school years.

Many of the programs described below are "pullout" programs in that the student is taken out of his regular class for a set number of periods every week to work with a specialist. These programs can be burdensome for students if they are not planned carefully and thus require some parental monitoring. If your child is participating in a pullout program, make sure that he is not missing crucial instruction, which may cause him to fall behind his classmates, and that he knows what to do when he returns to class. Also consider how many special programs your child is attending and whether he is missing too much regular class time.

Remedial Education

All schools offer some kind of remedial instruction to help children with learning problems. These programs may go by different names (for example, basic skills instruction or compensatory education) but they usually operate in a similar manner. Students typically qualify for these programs by falling below a cutoff point on a standardized test. Eligible students are usually pulled out of their regular classes two, three, or even five times a week to work in small groups for about thirty to forty-five minutes at a time. Remedial instruction is usually offered in reading, writing, and math. This extra help should supplement but not supplant the regular classroom instruction. The goal ultimately is to help children succeed in regular classes. Remedial instruction can sometimes be confusing to students as they are exposed to a new curriculum and a new set of learning activities.

Ideally the remedial program should dovetail with regular class instruction.

Remedial education is sometimes confused with special education. Remedial education is designed for students with mild academic deficiencies, while special education is intended for students with more severe deficiencies that meet the criteria of an educational disability, as defined in the state's special education code. Students do not usually receive remedial education and special education at the same time.

Remedial programs may be funded by the state or federal government. Chapter 1 is a federally funded remedial education program for schools with a large concentration of low-income families. School districts are required to involve parents of Chapter 1 students in the design and implementation of the program. The impact of this program has been limited by the relatively small number of students from poor families who receive help from this program. In addition, research suggests that Chapter 1 students tend to fall behind in the classes they miss.

English as a Second Language Instruction

English as a second language instruction, or ESL as it is commonly known, is provided to children who have limited proficiency in English. Students may receive as much as one to two hours a day of ESL instruction. The remainder of the day they attend regular English-speaking classes. The goal is to help students become proficient in speaking, reading, and writing English as quickly as possible by immersing them in classes taught in English. The underlying assumption of ESL instruction is that students benefit most if they spend the majority of their day in English-speaking classes and they are encouraged to speak English as much as possible. Children of Hispanic background make up the largest share of those receiving ESL instruction, although children of Asian background are being placed in this program in increasing numbers.

Bilingual Education

Students for whom English is a second language, numbering 2.8 million nationwide, may be placed in a bilingual education program rather than an ESL program. Bilingual education provides students with instruction in both languages. Basic skills—reading, writing, and math—are taught in their native language to ensure that students master these skills and keep pace with their English-speaking peers. As students become more proficient in English, they should receive increasing amounts of instruction in English-speaking classes. The ultimate goal is for students to attend a full-time English-speaking program.

Bilingual education aims to help students learn to speak English while preserving their native language skills as well as their own cultural heritage. In an effort to help children whose language might be a barrier to learning, the Bilingual Education Act of 1974 provided federal funds to local school districts to develop bilingual education programs. The 1984 amendment to this law expanded the scope of the law and gave parents the right to decline a bilingual placement. While the law does not mandate that states provide bilingual education, it encourages school districts to offer transitional programs for non-English-speaking students until they are prepared to enter English-speaking classes. By law, students can participate in transitional bilingual education programs for a maximum of three years unless an exception is granted allowing them to participate for up to two more years. Bilingual education programs are most common in urban districts. In suburban or rural districts, students whose first language is not English are usually taught in ESL programs. Some school districts with a large number of Spanish-speaking students have begun truly bilingual programs in which English-speaking students learn to speak Spanish and Spanish-speaking students learn to speak English.

Bilingual education has stirred heated controversy. Some say that bilingual education eases students' entry into the mainstream of American life; others say it postpones it. Supporters claim that bilingual education is essential for students to master basic academic skills and develop the foundation for more advanced academic work. They also contend that bilingual education promotes cultural parity by conveying respect for the customs and culture of people from other countries. Critics of bilingual education argue that students remain in bilingual education too long and thus do not develop fluency in English. They claim that as a result bilingual education keeps students from participating in the mainstream of American society and serves to divide students rather than unite them.

If your child is placed in a bilingual or ESL program, make sure that he is actually proficient in another language and not just deficient in English. If the latter is the case, then a remedial English class is called for rather than bilingual or ESL instruction. Monitor your child's bilingual education program to ensure that he is increasingly mainstreamed into English-speaking classes and is making visible progress in his ability to speak English. If not, make an appointment with your child's school to discuss your concerns. The school should provide an interpreter if necessary. A child who is kept out of the mainstream of school will likely be kept out of the mainstream of society. Parents should bear in mind that their child's progress will be hastened if they also make an effort to learn to speak English. In addition, their facility with English will enhance their ability to participate in their child's school life.

Speech and Language Therapy

It is not uncommon for schoolchildren to have problems with speech pronunciation or language usage. Many school districts have speech language pathologists to help students with these problems, specifically difficulties in articulation (for example, problems with the "r" sound), speech fluency (for example, stuttering), or voice characteristics (for example, volume). In addition, students may have problems expressing themselves or understanding what others are saying (for example, teacher directions).

Students with articulation problems are often self-conscious and insecure about their speech and thus early intervention can be crucial. If you suspect your child has a speech problem, call your school and ask how to arrange a "screening" or evaluation by the speech language pathologist. If she does not invite you in to discuss the results of the evaluation, request to meet with her. You are entitled to know the results. She will make a judgment as to whether the speech problem is developmental, suggesting that with time it will correct itself as many do by age eight or nine, or whether it warrants speech therapy. If the pathologist identifies a problem, find out what exercises, if any, you can do at home with your child. Whatever you do, make sure you do not draw undue attention to his speech difficulties or continually correct his mistakes.

Some school districts evaluate preschoolers exhibiting communication difficulties and provide help, if necessary. Preschoolers with speech problems are prone to behavioral difficulties because of frustration expressing themselves. Early speech intervention can sometimes minimize these problems.

Peer Teaching

Many schools have adopted an idea that was popular in the days of the one-room schoolhouse: students helping students. The contemporary version of peer teaching may take different forms. A fourth-grader may read stories to kindergartners once a week; a sixth-grader may tutor some second-graders in math; one-half of a class may learn a skill and then teach it to the other students; or a student may be asked to help a disabled classmate adjust to a regular class.

The purpose of peer teaching is not only to provide extra help to students but also to raise the self-confidence and self-esteem of the students doing the teaching. Peer teachers may derive self-esteem from being admired by the students they are teaching and satisfaction from doing something useful and important. They may also learn to lead a group and use skills that are not called for in other school activities. And, as studies suggest, they may even gain academically. As the old adage goes, he who teaches learns. In preparing for or conducting the lesson, peer teachers may develop a new and more profound understanding of the material. Being responsible for teaching others may provide special motivation for a student to master the material.

Vocational Education

Vocational education programs provide technical training to students so that they will be able to obtain skilled jobs upon graduation. It is intended for students who are not planning to go to a four-year college. Students who are unmotivated to do academic work often get a new lease on school life upon entering vocational school although the academic work can be demanding and highly technical.

All school districts offer some kind of vocational education although the programs vary in length and breadth. Students may begin a vocational program as early as ninth grade and as late as twelfth grade. They may attend a vocational school all day, in which case they take academic courses at the vocational school. Or they may attend vocational school for half the day and attend their regular high school for the academic portion of their program. Some regular high schools offer vocational programs within the school building. As part of their vocational program, advanced students may work at a related job for part of the day under the supervision of a skilled worker and receive credit. Special vocational programs are also available for students with disabilities of varying kinds.

If your child is a candidate for vocational school, begin the information-gathering process in eighth grade. Contact your child's guidance counselor and find out what programs are available and when the application must be filed. Parents should look for programs where teachers are up-to-date in their training and have recent experience in the field, where the equipment and technology are comparable to what is being used in the field, where meaningful work experiences are provided, and where the school is successful in placing students in their chosen vocations.

Alternative Schools

Some school districts offer alternatives to the regular public school. These are not special education schools for students with disabilities but rather schools that differ in their teaching approach from that offered in more traditional schools. They vary in their structure and student composition. Many alternative schools are designed for students who are alienated from school and at risk of dropping out. The rules may be more relaxed, the classes may be small in size, and the students may work at their own pace. Larger school districts may offer "magnet schools" that are organized around specific themes (for example, music and art or science), designed for a particular population (for example, gifted students), or characterized by a specific teaching approach (for example, open education). These magnet schools are typically open to children throughout the school district.

Home Instruction

If your child is unable to attend school for medical reasons for a significant period of time (for example, more than two weeks), the school district may provide temporary instruction at home by a certified teacher. If your child is in need of home instruction because of a lengthy illness or injury, call the school nurse to find out the procedure. The school district will probably require a letter from your child's physician to document the nature of the problem and support the need for home instruction.

TURNING POINTS: MAKING WISE DECISIONS

Schooling does not always proceed on an even course. Many students travel a rocky road through public school, encountering obstacles along the way that impede their progress. These obstacles may take the form of adjustment problems: students failing to adjust to the academic and behavioral requirements of schools or schools failing to adjust to the needs of students. Some of these issues may have a critical and lasting impact on your child's education so your involvement is crucial. This chapter takes a look at some of these educational crossroads, including repeating a grade, skipping a grade, school discipline, corporal punishment, school phobia, and changing schools. This information will help you safeguard your child's rights and ensure that decisions are made with her interests in mind.

REPEATING A GRADE

As spring nears, parents may receive a dreaded call from their child's principal. "I'd like you to come in for a meeting to discuss your child's progress," she explains. At the conference, your worst fears are confirmed: the school wants your child to repeat the grade. While you may feel distress and even anger upon hearing this recommendation, attacking the school or blaming the teacher will only complicate the problem. You play a key role in this decision and need to channel your energy into becoming informed.

Retention, the educational term for repeating a grade, is often advised for children who are having academic problems. This is most common in the early elementary grades and happens more frequently with boys than girls. The decision whether to retain a student is difficult for both the school and the parents. It requires weighing the benefit of another year to master the skills of that grade against the stigma and possible loss of self-esteem engendered by retention.

As with many issues in education, it is rarely clear which course to follow. Educators do not agree on the merits of retention. Some argue that retention provides slow learners with more time to catch up and claim it boosts students' confidence by providing a program in which they can keep pace with their classmates and in some cases even excel. Children who have not mastered grade-level skills are destined for failure in the next grade, educators maintain, since so much of learning is sequential. They argue that the threat of retention also motivates students who are otherwise unmotivated.

Opponents of retention contend that children who stay back gain little academically over the long term and bear emotional scars from the feelings of failure and humiliation. Those opposed maintain that retention lessens students' interest in school, even to the point that they may eventually drop out. Educators add that parents and teachers may place undue pressures on children to perform in order to avoid retention.

Educators have swung back and forth on the issue of retention. In the early 1900s almost half of all students stayed back at least once. With the advent of the progressive education movement in the 1930s, "social promotion," namely promoting a child to the next grade regardless of school performance, became the favored educational practice in order to spare the child emotional distress. The pendulum swung back in the 1970s with the back-to-the-basics movement. With the push for academic excellence and the public insistence on higher standards, schools returned to a policy of holding back students who did not make the grade. Some districts even went so far as to require the passing of a test to advance to the next grade. While schools have backed off somewhat from these arguably harsh policies, retention remains in wide use today. It is estimated that about 6 percent of public school children are retained every year.

While it is frequently used, retention is not a proven tool. Research has not demonstrated that retention is consistently beneficial. Studies have found that over the long term children who were retained generally did no better, and in some cases worse, than equally low-achieving children who were promoted. While most retained students performed better the second time through the grade, academic performance tended to lessen after a few years. Students repeating a grade were more likely to benefit if they came from suburban schools and received individualized instruction or were placed in smaller classes the following year.

So what is a parent to do whose child is recommended for retention when the experts can't agree and the research is inconclusive? First and foremost, recognize that you as a parent play a role in this decision. School districts differ about who makes the ultimate decision if the principal and parents cannot agree, but most districts will give weight to your views, especially if you are informed about the policies and programs of the district and the status of your child. Request a copy of the school's promotion and retention policies.

A recommendation of retention should not come as a total surprise. The teacher should have kept you informed of your child's difficulties during the course of the year. If the school is considering retention for your child, typically either the teacher or principal will call you in for a conference in the spring. Your agenda at this meeting should neither be to confront the teacher nor to unquestioningly accept the school's recommendation. Rather your goal should be to gain information to allow you to make an informed decision. You may be angry with the teacher, but blaming her will impede your ability to make an objective assessment. Remember that retention is stressful for teachers too and the teacher is trying to do what she feels is in your child's best interest. Your job is to obtain information on your child's skills, abilities, and maturity level. Make sure you get specific information. Do not settle for generalizations such as "He's performing below grade level" or "She's lazy." Ask for samples of her work (for example, handwriting tasks, compositions, tests, and drawings) and compare them with those of an "average" child in the class.

There is no need to make a decision at this meeting. In fact, it is advisable that you do not. You will need time to mull over the information given to you, perhaps speak with the principal to find out what other options are available, and talk with your spouse or friends. The final decision might be made as late as the summer.

The decision whether to retain your child should be based on a variety of factors and should not rely too heavily on one factor only (for example, test scores or a grade in one subject). You may also want to seek the advice of the school psychologist or guidance counselor. Ask them to observe your child in class and review her records. The following guidelines may help you in gathering information and in deciding which factors to consider:

WHAT GRADE IS YOUR CHILD IN? Retention is less stigmatizing if done in the early grades; it is highly questionable after third grade. By fourth grade, most children have a stable group of friends and will likely have difficulty adjusting socially to staying back. Retention at the middle school level is rarely effective and may discourage a child to the point that she falls even further behind and eventually gives up. High school students typically advance to the next grade only when they have accumulated sufficient credits.

HOW DOES YOUR CHILD COMPARE WITH HER CLASSMATES ACADEMICALLY, SOCIALLY, AND EMOTIONALLY? Retention is more appropriate for students who are "late bloomers" and lagging behind in most subjects than for those who are struggling in one subject. A child who is having difficulty in reading but is otherwise keeping pace with her classmates is more in need of extra reading help than retention. In assessing your child's academic skills and maturity level, consider the teacher's views, test scores, and work samples, but also factor in your own knowledge of your child. You may find it useful to observe your child in class.

WHAT IS THE CAUSE OF YOUR CHILD'S ACADEMIC PROBLEMS? Your child's school difficulties may be due to reasons other than being a late bloomer. She may have a learning disability, or a problem with her hearing or vision, or be emotionally upset and unable to concentrate. Her learning style may be out of synch with the teacher's instructional style. A sudden drop-off in academic performance may be the result of an emotional or physical problem that has come on recently. If so, confronting the problem directly is usually more effective than retaining the student.

IS THERE ANY EVIDENCE TO SUGGEST THAT YOUR CHILD HAS A LEARNING DISABILITY? If so, request testing by the school's evaluation team (see chapter 9). Retention is usually not appropriate for a learning disabled child and may even be harmful. Having a learning disabled child repeat the grade and relearn the same material with the same approach will probably have the same results: failure and frustration.

HOW BIG IS YOUR CHILD COMPARED WITH CLASSMATES? If your child is big for her age, she will stand out even more when she stays back and will feel even more different from her classmates.

HOW OLD IS YOUR CHILD COMPARED WITH CLASSMATES? All other factors being equal, a child who is chronologically young for her grade is a better candidate for retention than one who is not.

WHAT ARE YOUR CHILD'S FEELINGS ABOUT THE RETENTION? If your child feels strongly about moving on, this suggests that she feels up to the challenge and is willing to persist in the face of difficulties. On the other hand, if your child says that she wants to stay back, she is telling you that she doesn't feel ready to go on and is feeling overwhelmed by the classroom demands.

WHAT PROGRAMS ARE AVAILABLE TO HELP YOUR CHILD THE FOLLOWING YEAR? You may be less inclined to agree to retention if your child can receive academic support in the next grade. Your child may be able to get extra help from remedial instruction, after-school instruction, summer school, peer tutoring, assistance from a classroom aide, or private tutoring. Some school districts have what are sometimes called transition or pre-first classes after kindergarten for students who are not ready for first grade. After spending a year in this class, students usually go on to first grade the following year.

WHAT ARE THE STYLES OF THE TEACHERS IN THE NEXT GRADE? The style of the teacher can greatly affect your child's ability to succeed in the next grade. While school staff may be reluctant to talk candidly about teachers, other parents will not be. Ask them about the difficulty level, teaching style, homework demands, ability to individualize instruction, and flexibility of teachers in the following grade. You may even want to observe the teachers. This information may not only help you gauge whether your child can succeed if she moves on but give you ideas about which teacher to request.

If after reflection you decide it is best for your child to move to the next grade, say so. Assert your reasons and hold your ground. This is not an exact science and your opinions should carry weight. If you feel strongly and are insistent, your view should prevail.

Whether your child is promoted or retained, you will need to plan carefully for the following year and monitor her progress. Find out whether your child can receive extra help or will benefit from a different instructional approach. Speak with your child's teacher early in the year and let her know of your concerns, your interest in frequent contact, and your willingness to work with your child in areas of weakness. If your child is retained, find out how her school experience will be different next year. If there is more than one teacher at that grade level, you may want to request another teacher to give her a different experience.

Retention is not likely to be well received by your child. In a survey, students identified staying back as one of the worst things that could happen to them. Be prepared for a vigorous protest or even tears. She may feel that she has let you down. She may fear what other children will say. She may worry that she will be left back again. Your reassurance is important in helping her to deal with these issues. With your support, your child will gradually adjust to the retention, especially as she starts to do better in school, is looked up to as a leader, and makes new friends. Ask the teacher if your child can be a teacher's helper since she will likely know the routines of the grade.

When should you tell your child? In most cases, soon after the decision is made. Do not wait until right before school. She will need some time to get used to this decision. In talking with your child, explain in an honest, open manner the reason for the decision but be sure to frame it in positive terms. Of course, what you say will depend on your personal style and your child's situation, but you may want to start by saying something like the following: "Jennifer, your teacher and I have been talking about your schoolwork and it seems that you're having difficulty with some of the work. We both feel that it would help you to spend another year in first grade so you can catch up." You might mention that children learn at different rates and that staying back is not unusual. Highlight your child's strengths and accomplishments in other areas and restate how proud you are of her. As the school year approaches, help your child figure out something to say to other children when asked why she isn't moving on. A simple statement (for example, "My parents wanted me to get more help") will usually satisfy other children.

Retention can often be upsetting for parents, especially for those with high academic expectations. It is not uncommon for parents to feel that somehow they have failed their child or to see the retention as a reflection of their own weaknesses. You may feel disappointed with or even angry at your child, but expressing these emotions to her will serve no constructive purpose and may damage her self-esteem. If your child senses your anger and disappointment, she will feel she has let you down and may see the retention as punitive. On the other hand, if you convey your belief that this is a positive step and reassert your confidence and pride in your child, then she will be better able to accept and adjust to the retention.

SKIPPING A GRADE

Occasionally a child is performing so far above her classmates that she is recommended to skip a grade. Children who skip a grade typically enter a class two grades higher at the beginning of the next school year. In some cases, a child skips a grade by moving to the next grade during the course of the school year.

The decision about whether a child should bypass one year of public school is not an easy one. The school and the parents, who make this decision jointly, must weigh the pros and cons of skipping versus not skipping. A very bright child who is being taught material that she has already mastered may be bored in class. Finding schoolwork tedious and unchallenging, she may become turned off to school and start to underachieve. Even if she does the work, she may do so in a perfunctory manner, with little learning taking place.

Yet skipping a child also involves risks. A child who breezed through work previously may suddenly be faced with academic pressures for which she is unprepared. In addition, an academically advanced child may not be socially advanced to the same degree. A child who is moved ahead may be challenged academically but overwhelmed socially. She may be able to keep pace in the classroom yet feel out of place with her new classmates.

If your child is performing above grade level in all academic areas, she is not necessarily a candidate for skipping. Indeed, most classes have students who are performing above grade level. Elementary classes typically have at least a three-year span of academic levels in any subject: some children are a year or more above grade level; others are on grade level; and still others are a year or more below grade level. In some cases, students will perform several grade levels above their assigned grade on standardized tests. These results can be misleading, however. A second-grader who scores at the fifth-grade level in reading should not be assigned to a fifth-grade reading class since she lacks the experience, knowledge base, and maturity of fifth-graders.

The challenge facing the school and teacher is to provide educational programs that meet the diverse needs of students without moving them into socially inappropriate groups. The response of some schools to this problem has been to group students according to ability level rather than grade level. For example, a reading class might have second- and third-graders. A more common approach is to group by ability within a grade. For example, one teacher instructs the higher-level students while another instructs the lower-level students.

If you suspect that your child is not being sufficiently challenged, contact the teacher to see what changes can be made in the classroom. She may be able to provide more advanced work for your child while relieving her of the more mundane assignments. This should be work that stretches your child's understanding of the subject matter rather than busywork on topics she has already mastered. If you and the teacher agree on this strategy, monitor to ensure that the new work is not stressful or overwhelming. You might also talk with the principal to find out what programs are available outside the classroom. Your child may be eligible for the school's enrichment or gifted and talented program (see chapter 9). If your child is particularly advanced in one subject, she may be able to go to a higher grade for instruction in that subject. For example, a first-grader might go to second grade for reading but remain in first grade for all other subjects. Your school may have other options that are beneficial for your child. This is the time for you to be creative in coming up with strategies the school might adopt to enrich your child's education.

After reviewing these school alternatives, you may still believe that your child should be considered for skipping. If so, it is important to compare her to children in the next grade on a range of variables. These include the following:

LEARNING APTITUDE: Your assessment of your child's reasoning skills should draw from your own and the teacher's observations as well as testing results. Many schools administer intelligence tests as part of their group testing program.

ACADEMIC SKILLS: To evaluate your child's reading, math, and writing skills, review your child's report cards, work samples, and standardized test results.

WORK HABITS: Does your child work well independently? Can she concentrate for a sustained period? Can she prepare for tests effectively? Is she conscientious about completing homework?

ABILITY TO TOLERATE ACADEMIC PRESSURE: How will she cope with an increased workload? Will it upset her to no longer be the star of the class? How will she respond if she struggles in some subjects?

ENJOYMENT OF LEARNING: Does she enjoy learning new things? Will she pursue topics on her own that spark her interest?

SOCIAL MATURITY: Does she relate well to other children? How does she do with older children? Is she confident in social situations?

HEIGHT: A child who is short, especially a boy, may have difficulty if skipped because the size difference will be even greater in the next grade.

Also give weight to your child's views. If she is anxious at the prospect of skipping, she may not feel ready and may not be ready. If your child remains motivated in her present grade, is uncomplaining about the work, is comfortable with her classmates, and is uninterested in advancing a grade, think twice about having her skip a grade. In general, let caution be your watchword in making this decision.

After considering what the school can do to stimulate your child, you may conclude that any additional academic challenge and enrichment will need to come primarily from outside the school. This means that you will need to make a special effort to find ways of cultivating your child's talents and abilities. Visits to museums, plays, exhibits, and other cultural events are of course great ways of enhancing your child's education. In addition, find out whether your community or county provides weekend or summer enrichment programs. Some private tutoring programs also offer enrichment activities. Make sure, however, that you do not force your child to do something she doesn't want to do. A gentle nudge is okay, but insisting that she go to an academic or cultural enrichment program when she is strongly opposed will generate more resistance than learning.

SCHOOL DISCIPLINE

Surveys are conducted periodically to establish parents' school priorities. Invariably, discipline is near the top of their list. While there is a consensus about its importance, there is little agreement about the results. Some parents believe that schools go too far in disciplining students; others argue that schools are too lax.

Children misbehave in school for a variety of reasons. They may not have learned at home the proper respect for school officials or the importance of complying with school rules. They may be trying to gain the attention of peers or divert attention from learning difficulties. Misbehavior may also derive from feelings of anger or low self-esteem or distress about family problems. Some professionals contend that school discipline problems have risen due to increasing family problems and the lack of consistent supervision.

Parents have the right to expect that their child will be safe and secure in school and that classrooms will be free of frequent disruption. Children cannot learn in a class filled with unruly students. While students with behavior problems should be treated fairly and with sensitivity to their needs, the school's primary responsibility is to provide an atmosphere conducive to learning. By using various disciplinary measures, schools attempt to foster self-control. The purpose of discipline is thus to teach appropriate behavior rather than to punish. Indeed, the word discipline is derived from the Latin word *disciplina,* meaning instruction.

Discipline in any school system operates at three levels: the school district, the school building, and the classroom. The school district establishes general disciplinary policies that apply to all students in the district and that may be embodied in a written code of conduct. At the school building level, the principal is responsible for interpreting and applying these policies. Principals often have considerable leeway here. The teacher, of course, also has a large say in how and when students will be disciplined.

Effective School Practices

There is no simple how-to formula for disciplining students, but there are some features that characterize an effective school discipline program. These are described below.

THE DISTRICT HAS A CLEARLY WRITTEN CODE OF CONDUCT. The discipline code should clearly describe the school rules and the consequences for their violation. This code should be distributed to parents as well as to older students. Parents should be given an opportunity to help develop or revise the code. It should be neither too rigid nor too permissive and should reflect the values of the community. While parents may view the codes of some American schools as unnecessarily harsh, consider that in Japan students may be punished for such seemingly minor infractions as not wearing pants cuffs the proper width or styling their hair in a certain way.

SCHOOL STAFF WORKS CLOSELY WITH PARENTS. School discipline is much more effective when parents support the efforts of the school to maintain order. Principals and teachers need to enlist parents as partners in their efforts to discipline students. When a child has a behavior problem, the teacher will be better able to help the student if the parent and teacher have a good working relationship and if they are of one mind about how to respond to the problem.

THE SCHOOL REINFORCES GOOD BEHAVIOR. While many equate discipline with punishment, children can learn cooperation and responsibility through encouragement, praise, and incentives for good behavior. This is as important a part of any disciplinary program as consequences for misbehavior. The school may give awards to "students of the month" or "courtesy awards" or certificates to students with perfect attendance. In the classroom, the teacher has a myriad of opportunities for praising and rewarding students. A kind word, a special privilege, or a note home praising the student can work wonders in eliciting cooperation.

THE DISCIPLINE PROGRAM IS EDUCATIONAL. Students with behavior problems may benefit from learning alternative behaviors or problem-solving skills to prevent future problems. This may mean getting two students together who were in a fight to try to work out their differences, helping a student who has been playing the role of class clown to find better ways of gaining the attention of classmates, or counseling an acting-out student distressed about her parents' divorce. The goal is to try to deal with the student's underlying problem while minimizing classroom disruption.

THE PUNISHMENT FITS THE CRIME. The school's use of consequences should be in proportion to the severity of the student's action. Removing a student from a classroom is a last-resort measure to be used when other measures have proven ineffective or when there is a serious incident.

TEACHERS ARE AUTHORITATIVE RATHER THAN AUTHORITARIAN OR PERMISSIVE WITH STUDENTS. Teachers are most effective when they are in charge of the class in a way that is not domineering or intimidating. They command the respect of their students by valuing and respecting them. While teachers should allow students input on classroom concerns, they should also set and enforce reasonable standards of behavior. In addition, teachers with command of their subject are less likely to have behavioral problems.

TEACHERS ARE TRAINED IN DISCIPLINARY TECHNIQUES. Many teachers receive little instruction in discipline in their formal teacher training despite the abundance of research and the availability of formal classroom discipline programs. School districts should provide teachers with "in-service" education in this area.

THE SCHOOL RESPONDS SWIFTLY AND SERIOUSLY TO ISSUES OF SAFETY. The principal must take whatever steps are necessary to ensure the safety of the students. This should take precedence over other concerns.

How Schools Discipline Students

It is of course preferable that students regulate their own behavior but sometimes schools must impose consequences on students who violate school rules. The following are disciplinary measures commonly used by schools:

TIME OUT: A student given "time out" sits apart from other students for a short period and is not allowed to engage in any activity. This technique is most commonly used with young children and to help angry or acting-out children "cool down."

WITHDRAWAL OF PRIVILEGES: Misbehaving students may be denied school or classroom privileges ranging from being a line leader to attending a class trip.

DETENTION: You may know this better as "staying after." In some districts, students serve detention on Saturday mornings rather than before or after school. Elementary teachers often keep misbehaving students for detention during recess.

IN-SCHOOL SUSPENSION: This form of discipline requires students to go to a room in school where, under supervision, they remain all day and do assigned work.

OUT-OF-SCHOOL SUSPENSION: For more serious violations of school rules, students may be suspended from school and not allowed to attend for a specified number of days. In-school and out-of-school suspensions are more commonly employed with secondary school students.

Suspension has been used with alarming frequency by school districts, and sometimes for minor offenses such as skipping school or talking back to a teacher. According to the U.S. Department of Education, public school students received almost 2 million suspensions in 1990. Because of past abuses in the use of suspension and the willingness of parents to challenge school districts, the courts have imposed restrictions on school districts. To begin with, school districts must use "due process" in dealing with students and their parents in all serious disciplinary procedures, namely those where a student is not allowed to attend school. This means that the process of determining your child's guilt or innocence must be fair. At a minimum, fairness requires the provision of notice and an informal hearing. Thus, if your child is suspended, she must be informed either orally or in writing of the specific reasons for the suspension, told of the school rule that was violated, and given a chance to present her side. This hearing should be held prior to the serving of the suspension although the requirements of prior notice and a hearing can be delayed in the case of an emergency (for example, where there is a concern for the safety of students). Students may be allowed to make up missed work but are typically not permitted to participate in school activities during the suspension. Parents usually have the right to appeal school disciplinary actions to the superintendent or the board of education.

Suspensions should have a specific time limit. For example, a school district cannot keep a student out of school until she has paid for school repairs to damage she caused. In cases of a lengthy suspension (namely, longer than ten days) or expulsion (permanent exclusion from school), a more formal hearing is required in which the parents and the school have the right to use attorneys and call witnesses. A student being considered for expulsion may need to be evaluated by the school's evaluation team to determine whether she is educationally disabled and therefore legally entitled to public education in some form.

School districts have tried to be creative in designing effective disciplinary measures. Some have implemented alternative programs and special classes for disruptive students. Some have assigned misbehaving students to community service projects. In one suburban high school in Chicago, students serving after-school detention were made to listen to Frank Sinatra songs in an effort to make detention less desirable to the students (and perhaps more fun for the supervising teacher). Administrators looking to increase the effectiveness of the school's disciplinary program should pay heed to a recent survey of secondary school students: they identified Saturday detention and loss of extracurricular activities as the most effective punishments and verbal reprimands and corporal punishment as the least effective.

How Parents Can Help

Parents play a key role in school discipline. The messages they give to their children and the actions they take at home can shape the way students respond in school. The following are steps that parents can take to help their child become a cooperative student:

SET AND ENFORCE REASONABLE LIMITS AT HOME. The discipline your child learns at home sets the tone for the way she behaves in school. A student who is first exposed to firm limits in school is bound to have problems.

TEACH RESPECT FOR THE AUTHORITY OF SCHOOL STAFF. Avoid criticizing or otherwise undermining the authority of the school in the presence of your child. Your disrespect for school authority figures may engender your child's disrespect.

CONVEY RESPECT FOR THE SCHOOL'S RULES. Obtain a copy of the school's disciplinary code (it may be in the student handbook) and let your child know that you are reading it. Inform your child that you expect her to abide by the school's rules. Review specific rules with your child that may be troublesome for her and discuss ways of handling them. Make sure that you don't set a bad example for your child by violating school rules (for example, writing a false excuse when your child skipped school for a day).

MAINTAIN GOOD COMMUNICATION WITH THE TEACHER. Develop a rapport with your child's teacher. Let her know about family or home concerns that may affect your child's school behavior so that she can respond sensitively to your child's needs.

If your child has been disciplined in school, it is important that you support the school's action if you believe it was appropriate. Listen to your child's view of the problem, but be careful about coming to her rescue or condoning what she did. Contact the principal or teacher if you are unclear about what happened. If you believe that the school action was unfair or unjustified, say so but quickly move from a blaming mode to a problem-solving mode. You might inquire what other steps were taken to deal with the problem and suggest how it might be handled differently in the future.

If your child is having frequent disciplinary problems, it is important to meet with school staff to obtain their perspective and to work together to solve the problem. This meeting may include the principal, guidance counselor, and teacher. If you and the school can agree on how to handle your child, it may be useful to bring her into the conference and allow her to see that you and the school are united about how future problems will be handled. If your child continues to have significant behavioral problems, testing by the district's evaluation team may be warranted (see chapter 9).

Children with educational disabilities may require different disciplinary standards and strategies than other students. Federal law bars special education students from being disciplined for behavior that is a direct consequence of their disability. For example, the school cannot punish a student with an attention deficit disorder for being restless and distractible. The school and parents may decide to use alternative disciplinary methods with a disabled student. If so, they should be spelled out in the student's Individualized Education Program (IEP), which the district is obligated to follow.

CORPORAL PUNISHMENT

Some school districts use corporal punishment as a means of discipline. Corporal punishment is physical punishment intended to change the behavior of a student (most commonly an elementary school boy) and does not include actions taken by a school staff member to protect herself or other students. Typically, this takes the form of spanking the student or paddling her with a wooden board. And corporal punishment is not uncommon. In 1986, according to the Federal Department of Education, over one million public school students received physical punishment. This number has been declining over the last decade as opposition has mounted to corporal punishment.

The United States Supreme Court ruled in 1977 that school districts can use corporal punishment if deemed necessary to maintain order. States maintain the right to prohibit its use, which twenty-six states have done. In the twenty-four states that permit corporal punishment, school districts may enact a policy barring its use. Many of the states permitting this form of discipline are in the South, where the "spare the rod, spoil the child" philosophy is arguably more rooted in the culture.

School districts that permit corporal punishment may restrict the way in which it is administered. Typically, local statutes require that the punishment be imposed "in good faith" and not be "unduly severe." School districts may place other restrictions on its use, such as requiring parent consent in writing before a school can physically punish their child, mandating that a school administrator mete out the punishment, or requiring the presence of a witness. Districts may also restrict the use of corporal punishment to select misbehaviors. While it is usually reserved for extreme misbehavior, students have received physical punishment for failure to complete homework, use of insulting language, and truancy.

Proponents of corporal punishment argue that the threat of physical punishment is necessary to maintain order in the schools. It is depicted as a last-resort measure for children who do not respond to other forms of discipline. They claim that it deters future misbehavior effectively and is superior to out-of-school suspension because it keeps the student in school.

Despite these claims, a consensus has been growing among educational and medical groups to abolish corporal punishment in the schools. The National Education Association, National Association of School Psychologists, National PTA, and American Medical Association have all taken stands opposing corporal punishment. In addition, Japan, Israel, and many European nations have abolished it.

The arguments opposing its use are persuasive. Corporal punishment can be both physically and psychologically damaging to students who have experienced it firsthand. Students who have been paddled are more likely to lose self-worth than to gain self-control. Moreover, well-behaved students may go through school fearful and anxious at the possibility of being paddled. This is hardly a setting conducive to learning.

The use of corporal punishment conveys an unhealthful message to students: aggression is the way to solve problems. Indeed, many believe that students who are paddled are actually more likely to be aggressive as a result of the punishment. As an example of how corporal punishment can beget violence, in Georgia a thirteen-year-old student stabbed to death a school principal who had paddled him two days earlier.

Research on corporal punishment raises questions about the way it is administered and its effectiveness. School authorities often do not exhaust other options before resorting to corporal punishment. Moreover, minority students and students with emotional and learning disabilities are more likely to receive physical punishment. In terms of effectiveness, studies indicate that districts using corporal punishment are no more successful in deterring misbehavior than those not using it. Nor is there any convincing evidence that it promotes development of internal controls. While corporal punishment may suppress misbehavior temporarily, it does not teach more appropriate behavior. Many psychologists believe that a positive approach to discipline focusing on self-esteem and providing incentives for appropriate behavior is more likely to elicit cooperation from students.

Giving license to school authorities to physically punish students raises the potential for physical harm. This potential is heightened when the person doing the paddling is angry or frustrated, as is sometimes the case. Injuries do happen, and sometimes they are serious. Some of these injuries would result in charges of child abuse if done by parents. School officials, however, have generally been immune from charges of excessive punishment. This may be changing as parents have been more willing to take legal action and courts have been more willing to hold school officials accountable for excessive corporal punishment.

Even in districts where corporal punishment is permitted, there is no justification for its frequent use. If this is the case, it suggests the need for further education for school staff. Teachers typically receive minimal training in discipline during their schooling so that school districts may need to provide "in-service" education to their teachers about various approaches to discipline. There are a variety of alternatives to corporal punishment, including counseling, parent conferences, reward or incentive programs, denial of school privileges, time out, after-school or Saturday detention, and in-school and out-of-school suspensions. There are also various published approaches to classroom discipline that have been found effective. Assertive Discipline, a formal program of classroom discipline employing positive and negative consequences, is one such approach.

If you live in a school district that permits corporal punishment, ask for a copy of the district's disciplinary code. If there is none, request that the district write one. Review the section on corporal punishment to find out under what circumstances it can be used and in what manner. There should be some specific safeguards to lessen the possibility of physical harm to a student. Also, the code should identify the specific behaviors that warrant the use of corporal punishment. Check whether the code contains a scale of increasing punishments to be used prior to corporal punishment as well as rewards or incentives for positive behavior.

If your child is administered corporal punishment by a school official, consider asking the following questions:

- Did the staff member anticipate the problem, and if so, what steps were taken to avoid it?
- Did the staff member consult with school professionals (for example, the school psychologist) to try to resolve the problem?
- Did the staff member use less severe disciplinary measures prior to using corporal punishment?
- Did the school comply with the district's requirements for administering corporal punishment?
- What can school staff and parents do to avoid a similar problem in the future?

If your state and district permit corporal punishment and you wish to change this policy, you have your work cut out for you. But this is not a futile cause, inasmuch as the winds of change are blowing in your favor. Since 1987, eleven states have banned corporal punishment. Bear in mind that your community can pass a local statute prohibiting its use even if your state does not do so. If you are unsuccessful in prohibiting its use, work to ensure some safeguards are built into the district's corporal punishment policy, most notably a requirement that parents consent in writing before their child can be administered corporal punishment.

SCHOOL RESISTANCE

If your child is like most others, she has occasionally woken up on a school day and complained of not feeling well despite no outward signs of sickness. While you suspect that she is looking for a way not to attend school, you are eager to avoid a battle and allow her to stay home for the day. Mysteriously, your child's ailments clear up almost immediately and your suspicions are aroused even further.

Parents are often concerned that school resistance portends deep, long-lasting problems, but there is no need for panic. In most cases, this problem can be resolved and the child returned to school quickly with teamwork by the parents and teacher. In a minority of cases, however, school resistance can turn into a prolonged problem requiring professional help. At its most extreme, resistance to school may take the form of school phobia or school refusal. This is an intense anxiety reaction that results in a determined refusal to attend school. School phobia, which differs from truancy, affects up to 3 percent of schoolchildren and is as common in boys as it is in girls.

Making a judgment about whether your child is resisting school requires the skills of a detective. Signs of school resistance may be physical: your child may frequently complain of stomachaches, headaches, or nausea on weekday mornings (but rarely on weekends) or go to the school nurse often with similar complaints. The signs may be behavioral: your child may seem unusually listless, withdrawn, or irritable before or after school. The signs may be verbal: your child may tell you directly she is not happy in school. Or nonverbal: she may give you more subtle clues that all is not right in school. These signs may be especially evident as the weekend or a school vacation comes to a close.

A rare request by a child to stay home despite no outward evidence of illness should raise little concern for parents. Frequent requests are another story. Honoring these requests routinely can not only interfere with your child's academic development but also set the stage for more serious problems of school resistance. Rather, you need to find out why your child may be resisting school and, if necessary, take action to quickly stem the problem. For some children, the answer lies in what is happening in school. For others, curcumstances at home hold the key to understanding their school resistance.

It is not unusual for young children to resist attending school. After all, they may be leaving a comfortable, secure setting with a nurturing adult whom they can trust for an unfamiliar place with an adult and children they may not know. Chapter 4 offers steps you can take to help your child feel more comfortable in school. Older children, even those in middle and high school, may also resist going to school, but their stress is usually due more to school- or peer-related problems than difficulty separating from their parents.

If your child has suddenly become anxious about school after seeming happy and secure about attending, it is likely that something specific has happened in school to arouse her anxiety. Give thought to what has changed for your child. School transitions are particularly difficult for children. Going from elementary to middle school, for example, means adjusting to larger classes, more teachers, new students, greater academic demands, more peer pressures, and a less personal relationship with the teacher. It is no coincidence that school resistance is most common at about age eleven when children are often adjusting to these changes. Other anxiety-provoking situations in school include the following:

- academic difficulty
- feeling overwhelmed by academic pressures
- fear of talking in front of the class
- bullying by another child
- teasing from classmates
- feeling left out by classmates or not having friends
- losing a close friend
- fear of a strict or intimidating teacher
- problems on the school bus or at the bus stop
- fear of a toileting accident
- anxiety about changing for gym or showering after gym
- moving to a new school district and not knowing anyone
- returning to school after a long illness

The first place to start in understanding school resistance is with your child. During a calm moment ask her directly if something or someone is bothering her in school. Your child may not be able to put into words her concern or may be embarrassed to tell you. If so, go through a list of possible situations (the above list is a good starting place) and ask your child whether any of these is a problem area. You may get some clues from watching her response: she may look away, pause, or become teary eyed when you mention a sensitive area.

The teacher is your next stop. If she doesn't have any ideas about what may be troubling your child, ask her to pay close attention to your child over the next couple of weeks to see if she can note any trouble spots. You may also want to talk with other parents if your child is complaining about the teacher's style or other classmates to find out whether other children are experiencing similar problems.

School phobia, an intense form of school resistance, often has less to do with what is happening in school than what is happening at home. For these children, the term "school phobia" is a misnomer. Many children resist going to school because they have great difficulty separating from their parents, usually their mother. They have what psychologists call separation anxiety, which often results from an overly close relationship between parent and child. This may manifest itself in ways other than a refusal to attend school. They may be reluctant to go over to friends' houses, to be left with a baby-sitter, to join community activities, or to go to bed by themselves. They may lack the inner resources to act independently of their parents.

School-phobic children may dread attending school because of a fear that some harm or catastrophe will befall their family, particularly the parents. They may also fear abandonment. A family event or circumstance such as the birth of a baby, the illness or death of a parent, parental conflict, divorce, or even the death of a pet may trigger their fear of leaving home. Staying home may be the child's way of protecting a family member, preserving family stability, or obtaining attention for herself that is unavailable at other times.

The first and foremost goal with a child who is school phobic is to get her back in school as soon as possible. The longer your child stays out of school, the harder it will be to get her back in, so don't waste time. Confronting and resolving the problem may call upon all your resources as parents, but your failure to face the problem will only prolong it. The following are strategies that you may find helpful. Some are more appropriate for milder problems; others are designed for more serious cases of school phobia.

OBTAIN A MEDICAL EXAMINATION. If your child is complaining of physical problems, be certain that she is not genuinely sick. Make sure the examination includes a check of her vision and hearing. A clean bill of health from the doctor suggests that your child's physical complaints, while perhaps reflecting actual discomfort, are due to stress and anxiety. If so, you need to help your child confront the source of that stress.

INSIST THAT YOUR CHILD ATTEND SCHOOL. Take a firm stand. Let your child know this is not only your requirement but a legal requirement as well. Ready yourself for a vigorous protest from your child. This may take the form of a tantrum, an episode of crying, or an increase in physical complaints. These behaviors are likely your child's way of testing your resolve. Stay the course and resist your impulse to give in to your child. You may need the help of your spouse or perhaps another family member. If your child cries as you drop her off at school, do not stick around except in a case of extreme distress, in which case you may want to stay until she settles down. The teacher has no doubt dealt with similar situations in the past, and your child will likely stop crying soon after you leave.

ADJUST YOUR INTERACTIONS WITH YOUR CHILD. Let your child know that you understand her distress but reassure her that school will get a little easier each day. Focus on the positive aspects of school. Keep discussion with your child of her feelings and complaints to a minimum. Avoid excessive sympathy since this will reinforce her impulse to stay home. At the same time, avoid going to the other extreme of lashing out in anger. This will only intensify your child's anxiety and fortify her school resistance. In the morning, try to deal with your child in a calm, matter-of-fact manner while maintaining your resolve. (That will be a challenge!) When your child returns home from school, let her know how proud you are that she attended school.

CONSIDER AN ABBREVIATED SCHEDULE. While it is preferable to have your child return to school for a full day, you may have more success getting her back in school if she initially attends for part of the day and then gradually increases her time until she is attending all day. Strongly resist suggestions to place your child on home instruction. This will further entrench her school resistance.

PROBLEM-SOLVE WITH YOUR CHILD. Ask your child what ideas she has for making the problem better. After you have given her a chance to come up with some ideas, offer some of your own. Review the pros and cons of each idea and together come up with a realistic plan. Try role-playing aspects of the plan with your child. The older the child, the more you will want to encourage her to solve the problem on her own. This will increase her coping skills and give her a sense of accomplishment.

INVOLVE THE TEACHER AND, IF NECESSARY, OTHER SCHOOL STAFF. The teacher will likely need to be made aware of whatever is upsetting your child and involved in the plan to get her back in school. Don't hesitate to suggest to the teacher ways of easing your child's worries. If the teacher reports that your child is crying less or participating more, take this as an encouraging sign that your child is adjusting to school even if you are still battling with him in the morning. The principal or guidance counselor should be called upon if another child is bullying your child or there are problems on the bus.

MAINTAIN CONTACT WITH YOUR CHILD DURING THE DAY. Young children who are unhappy separating from their parents may benefit from calling them during the day at a prearranged time. This tactic should be used with discretion since a call to a parent may be more upsetting than helpful. Another way of easing the separation is to give your child an item to carry during the day that reminds her of home. This may be a picture of the family or a favorite toy, book, or doll.

USE BEHAVIOR MODIFICATION. Consider working with the teacher and the school psychologist to devise a program of incentives for your child to come to school. For example, your child may receive points for participating in class, not crying in school, attending all day, and completing assignments. These points could be exchanged for special privileges or tangible rewards in school or at home. The hope is that by increasing your child's attendance and involvement through incentives you will help her to gradually feel more comfortable in school and less resistant to coming.

SEEK PROFESSIONAL HELP. If your best efforts to get your child back in school are unsuccessful, seek help from a mental health counselor. The guidance counselor, social worker, or school psychologist at your child's school should be able to recommend either a community agency or a private counselor. Keep in mind that the focus of this counseling should be on getting your child back in school as quickly as possible. Be prepared for the counselor to work, at least some of the time, with the whole family. It is not appropriate for a counselor to see your child for weeks on end while she stays home. The initial focus should be on helping the family help their child return to school. In severe cases of school phobia, some physicians have prescribed antidepressants to help the child return to school.

MOVING TO A NEW SCHOOL

It is estimated that one out of five families moves every year. If your family is like most, your child will probably change schools at least once prior to graduation. A change in schools can be as stressful for children as a change in jobs and communities is for their parents. For many children, their school is the center of not only their educational life but their social and recreational life as well. Older children generally have a more difficult time adjusting to a school change because their peer relationships are more firmly established.

While moving to a new community holds the promise of something new and different, school-age children are often more worried than excited. They will likely not want to leave their friends behind or go from a familiar setting to an unfamiliar one. They may fear that they will not like the kids in their new school or, even worse, that the kids will not like them. They may worry that the work will be too hard or that their new teacher will be too strict. They may fret that their clothes will be out of style.

These jitters are natural and should be expected. You will not be able to completely put your child's fears to rest by soothing words of reassurance. Only experience can do that. And the adjustment will take a little while.

With the myriad concerns that parents must attend to during a move, it is easy for them not to give the school change the attention it deserves. There are some steps, however, that parents can take to smooth out the unsettling bumps their children may face during the first few days in their new school. They are described below.

DO YOUR HOMEWORK ON POSSIBLE SCHOOLS FOR YOUR CHILD. Chapter 1 describes ways to evaluate a school system and factors you should consider. Listed in appendix A is a service called SchoolMatch, which offers specific information on public schools nationwide.

TRY TO MOVE BEFORE THE START OF SCHOOL. You may not have control of the timing of your move, but if you do, aim for an early summer move. The school transition is considerably easier for children if they begin the school year in their new school. Other children new to the school will also be starting at the beginning of the year. In addition, if your child moves in the middle of the year, she can sometimes miss out on learning critical skills because of the differences in the two schools' curricula. The move may also be easier for your child if the students in her grade are also entering a new school (for example, if they are going from elementary to middle school).

ACKNOWLEDGE YOUR CHILD'S WORRIES BUT LOOK FOR THE SILVER LINING. Give your child a chance to express her fears and anxieties. Be respectful of her feelings and be extra patient with her during the first few days of school when she is likely to be on edge. Let your child know that you understand her worries and assure her that it is very normal to feel nervous about changing schools but don't feel that you have to offer solutions. What your child is looking for is a sympathetic ear. At the same time, reassure her that it will take a little while but with time she will feel comfortable in the new school. (This is especially important with young children who may not understand that unsettled feelings gradually fade with time.) Be upbeat in discussing the advantages to your child of the move. Your positive attitude will help your child feel more confident in the move.

VISIT THE NEW SCHOOL. Try to arrange a visit to the school with your child before she is scheduled to begin. Call in advance and ask if you can meet with the principal. The purpose of this meeting is not only to establish a rapport with the principal but also to obtain specific information. Make sure to confirm that this is the school your child will be attending. In some communities, students are bused to schools outside of their attendance area to ease overcrowding or achieve racial balance. You will also want to know about school hours, lunch policy, bus arrangements, and the school calendar, but most important you will want to inquire of the program options. If your child has any special needs, make sure to talk with the principal about them. Ask what specific school records the new school will need and what information you will need to bring in when enrolling. (You will likely need to be living at your new address before you can enroll your child.) Most likely, you will need proof of your child's age, proof of residency, and health records. Ask if you can have a brief tour of the school. While walking around, make note of the other students' dress so that you can help your child to dress in a way that helps her to fit in. If your schedule allows, volunteer for some school activities. This is not only a way of getting to know your child's school better but also of meeting other parents, who will give you vital information about the school that you will not hear from the principal. Before leaving, make sure to introduce yourself to the school secretary. She is a key member of the school staff whose help you will likely need at some point.

REVIEW SCHOOL RECORDS BEFORE THEY ARE SENT. Make sure that your child's records are accurate, complete, and current, and include grades for the most recent marking period. If the records contain inappropriate comments, ask that they be removed from the file (see Chapter 1 for a discussion of school records). It may help the new school if the old school can send some of your child's work samples along with the other records. It is even better if the teacher from the previous school can send to the new teacher a description of your child's strengths and weaknesses as well as skills covered. If your child is in a special education program, arrange for the Individualized Education Program (IEP) document and evaluation reports to be sent before your child enrolls so there is minimal delay in your child's beginning school. If your child is in a special education program, the new school may not allow your child to begin until it has reviewed the evaluation reports and IEP from the previous district and developed its own IEP.

HELP YOUR CHILD MEET OTHER CHILDREN. Your child will feel more comfortable going to a new school if she knows at least one other student. If you move during the summer, find out the names of children the same age as your child who live nearby. The principal may be willing to give you some suggestions. Put aside social inhibition and try to arrange some dates for your child to play with other children. This will also offer you a chance to meet other parents. These social connections will be important in your child's overall adjustment to school, so be flexible about allowing your child to invite other children to the house even if boxes are still unpacked and the curtains are not yet hung. Also, arrange for your child to join a reasonable number of school or local activities soon after moving into the community (for example, sports teams, clubs, chorus, Scouts, dance lessons, or gymnastics).

CHAPTER ELEVEN

MEETING YOUR FAMILY'S SPECIAL NEEDS

We are living in a society where the traditional nuclear family in which the biological parents live in the same household, the father works, and the mother stays home can no longer be assumed. Indeed, this white picket fence, "Leave It to Beaver," arrangement is more the exception than the rule. Only about one in every four families with children under eighteen fits this description. Today families come in many shapes and sizes: dual-earner families, single-parent families, stepfamilies, blended families, extended families, foster families, adoptive families, and families with gay and lesbian parents. In some cases, it is the woman who is bringing home the bacon while the man is home cooking it. John Naisbitt, describing the diversity of today's family arrangements in his book *Megatrends,* called it a "Rubik's cube of complexity."

ADAPTING SCHOOL PRACTICES

These changes in the family landscape call for changes in school practices. Not all school districts have answered this call. Some still operate on old assumptions and persist with outmoded practices. The results have at times been embarrassing and awkward for both parents and children: a girl living with her mother is told by a teacher to ask her father for help with a science project; a stepmother has no place to sign her name on a school enrollment form; a noncustodial father is denied the right to see his daughter's school records; and a boy is put in the position of choosing whether he will invite his father or stepfather to a father-son school activity.

These kinds of incidents can make children feel like second-class citizens or outcasts from defective families. (Some educators even persist in using the phrase "broken home" to describe a family where the parents are divorced.) Yet most of these awkward moments can be avoided if schools learn to be sensitive to these diverse family arrangements and adjust their practices accordingly. Whether or not your child's school has adjusted its practices, it is important that you keep the school abreast of your family's needs. Meeting the needs of families is thus a shared responsibility: schools need to be sensitive to their students' family situations while parents need to communicate with schools about their circumstances and needs. Helping a school adapt its practices to the changing family scene may be a project for the PTA.

Divorced Parents

It is projected that nearly half of today's marriages will end in divorce. Children whose parents are not living together may display a range of reactions in school. Some may show little overt distress. Some may withdraw. Some may act out in class. Some may have trouble focusing on schoolwork. The teacher's ability to respond in a supportive and nurturing manner depends partially on her understanding of what is troubling the student. If you are recently separated or divorced, let the teacher know, though you should not feel obligated to explain or justify your family status. This knowledge of your situation will enable the teacher to be sensitive to your child's feelings and avoid potentially embarrassing situations. If you do not tell the teacher and encourage your child to keep the separation or divorce a secret, you are giving him a message that this is something he should feel ashamed of.

Noncustodial parents often feel shut out of much of their child's life. Schools reinforce this situation when they communicate exclusively with the custodial parent. In most districts, school mailings and report cards are sent to the custodial parent only and school conferences are usually held with the custodial parent. In fact, noncustodial parents are entitled to attend school conferences and have the same rights as custodial parents to receive and review records on their child, including the report card. This right to review school records is granted to them by the Family Educational Rights and

Privacy Act, a federal law (see chapter 1). The only way that noncustodial parents can be denied the right to see their child's school records is if a court order prohibits this access, a rare occurrence. A custodial parent cannot deny a noncustodial parent this right.

If you are a noncustodial parent and wish to have school involvement, request that the school send you copies of the same school mailings that are sent to the custodial parent, including invitations to meetings and school events. Be insistent. All that you are really asking is to be added to the mailing list, hardly a burden to the school. You might even offer to supply the school with stamped, self-addressed envelopes to facilitate the process.

Noncustodial parents also have the right to attend school events as well as meetings with their child's teacher. A joint meeting with both parents is preferable so that any decisions can be made together, but if such a meeting is awkward, the school will likely agree to hold separate meetings. Other options include the teacher conferring with one parent in person and one by phone, the parents alternating attendance at parent-teacher conferences, or one parent attending and taking notes to be shared with the other.

Stepparents

Being a stepparent defines the word awkward. The awkwardness that stepparents may feel in their new family is paralleled by the awkwardness that they may feel in their contact with their stepchild's school. They may not be sure what their role is or what the school's expectations are. Is it okay for them to attend conferences? Can they write a note to school when their stepchild is sick? Can a stepparent assume the role of room parent? While the answer to these questions is an unequivocal yes, nonetheless many stepparents are very tentative in their dealings with schools. They may back off from school involvement and as a result may fail to gain the experience and confidence they need to deal effectively with the school. Given that one out of every four children is a stepchild, schools must put out the welcome mat for stepparents and help them feel comfortable in the school setting.

Single Parents

It is estimated that one out of every four families with children under eighteen and at home is led by a single mother. Whereas most single parents used to move in with their own parents upon divorcing, now most go it alone. While most schools have adjusted their thinking and practices, many districts still communicate with parents on the assumption that the household consists of two parents. This can be embarrassing for both parent and child and thus demands that schools monitor how they communicate with parents. Schools also need to adopt practices that allow single parents to participate in school affairs. This may mean holding parent-teacher conferences and parent organization meetings in the evenings or on Saturdays as well as offering child care during these meetings.

Working Parents

There has been a dramatic increase in recent years in families in which both parents work. The number of mothers who work outside the home rose by 225 percent from 1960 to 1985. At present in about one-third of families with children under the age of eighteen both parents are employed full-time. Such arrangements require considerable advance planning as well as sacrifices by family members to accommodate everyone's needs.

Working mothers may feel guilty that they are neglecting their children's needs, but the research shows otherwise. Studies suggest that children in families where mothers are employed generally fare well both academically and socially. A five-year study by Kent State researchers indicated that children in dual-career families performed better than children in single-career families on a variety of measures of academic and social performance. Children of divorced working mothers also performed better academically than children of divorced mothers who did not work outside the home. Thus, the assumption that children of working parents are more likely to experience stress and suffer academically has not proven to be the case.

This is not to say there are not pressures in families where both parents work. There are, but these tensions can be eased with some careful planning. Some school-related suggestions follow:

TAKE STEPS TO MAKE WEEKDAY MORNINGS LESS FRENZIED. Do school tasks the night before rather than leaving them for the morning, including setting the breakfast table, making lunch, checking homework, and signing permission slips. Also have your child lay out his clothes the night before. If your child buys lunch in school, you might have a box with money easily accessible to him. If you still find that the morning is too rushed, try having everybody get up fifteen minutes earlier.

BE AVAILABLE TO THE SCHOOL BY PHONE. Make sure the school has the work numbers of both parents. If one parent is more accessible, inform the school which parent should be contacted first.

REQUEST TIME OFF FROM WORK. If your work schedule conflicts with the school day, consider asking your employer in advance for release time to allow you to attend school events or conferences. This might even be included in union contracts.

MAKE TIME DURING THE EVENING TO TALK ABOUT SCHOOL. If your child talks about his school day, listen attentively and show interest in what he is saying. You will have more success engaging your child in a discussion with open-ended questions than yes or no questions. But don't push if your child does not feel like saying much.

BEFORE- AND AFTER-SCHOOL CHILD CARE

Working parents are often faced with the anxiety-provoking problem of finding child care before or after school. Some communities have responded to this need by offering child care for a fee in the schools. This idea is not new—California has had school-based child care since World War II—but it is unavailable in many communities.

School-based child care has many advantages. It allows children to be cared for in the school that they attend, in a setting designed for children, and usually with children they already know. While the programs vary, a typical program is run by a community agency (for example, the town recreation department or the local Y) and may open its doors as early as 7:00 A.M. and close them as late as 6:00 P.M. Child care may be offered during school vacations. Some programs offer classes in areas of interest to children.

If such a program does not exist in your community, consider forming a committee with other parents to organize one. This program might be sponsored by the school or a community agency. The school district may opt not to charge a fee for the use of the facility although the sponsoring agency will likely be required to purchase separate insurance. Talk with the principal of your child's school to find out which school official is authorized to approve this kind of program. Once you get approval, work with the principal at each step of the way. Further information and technical assistance on child care programs can be obtained from the School-Age Child Care Project (see appendix A).

Where school-based child care is not available or the program is inaccessible because of time or geographical considerations, parents in need of child care must make other arrangements. In their efforts to come up with alternatives that meet their needs, parents of school-children have developed a diverse array of child care choices. Some parents choose to have someone come into their home when they are absent (for example, a relative, neighbor, housekeeper, or baby-sitter). Others opt to have their child cared for in a child care center or in someone else's home if transportation to and from school can be worked out. The school district will likely be willing to have the school bus drop your child off at a stop near the baby-sitter's home, if it is on the route. Others choose to work at home or hold part-time jobs that allow them to be home when their child is home. Some companies have allowed employees to stagger their hours so that they can be more available to their children. Some parents have joined forces with other parents and organized an after-school cooperative, with each member responsible for child care on a rotating basis. And still others choose self-care, namely, they allow their child to stay home alone before or after school. These are the so-called latchkey children.

LATCHKEY CHILDREN

Latchkey children are those who regularly care for themselves before or after school because their parents are working. For these children, *Home Alone* is not just a movie, it is a reality. While precise information is not available on the number of children in what is called self-care (estimates range from 2 to 7 million), according to a recent survey, 41 percent of parents said that their child was often left alone from the end of school to 5:30 P.M. Some children in self-care relish the independence and easily handle the responsibility while experiencing little anxiety. Others may be fearful, lonely, or bored staying home alone and may comfort themselves by watching television and doing little else.

There is no simple formula for deciding whether your child is ready to stay home alone, nor is there a consensus at what age a child should be allowed to be at home without adult supervision. Five- and six-year-olds should not, in the judgment of virtually all experts, be left home alone. Many contend that parents should not leave a child under the age of ten alone for an extended period. By the time a child reaches twelve or thirteen, he can usually be relied on to be responsible without adult supervision.

In deciding whether your child is ready to be left home alone, consider the following factors:

- his comfort level while home alone
- his responsibility and resourcefulness in solving problems
- the length of time he is to be home alone
- your accessibility by phone
- his ability to use the telephone and communicate with adults
- the availability of a nearby familiar adult in case of emergency

If you are unsure whether your child is ready for self-care, consider some dry runs: have your child stay alone on a few occasions while you do an errand, starting with perhaps ten minutes and then gradually increasing to an hour or so. Talk with him afterward about how he felt. If he expresses or even hints at being afraid or upset, he is not ready to be left alone.

If you decide to have your child care for himself either before or after school, consider the following strategies:

SET OUT CLEAR RULES FOR YOUR CHILD TO FOLLOW. Safety concerns should be paramount. The rules might include coming home right after school, locking the door, not allowing strangers into the house, not using the stove and sharp knives, limiting the length of phone calls (in case you want to call), and not informing callers that he is home alone (teach your child to say that you can't come to the phone). Post these rules in a prominent place and review them on occasion with your child. Be clear with him about your policy regarding having visitors over to the house after school or his going over to a friend's house. Make sure he knows where the first aid kit is and how to use it for basic problems. To give you peace of mind and your child some practice in problem solving, ask him some "What would you do if . . . ?" questions. Call around to see if your community offers a course in "survival skills" for children in self-care.

MAKE SURE YOUR CHILD CAN USE THE TELEPHONE. If he needs help, unplug the phone and have him practice. Post in a prominent place key numbers (your place of work, police and fire department, neighbors, and relatives). Consider getting a phone that can be programmed automatically to dial a number at the press of a button.

MAKE SURE YOUR CHILD'S SCHOOL AFFAIRS ARE IN ORDER THE NIGHT BEFORE. If your child gets himself off to school in the morning, you may not have a chance in the morning to give your child lunch money, check homework, make sure it is in his book bag, and sign permission slips.

SET AN ALARM TO GO OFF WHEN YOUR CHILD IS TO LEAVE FOR SCHOOL. Or you might call from work. Children in self-care are not always reliable about leaving on time and risk missing their bus. If your child walks to school, ask the school to let you know if he is frequently late to school.

HAVE YOUR CHILD KEEP THE HOUSEKEY HIDDEN FROM VIEW. Wearing a key around their neck, as some latchkey children do, invites trouble by advertising their "home alone" status. Encourage your child to keep it out of view. Never add name or address to the key. If he puts it into his book bag, have him attach it to something that is easy to find (for example, a shoe lace). Also, parents should hide a key outside the house or give one to a neighbor just in case their child loses his key.

HAVE YOUR CHILD CALL YOU WHEN HE GETS HOME. Leave instructions for your coworkers to put your child through or, if necessary, to track you down. The call need not be long—just enough time for you to gain peace of mind and perhaps discuss your child's after-school plans. If you are unavailable and your child needs to speak with an adult, make sure he has another familiar adult he can call. Some communities provide telephone services (often called "phone friends" or "warm lines") for children who are staying alone and need to talk to an adult.

MAKE OCCASIONAL AFTER-SCHOOL ARRANGEMENTS FOR YOUR CHILD. Try to arrange for your child to go over to a friend's house or participate in a community or extracurricular activity one or two afternoons a week as a way of breaking up the monotony of self-care. You may have to prevail on a friend or neighbor to transport your child. If so, find ways of reciprocating on the weekend. Older children may be able to volunteer after school within the community. On days your child is home, you might assign chores or set out games or projects for him to do when he gets home.

BE HOME WHEN YOUR CHILD EXPECTS YOU. Your child will likely worry if you are late. If you are delayed, call your child to reassure him. If your budget allows, consider getting a car phone so you are more accessible to your child.

PARENT GROUPS

Parents can receive information and support on school- and child-related issues from a wide variety of organizations. These groups may be based at the local, county, state, or national level and are usually organized around specific concerns or issues. Appendix A lists national organizations of interest to parents. Some of these national organizations have local chapters.

While these organizations provide a place for parents to turn for answers to questions about a wide range of concerns, parents can also be helpful to each other. Parent groups can be oases of support that provide an opportunity to share your concerns, questions, struggles, and successes with other parents who are likely to identify with and understand your situation. In addition, other parents can provide you with a gold mine of experience-based information about how to solve problems, obtain specific services, and negotiate the bureaucratic maze. Hearing how other parents solved problems may suggest solutions to problems you are facing. The group may take different forms, from loosely structured to more formal, and serve various purposes, from providing a support system for parents to training parents in specific skills to taking action in areas of concern.

How do you start a parent group? The first step is to identify what resources are already available. Check the PTA to find out whether such a group is offered and, if not, whether the PTA would sponsor it. You may find that your focus is too specific for the PTA's active support and thus you may need to serve as the group's organizer. This task may seem daunting but in fact parent groups are not difficult to start. Strategies for finding participants depend on the group's focus. The school may assist you by sending out fliers to a specific segment of the parent population, for example, parents of special education students, or allow you to post notices of the meeting within the schools. Also consider putting up notices in the public library, churches, synagogues, and retail establishments. You might even advertise in the classified section of your local newspaper. While these efforts are important, word of mouth will likely be your best information source.

The size of the group is an important consideration. Parents are likely to be much more comfortable participating in a group of twenty or fewer. Ten is about the maximum if the group is dealing with sensitive issues such as their child's learning or behavioral problems to both promote bonding and encourage sharing. Small group meetings may be held in the home of a group member, with this responsibility shared among the members. With larger groups, you will likely be able to use a school or community building such as the public library at no charge.

Whatever the size or theme of the group, remember that you need to identify the needs of the group's members. Thus, at least the initial meeting should be devoted to hearing from those in attendance to delineate common concerns. Sharing will be facilitated by a nonjudgmental, accepting environment. As the group develops a consensus about its goals, it will be helpful to put in writing the group's mission in broad terms to enable other parents to determine the group's relevance to them. When you have agreed upon the group's purpose, you can move on to talk about some of the following nuts-and-bolts issues:

- What will the group be called?
- Where will the group meet? How often?
- What will be the format?
- Will new members be allowed into the group after it begins?
- Who, if anyone, will serve as leader or facilitator? Will this role be rotated? Are officers needed?
- Will funds be needed and, if so, how will they be obtained?
- Will child care be provided? By whom?
- Should the group keep a written record of its meetings and disseminate this information to members?

You may want to begin a local branch of an already established organization. The umbrella organization can provide you with ideas for starting the group, suggested activities, a source of information for members, a newsletter, and media recognition. It may also enhance your ability to recruit group members. Whatever decision you make, keep in mind that the group belongs to its members and should be designed to meet their needs.

CHAPTER TWELVE

IT'S ON TO MIDDLE SCHOOL

Sixth or seventh grade is a time of transition for most students. In addition to facing many personal changes, they are also likely to be changing schools. Most will enter a middle school, which typically serves sixth- through eighth-graders. Others will enter a junior high school, which typically serves seventh- through ninth-graders. Whichever school students attend, the move from elementary school presents many challenges. Students are most likely leaving a small, familiar school where they have one primary teacher and entering a large, impersonal school where they have as many as six or seven teachers. They may be leaving a school where they spend almost all day in one class at one desk with the same classmates and entering a school where they move from class to class with a different mix of students in almost every class. They are leaving a school where they are the oldest students and entering a school where they are the youngest. These changes can be jolting for many students.

Just as their child may feel lost and confused upon entering middle school, so too parents may feel like strangers in a strange land. This chapter will take a close-up look at the middle school program, paying particular attention to the kinds of changes students will experience and how parents can help them bridge the gap between elementary and middle school.

THE SCHOOL ORGANIZATION

When you were in seventh or eighth grade, you probably attended a junior high school. Junior high schools became popular in the 1920s and 1930s and continued through the 1960s as the primary setting for educating early adolescents. These schools were intended to help students make the transition to high school, so many were modeled after high schools. They were completely departmentalized, meaning that students had a different teacher for every subject and moved from class to class. Many junior high schools continue to follow this model today, even though students sometimes have problems adjusting to this kind of setting after coming from the secure and protected cocoon of elementary school.

Today most early adolescents are educated in middle schools rather than junior high schools. There are over 8000 middle schools in this country compared with about 4500 junior high schools. Many districts started middle schools because declining enrollments forced a school reorganization. Others went this route because it made educational sense. Educators came to view youngsters as maturing at an earlier age than youngsters in the past. Ninth-graders were seen as ready for the academic and social demands of high school while sixth-graders were seen as able to benefit from the more diverse structure of middle school. Some middle schools include fourth- and fifth-graders although many educators and parents believe that students in these grades are more suited to elementary school. They worry that in middle school these students will be hurried along at too quick a pace and exposed to concerns not appropriate for their age.

Some smaller school districts provide instruction to students in the middle grades in "K to 8" schools, namely those that accommodate students from kindergarten through eighth grade. This kind of school organization will likely influence the kind of education middle grade students receive. There may be fewer course offerings, and instruction may focus more on rote learning and less on applied learning.

THE MIDDLE SCHOOL PHILOSOPHY

The middle school years (ages 10 to 14) are critical to a child's academic, social, and moral development. Children are beginning to formulate their values during this time as well as their attitude toward education. Students who eventually drop out in high school are often turned off to academics in middle school. Despite its importance to their later adjustment, middle school has not always received the attention it deserves from the educational community. Just as middle children are squeezed for attention by their older and younger siblings, so too middle schools have been overshadowed by elementary and high schools. Just as middle children grapple to find their place in the family, so too middle schools have struggled to define their educational mission.

The central tenet of middle school education is that the educational program should be keyed to the needs and characteristics of the students. Middle school educators attempt to strike a balance between providing challenging academic instruction and promoting self-esteem. In serving as a bridge between elementary school and high school, middle schools try to retain some of the more nurturing aspects of elementary school while gradually introducing students to the subject orientation of high school. Middle schools are often divided into smaller units or teams, in effect schools within a school, in an effort to make the school setting less impersonal and isolating. Traditional junior high practices such as departmentalization, tracking, teacher-centered learning, and lecturing may give way in middle school to approaches designed to promote a sense of belonging and positive peer interaction, which are so important to students of this age. Athletics may take the form of intramurals rather than interscholastic competition. In sum, the middle school climate is intended to be more supportive and relaxed than that found in a traditional junior high school. In line with this approach, some middle schools are even using new ways to evaluate and grade students that are less anxiety-provoking and more meaningful (for example, portfolio assessment in which a student's performance in a subject is based on a cumulative review of her work in the course).

While this philosophy is more often identified with middle schools, junior high schools may also embrace this approach in an effort to make the school less impersonal to its students. Indeed, studies indicate that junior high schools that have adopted practices strengthening the connection between teacher and student (for example, interdisciplinary team teaching) have been successful in curtailing the dropout rate.

UNDERSTANDING THE MIDDLE SCHOOL CHILD

Students in the middle grades are changing more than their schools. They are undergoing dramatic personal changes as well.

Indeed, it is not an exaggeration to say that early adolescents are changing more than at any point in their life other than infancy. These changes can be awkward and unsettling for the students and for their parents.

They are changing physically. Around the age of ten or eleven, hormones begin to be released, stimulating significant bodily changes. The growth patterns are often inconsistent and may give rise to physical awkwardness. They are changing socially. They are beginning to move away from their parents and toward their peers. Being accepted by their peers is now a paramount concern and may dominate their thinking. Conformity is near or at its peak as they strive to look, talk, and act like their classmates. They are also changing emotionally. Their quest for independence may be accompanied by rebelliousness and defiance. They may challenge your values and reject your ideas. At the same time, their self-confidence may be shaky, and they may experience moodiness and feelings of inadequacy. Even seemingly minor issues can prove overwhelming and cause them to lose perspective. Your reassurance and nurturing will likely continue to be in demand. Their behaviors and emotions reflect an in-between status: They want the freedom and independence of older adolescents but in other ways they are still children. Dr. Katherine V. Goerss, a middle school principal in New Jersey, tells the story of a seventh-grader who was observed getting a haircut. He gave the barber detailed instructions about how to style his hair. After the haircut was completed, he paused in front of the mirror admiringly and then turned to the barber and asked, "May, I have my lollipop?" Growing up, it would seem, entails taking two steps forward and one back.

The school adjustment difficulties of some middle schoolers are understandable and predictable. At the same time that students are entering a large, impersonal school where they may feel isolated and unsupported, they are also entering a stage filled with self-doubts and insecurities. As they are exposed to new students, new activities, new ways of acting, and new demands from adults, their coping skills may be taxed to the limit. In their preoccupation with social concerns, academic achievement may take a back seat to peer acceptance. Indeed, many students who excelled academically in elementary school are ambivalent about excelling in middle school for fear of being ostracized by their peers and labeled a "nerd."

Some have difficulty adjusting to the academic expectations of middle school. They may find the work more demanding, the assignments longer, the grading stricter, and the teachers less nurturing. Some of their teachers may have been trained as high school teachers and may conduct their classes more like high school than elementary school. The work habits that allowed students to get by in elementary school may be inadequate for success in middle school. These difficulties may be reflected in declining grades, lowered motivation, and a drop in self-esteem. Middle school students overwhelmed by academic demands may even begin to exhibit behavior problems. In an effort to keep parents informed, many middle schools send home mid-marking period notices to parents if their child is having difficulty in one or more subjects.

Most students in middle school eventually find their way. They gradually master the layout of the school, memorize their schedule, learn to negotiate the academic maze, and find ways to sidestep the social minefields. Schools can help ease students' passage through middle school by providing a program that considers their special needs and characteristics.

TEACHING THE MIDDLE SCHOOL CHILD

The challenge for middle school educators is to provide instruction that matches the developmental needs of the students. This instruction should reflect students' enhanced ability to think abstractly and do complex learning tasks. The key to meeting this challenge is to use a variety of teaching methods to make the lessons meaningful. Classroom instruction must go beyond lecturing, reading, and memorizing to include tasks stressing applied learning and higher-order thinking. A skilled middle school teacher will use diverse approaches to enhance understanding and retention such as cooperative learning, hands-on activities, student-led instruction, simulations, computer-assisted instruction, and community service projects. By involving students in the learning process and relating instruction to their own life as well as real problems, teachers can create a genuine excitement for learning.

The job of a middle school teacher is as demanding as that of any teacher. Middle school teachers must strike a balance between the subject orientation of high school, in which the focus is on mastering subject matter, and the child orientation of elementary school, in which the focus is as much on fostering positive feelings about school as it is on academic skills. They must also bring special qualities to their work with middle school students if they are to be successful, including being flexible, understanding, accepting, encouraging, and enthusiastic. Despite the special requirements for being a successful middle school teacher, many teacher training programs do not provide specific courses in middle school education, although that is beginning to change. Currently, twenty-eight states have certification programs for middle school teachers.

Middle schools vary considerably in their organization, programs, course offerings, and report card system. The remainder of this section discusses educational practices followed by many middle schools.

The Middle School Curriculum

Middle school is an opportunity to expand students' horizons by exposing them to a diversity of topics and skills. This goal is sometimes undermined by pressures on middle school staff to follow the curriculum guide and focus on basic academic skills in the hopes of raising standardized test scores.

Most middle schools offer reading in addition to English. Whether or not it is offered as a separate course, reading does not receive the attention in middle school that it does in elementary school. Middle school teachers assume that students have mastered the basics of reading and are able to read independently with comprehension and to elicit information. Middle school students with reading difficulties are likely to have problems in various subjects. If your middle school child is struggling with reading, find out about remedial reading options available in her school or consider obtaining help outside the school.

In many middle schools, math is the only subject in which students are grouped by ability. The justification for homogeneous math classes is that math is organized more sequentially than other subjects. Failure to master earlier math skills will make it difficult to succeed at higher-level math tasks. Algebra may be given to advanced math students as early as seventh or eighth grade. Most students begin algebra in ninth grade, followed by a year of geometry and a second year of algebra (often called Algebra II).

Middle school students will, of course, take science and social studies. Nonacademic courses will comprise about a quarter of the students' school day. They may be assigned to some of the following "specials": art, music, physical education, health, industrial arts, computer education, and home economics. Some middle school students may also take a foreign language. Common sense dictates that the earlier students begin studying a foreign language, the more proficient they will become. Some students (about 5 percent nationwide) even receive foreign language instruction in elementary school.

Students in middle school may also be given instruction for part of the year in various topics, to allow them to explore new areas and discover unknown talents. These minicourses, taught by school staff or members of the community, might be offered on such topics as study skills, outdoor education, drawing, dance, drama, and photography.

Interdisciplinary Team Teaching

Interdisciplinary team teaching is one of the cornerstones of middle school education. In middle schools that employ this practice, students are assigned to a teaching team. An interdisciplinary teaching team is made up of approximately 100 to 125 students as well as teachers of different subjects who instruct only the students on that team. Thus, all the students on a particular team will have the same English, math, science, and social studies teachers. By being part of a team, students develop a sense of belonging and identity. The team is, in effect, a school within a school.

A student may also have a teacher on the team for more than one subject. This practice charts a middle course between the self-contained classroom of elementary school and the departmentalized approach of high school, where students have a different teacher for every subject. The middle school student may thus have three or four teachers as opposed to six or seven in high school. This helps prepare students for high school but also provides them with a close connection with one teacher whom they see for much of the day.

This sharing of students provides the teaching team with considerable flexibility in scheduling classes and coordinating instruction. Teachers are not ruled by the school bell in planning lessons. If a science teacher wants to have a double period because the students are doing an elaborate experiment, this can be arranged with little difficulty. If the English and history teachers want to teach a class together, this too is easily done. A teaching team can also work together to plan instruction around a particular theme, which can then be integrated into each of the subjects. For example, a student may do an experiment in science class, perform the related calculations in math class, and then write the report in English class. This kind of integrated instruction helps students make connections between different subjects. The teachers on a team may also coordinate schoolwork so that students are not overwhelmed with a number of demanding assignments or tests at the same time.

Team teaching also helps teachers deal with individual problems. Because they share the same students, teachers on the team can talk about students who are having difficulty and develop joint problem-solving strategies. Problems can be recognized early and resolved before they become larger problems.

Communication and training are the keys to an effective teaching team and are facilitated when teachers on a team have a common planning period. This planning period enables teachers to coordinate instruction and problem solve, but it also provides them with a support system that is often lacking in secondary schools. Teachers also need to receive training in working as part of a teaching team to maximize the team's effectiveness.

Cooperative Learning

Another instructional approach designed with the middle school student in mind is cooperative learning. Teachers using this approach assign students of mixed ability to small groups to work on a specific task. This may culminate in a project or group report. The teacher's role is to promote group interaction and ensure that all members of the group participate and that no one student dominates the group. The basic premise of cooperative learning is that students learn not only by listening to one another but also by teaching one another. It also fosters self-esteem and helps students of different backgrounds learn to get along with one another.

TRACKING

Students enter middle school with widely varying levels of academic performance. Some are achieving well above grade level while others are well below grade level. Meeting the needs of this academically heterogeneous group while maintaining motivation and self-esteem is a difficult challenge for middle school educators. Many middle schools attempt to deal with this problem by grouping students according to ability, what is commonly called tracking.

This is not a new practice. Indeed, tracking has been a part of the American public school scene for over a century. And most school districts continue to adhere to this tradition. Experts estimate that about 80 percent of all secondary schools use some form of tracking. In middle schools that use tracking, it is more likely to be used in the higher grades. About 75 percent of all eighth-graders are tracked for at least one subject.

Students can be tracked for all or some of their academic classes. With rigid tracking, where students are placed in one track for all academic classes, the determination of who is placed in which track is often based on grade-point average or a single test score such as a composite achievement or reading test score. This sometimes gives rise to inappropriate placements. For example, a student placed in the high track for all subjects because of a high score on a reading test will be in the high-level math class even though she may be an average math student. In some cases, students will be assigned to a low track not because of poor academic achievement but because of disciplinary problems. Where students are grouped by ability for specific subjects only, assignment to a class is usually based on teacher recommendation or standardized test performance in that subject. The most likely subjects to be tracked are math and reading; the least likely are science and social studies.

Advocates of tracking claim that ability grouping allows teachers to better tailor instruction to the needs of students so that they are continually challenged and move at their own pace. They contend that faster students will not be held back and slower students will not fall behind. According to its proponents, tracking allows slower students to participate in class and not be overshadowed by the more advanced students, preserving self-esteem and boosting self-confidence.

Critics of tracking claim that it goes against the philosophy of providing equal educational opportunities for all students and is thus incompatible with democratic notions of fairness and equity. They argue that students in the low track come to think of themselves as dumb and experience a lessening of self-esteem and motivation. Once a student is placed in a low track, it may be difficult for her to move to a higher track, so discouragement and apathy may set in. Critics also question the accuracy of tracking decisions, which are often based on standardized test scores. They point out that two children with very small differences in test scores can be placed in two different academic tracks, which can have very large differences in ability level and can set the stage for divergent career paths. In its most extreme form, tracking can give rise to an academic caste system.

While those who want to derail tracking accentuate its effects on students at the bottom of the learning curve, they also claim that high achievers benefit little, if at all, from tracking. They argue that students in the top track may come to think of themselves as members of an elite group and become intolerant of less able students. The only time students of different tracks may interact is in lunch, gym, and nonacademic courses. Social harmony, an important goal in middle school, may thus be a casualty of tracking.

While tracking continues to be used widely in middle schools across the country, the weight of research is on the side of those who oppose tracking. Studies indicate that students in low tracks experience low self-esteem and elicit low teacher expectations. And research on teacher expectations points to one conclusion: when teachers expect less, students produce less. One study indicated that eighth-graders assigned to the low track for all academic subjects performed much worse in tenth grade than eighth-graders with comparable test scores and demographic characteristics who were in heterogeneous classes.

The absence of compelling research supporting tracking as well as the studies suggesting the demoralizing effects on students in low tracks has led many prominent educators and groups to take a strong stand against tracking. Recently the Carnegie Council on Adolescent Development called for an end to middle school tracking, describing it as "one of the most divisive and damaging school practices in existence." The National Education Association reviewed the research and concluded that "rigid academic tracking creates academic problems for many students from all socioeconomic and ethnic groups."

While rigid tracking in middle school, in which students are placed in either a high or low track for all academic subjects, is at best a questionable practice, nonetheless schools must make an effort to meet the needs of students of varying abilities and skill levels. Where tracking is used, schools should ensure that the most skilled teachers are divided equally among the tracks. Rather than track students for all subjects, schools might track only those subjects that require a certain level of skill development to succeed, such as math. Also, track assignments should be based on a student's performance in that subject rather than a general test of learning aptitude. Thus, placement in a math class should be based on previous math grades, standardized test results in math, or a recommendation from the student's math teacher. Parent views should also be considered in determining the student's class assignment.

School districts that opt to use heterogeneous grouping must be sensitive to the needs of lower-level students. Extra help should be available to those who are struggling. Cooperative learning, discussed previously, has shown potential for being effective with both high- and low-ability students. In addition, grades for low-level students should reflect not only their achievement but their effort and progress.

Parents need to pay careful attention to how tracking works in their district. If their school groups students by ability, they will want to ask questions such as the following:

- How many tracks are there?
- How are students assigned to a track? Is it based on teacher recommendation? Grades? Test performance? What kind of test? Do parents have a say? Can parents override the school's recommendation?
- Do teachers of the different tracks use the same textbooks and teaching materials?
- Once a student is placed in a track, how difficult is it to move her to another track? What factors are considered? Is there a formal process for reviewing tracking decisions yearly?
- How are teachers assigned to different tracks? (In some districts, the less experienced and less skilled teachers may be assigned to teach the lower tracks.)

PERSONAL AND SOCIAL DEVELOPMENT

Early adolescents may yearn for independence and freedom to make their own decisions, but they continue to need support and guidance to deal with the pressures of their age and their changing needs. Indeed, research suggests that many youngsters entering middle school experience a drop in self-esteem, confidence, and motivation. Middle schools face the challenge of offering a program that is academically demanding but also responds to students' social and emotional needs and promotes their moral development. In sum, middle schools need to deal with what the educational psychologist John Dewey called the "whole child." In middle school, this kind of support may be offered by sensitive and understanding teachers as well as by programs outside the classroom such as advisory programs and guidance counseling.

Advisory Programs

Advisory programs play an important role in responding to students' personal needs and promoting a sense of belonging to their school. These programs may take different forms but they share the same goal: to provide students with the support and guidance of an adult in school on a regular basis. This adviser is the student's primary link with the school and may also be the contact person for parents. Students may meet with their adviser individually or in a small group. They may talk about a range of subjects, from developing good study habits to handling peer pressure to dealing with a strict teacher to identifying career possibilities. In the process, students may improve their decision-making ability and social skills as well as gain personal insight.

Guidance Counseling

Middle school guidance counselors are also crucial to helping students adjust to middle school. While scheduling continues to be an important part of their responsibilities, many middle school guidance counselors will do what they have been trained to do: counsel students. They may run groups or see students individually about school or personal concerns. They may also help their counselees develop effective study skills. The time available for counseling will depend on their student load. Professional organizations recommend a ratio of one school counselor for every one hundred students although this ratio is rarely achieved. Parents should be concerned with high ratios because counselors are then less available to help students with personal issues.

MAKING THE MOVE TO MIDDLE SCHOOL

Almost all students making the move to middle school have some trepidations. Some worry that they won't be able to find their way around school. Some worry that they will be unable to open up their locker. Others worry that they will be picked on by older students. And still others worry about almost everything. Parents and school staff play important roles in preparing students for the school change and easing their worries.

Preparing for middle school is a year-long process. During your child's last year of elementary school, her teacher should be getting her ready for middle school by helping her become more independent and emphasizing study skills. Basic skills should be reviewed and writing should receive considerable attention. As one elementary teacher observed: "Sixth grade is the last stop for gas before the beltway."

Most schools provide activities to orient students to their new school. During the spring of your child's last year in elementary school, she and her classmates may visit the middle school they will attend, to take a tour and hear a presentation by staff. In some districts, middle school students will visit elementary schools to talk about the middle school program and answer questions. Some school districts hold orientation days during the summer, when students can pick up their schedule, obtain a locker, and tour the building. Parents should also be included in this orientation process. Many districts invite them in the spring or summer to an evening program describing the policies and practices of the middle school.

Once students begin middle school, they should be given an opportunity to meet their guidance counselor. They may also be paired with older students who will guide them in the ways of middle school life.

If these kinds of transition activities are not offered in your district, you should urge your district to provide them. If your school district does not arrange for your child to visit the middle school, you might want to visit the school with her during the summer. (Be sure to call in advance.) Seeing some classrooms and finding out where the guidance office, cafeteria, and gymnasium are located can help relieve your child's anxieties.

HOW PARENTS CAN HELP

Parents' involvement in their child's schooling gradually declines after first grade and drops dramatically when their child enters middle school. Yet research suggests that parent participation continues to be important in promoting school success throughout public school. Keep in mind, however, that parent involvement at the middle school level may take a different form from parent involvement at the elementary school level. The following strategies may guide you in helping your child adjust to middle school and helping you adjust to the ups and downs of early adolescence.

BE ON CALL EARLY IN THE YEAR FOR TROUBLE SHOOTING AND REASSURANCE. Your child may be anxious and confused during the initial days of school. Most of the problems first-year middle schoolers encounter are common and resolve themselves with time and practice: opening up their locker, finding a classroom, making it to class on time, remembering whether it is day one or day two, and keeping track of their schedule. Other problems may take more time to resolve and may call for your reassurance and encouragement. The initial adjustment may be especially hard for your child if many of her friends are attending a different middle school.

ENCOURAGE INDEPENDENCE AND RESPONSIBILITY. By the time your child enters middle school, she should be responsible for keeping track of homework, test dates, and project deadlines. Do not assume this responsibility for her. This is her job. If you find out from teachers that she is not handing in homework consistently or is not meeting deadlines, this is the time to step in. Similarly, if your child has a problem with a teacher, let her try to work it out unless its seriousness calls for your involvement. Your child should be able to handle most classroom problems without your help, including clarifying instructions from the teacher, asking for extra help, or questioning a grade. If a problem calls for your meeting with a teacher or counselor, consider inviting your child to the meeting and giving her an opportunity to speak.

BE AVAILABLE AND SUPPORTIVE. While your middle school child may be determined to handle many concerns on her own, your guidance remains crucial, especially since she will be experimenting with new friends, experiences, and interests. Don't expect her to trust your taste in music or clothes, but your views will still carry weight in dealing with more personal matters and developing more enduring values. Even if your child overtly rejects your advice, she may still give it serious consideration. With regard to schoolwork, your child will likely be less receptive to your help in middle school than she was in elementary school. Don't insist on working with her unless she is performing poorly, but be available if she asks.

BE PREPARED TO ACT IF PROBLEMS EMERGE. If your child's grades or motivation drop drastically, take a close-up look. She may be overwhelmed by the work or distressed by other concerns. With middle school students, peer issues are often the culprit. Also take a look at your child's study habits (see below). If your child's school problem persists, contact her guidance counselor or her primary teacher, who should be able to arrange a meeting with the other teachers.

PROMOTE GOOD STUDY HABITS. It is important to lay the groundwork for high school by helping your child develop good study skills during her middle school years. This means setting limits on the use of the television and telephone, both prominent activities of middle schoolers, and, if necessary, teaching your child how to budget her time and organize her workspace. In addition, encourage your child to keep track of homework by using an assignment pad, and project and test dates by using a calendar. Also encourage a regular time for reading every night.

ENCOURAGE PARTICIPATION IN EXTRACURRICULAR ACTIVI-TIES. Middle school may be your child's first opportunity to participate in after-school activities. Help her choose some activities that interest her and that are not burdensome in terms of time and stress. Middle schools vary in their after-school program offerings. Typical programs include intramural sports, student government, student publications, and community service. These programs not only give your child a chance to interact with classmates in enjoyable activities but also promote leadership and responsibility. Encourage your child to participate even if she is doing poorly in school. These activities may help her develop some positive connection with school and her classmates. Studies suggest that students who participate in school activities generally do well academically and learn to manage their time effectively.

CHOOSE YOUR BATTLES CAREFULLY. If you are like many parents, you will find early adolescence to be tough going. Your child may do things that you find objectionable and she may be especially contentious during these years. Avoid getting into battles over every issue. If you choose to fight every battle, you are assured of fighting a larger war. Be discriminating about the issues you tackle with your child and try not to sweat the small stuff. There will be times when you will have to bite your tongue. Reserve your expressions of concern or annoyance for the issues that really matter to you. Your relationship with your middle school child will call for a mix of tenderness, firmness, understanding, patience, restraint, and a sense of humor.

GIVE YOUR CHILD MORE OF A SAY AT HOME. Early adolescents need and deserve opportunities to make decisions and be responsible. Give them a chance to have a say in family rules and activities. With decisions that belong to you, make it clear that the final decision is yours but give your child a chance to offer her opinion.

RESPECT YOUR CHILD'S PRIVACY. You may find that the child who couldn't stop talking in elementary school is suddenly tight-lipped upon entering middle school. Your question "How was school today?" may be answered with a nonresponsive "fine." Asking "What happened in school today?" may elicit a curt "nothing." This may be your child's way of asserting her independence and separating emotionally from you. Try making your questions more specific (for example, "What are you working on in art class?"). Asking a few questions is fine but curtail your impatience and anger if you don't get much of a response. When your child does talk with you about personal matters, make sure to be attentive and concerned but monitor your questions to avoid being intrusive.

APPENDIX A
ORGANIZATIONS

American Association for Gifted
  Children
Duke University
1121 W. Main Street, Suite 100
Durham, NC 27701
919-683-1400

American Association on Mental
  Retardation
1719 Kalorama Road NW
Washington, DC 20009
202-387-1968

American Speech-Language-Hearing
  Association
10801 Rockville Pike
Rockville, MD 20852
301-897-5700

The ARC (formerly Association for
  Retarded Citizens)
500 E. Border Street, Suite 300
Arlington, TX 76010
817-261-6003

Center for Law and Education
955 Massachusetts Avenue
Cambridge, MA 02139
617-876-6611
*Provides legal advice and services to
educational organizations and
advocates throughout the country.*

Center for Talented Youth
Johns Hopkins University
3400 N. Charles Street
Baltimore, MD 21218
410-516-0337
*Conducts a talent search for gifted
children in second grade and above and
offers educational programs during the
school year and summer.*

Center for the Study of Parent
  Involvement
JFK University
370 Camino Pablo
Orinda, CA 94563
510-254-0110
*Provides training and technical
assistance to educators and community
leaders to promote parent involvement
in the schools.*

Center on Parent Involvement
Johns Hopkins University
3505 N. Charles Street
Baltimore, MD 21218
410-516-8800
*Conducts research and disseminates
information about how families,
schools, and communities can promote
children's learning.*

Children's Book Council
568 Broadway
New York, NY 10012
212-966-1990
Promotes the reading and enjoyment of children's books.

Children's Defense Fund
25 E. State Street NW
Washington, DC 20001
202-628-8787
Provides long-range advocacy on behalf of children and youth.

Council for Exceptional Children
1920 Association Drive
Reston, VA 22091–1589
703-620-3660
Offers information, workshops, and advocacy services dealing with children with special needs.

Family Policy Compliance Staff
Office of Human Resources and
    Administration
U.S. Department of Education
L'Enfant Plaza, 2100 Corridor
400 Maryland Avenue SW
Washington, DC 20202–4605
202-732-1807
Offers advice and information on issues relating to school records, including parent rights and privacy concerns.

Federation for Children with Special
    Needs
95 Berkley Street, Suite 104
Boston, MA 02116
617-482-2915

Institute for Responsive Education
605 Commonwealth Avenue
Boston, MA 02215
617-353-3309

Works to enhance citizen participation in educational decision making.

International Reading Association
PO Box 8139
800 Barksdale Road
Newark, DE 19714–8139
302-731-1600

Learning Disabilities Association of
    America
4156 Library Road
Pittsburgh, PA 15234
412-341-1515

Math/Science Network
Preservation Park
678 13th Street, Suite 100
Oakland, CA 94612
510-893-6284
Fosters the participation of girls in math, science, and technology.

MegaSkills Education Center
The Home and School Institute
1500 Massachusetts Avenue NW
Washington, DC 20005
202-466-3633
Trains individuals to provide workshops to parents on how to enrich their children's education.

National Association for Gifted
    Children
1155 15th Street NW, No. 1002
Washington, DC 20005
202-785-4268

National Association of Partners in
    Education
209 Madison Street, Suite 401
Alexandria, VA 22314
703-836-4880
Promotes the value of and provides information about school volunteering.

National Center for Learning
  Disabilities
99 Park Avenue, 6th Floor
New York, NY 10016
212-687-7211

National Center for the Study of
  Corporal Punishment and
  Alternatives
Temple University
253 Ritter Annex
Philadelphia, PA 19122
215-204-6091

National Clearinghouse on Bilingual
  Education
1118 22nd Street NW
Washington, DC 20037
800-321-6223

National Coalition against Censorship
275 7th Avenue, 20th Floor
New York, NY 10001
212-807-6222

National Coalition for Parent
  Involvement in Education
PO Box 39
1201 16th Street NW
Washington, DC 20036
202-416-0300

National Coalition for School Bus
  Safety
PO Box 781
Skokie, IL 60076
708-679-2694

National Coalition for Sex Equity in
  Education
1 Redwood Drive
Clinton, NJ 08809
908-735-5045

National Coalition to Abolish Corporal
  Punishment in Schools
6350 Frantz Road, Suite D
Dublin, OH 43017
614-766-6688

National Committee for Prevention of
  Child Abuse
332 S. Michigan Avenue, Suite 1600
Chicago, IL 60604–4357
312-663-3520

National Congress of Parents and
  Teachers (National PTA)
700 N. Rush Street
Chicago, IL 60611
312-787-0977

National Education Association
1201 16th Street NW
Washington, DC 20036
202-822-7200

National Homeschool Association
PO Box 290
Hartland, MI 48353-0290
313-632-5208

National Information Center for
  Children and Youth with Disabilities
PO Box 1492
Washington, DC 20013
703-893-6061

National Middle School Association
4807 Evanswood Drive
Columbus, OH 43229
614-848-8211

National Peer Helpers Association
PO Box 2684
Greenville, NC 27858
919-757-6923

Orton Dyslexia Society
Chester Building, Suite 382
8600 LaSalle Road
Baltimore, MD 21286–2044
410-296-0232
*Gives information and training on
reading and language disabilities.*

Parents Anonymous
520 S. Lafayette Park Place, Suite 316
Los Angeles, CA 90057
800-421-0353
*Offers support services to parents in an
effort to prevent and treat child abuse.*

Parents as Teachers National Center
9374 Olive Boulevard
St. Louis, MO 63132
314-432-4330
*Trains parent educators to visit with
and educate parents of young children.
Sponsors 1300 parent education
programs in 44 states.*

School-Age Child Care Project
Wellesley College
Center for Research on Women
Wellesley, MA 02181
617-283-2547
*Provides a broad range of services to
support the start-up and improvement of
school-age child care programs.*

SchoolMatch
5027 Pine Creek Drive
Blendonview Office Park
Westerville, OH 43081
800-724-6651
*Provides information for a fee on all
American public school districts and
accredited private schools throughout the
world.*

Sex Information and Education Council
    of the U.S.
130 W. 42nd Street, Suite 2500
New York, NY 10036
212-819-9770

Single Parent Resource Center
141 W 28th Street, Suite 302
New York, NY 10001
212-947-0221

US Department of Education
400 Maryland Avenue SW
Washington, DC 20202
202-708-5366

Work and Family Information Center
845 3rd Avenue
New York, NY 10022
212-759-0900
*Does research and provides information
on changes in work and family
relationships.*

APPENDIX B

FOR FURTHER INFORMATION

Computers

Blank, M., & Berlin, M. 1991. *The parent's guide to educational software.* Richmond, WA: Microsoft Press.

Raskin, R., & Ellison, C. 1992. *Parents, kids and computers: An activity guide for family fun and learning.* New York: Random House Electronic Publishing.

Salpeter, J. 1992. *Kids and computers: A parents' handbook.* Carmel, IN: Sams/Prentice-Hall Computer Publishing.

Corporal Punishment

Hyman, I. A. 1990. *Reading, writing, and the hickory stick: The appalling story of physical and psychological abuse in American schools.* New York: Free Press.

Evaluating Your Child's School

Thomas, M. D. 1982. *Your school: How well is it working?* Washington, DC: National Committee for Citizens in Education.

Unger, H. 1991. *What did you learn in school today? A parent's guide for evaluating your child's school.* New York: Facts on File.

Family Matters

Brazelton, T. B. 1992. *Working and caring.* Reading, MA: Addison-Wesley.

Dana, T. K. 1988. *Safe and sound: A parents' guide to the care of children home alone.* New York: McGraw-Hill.

Elkind, D. 1984. *The hurried child: Growing up too fast too soon.* Reading, MA: Addison-Wesley.

Eyre, R., & Eyre, L. 1993. *Teaching your children values.* New York: Simon & Schuster.

Olds, S. W. 1989. *The working parents' survival guide.* New York: Bantam.

Planned Parenthood of America. 1986. *How to talk with your child about sexuality: A parents' guide.* Garden City, NY: Doubleday.

Smith, D. 1991. *Parents' guide to raising kids in a changing world.* New York: Prentice Hall.

Gifted Children

Alvino, J. 1985. *Parents' guide to raising a gifted child.* Boston: Little, Brown and Company.

Eby, J. W., & Smutny, J. F. 1990. *A thoughtful overview of gifted education.* New York: Longman.

Smutny, J. F., Veenker, K., & Veenker, S. 1991. *Your gifted child: How to recognize and develop the special talents in your child.* New York: Ballantine.

Home Schooling

Guterson, D. 1992. *Family matters: Why home schooling makes sense.* New York: Harcourt Brace Jovanovich.

Hendrickson, B. 1988. *Home school: Taking the first step.* Kooskia, ID: Mountain Meadow Press.

Holt, J. 1982. *Teach your own.* New York: Delacorte.

Wade, T. E. 1988. *The home school manual: For parents who teach their own.* Auburn, CA: Gazelle Publications.

Homework

Clark, F., & Clark, C. 1989. *Hassle-free homework.* New York: Doubleday.

Levine, F. M., & Anesko, K. M. 1987. *Winning the homework war.* New York: Arco.

Radencich, M. C., & Schumm, J. S. 1988. *How to help your child with homework.* Minneapolis: Free Spirit Publications.

Rosemond, J. 1990. *Ending the homework hassle.* Kansas City: Andrews and McMeel.

Kindergarten

Eberts, M., & Gisler, P. 1991. *Ready for school? What every preschooler should know.* Deephaven, MN: Meadowbrook Press.

Marzollo, J. 1987. *The new kindergarten: Full day, child centered, academic*. New York: Harper Collins.

Perrone, V. 1993. *101 educational conversations you should have with your kindergartner and first grader*. New York: Chelsea House.

Robinson, J. 1990. *Is your child ready for school?* New York: Arco.

Sobol, T., & Sobol, H. 1987. *Your child in school: Kindergarten through second grade*. New York: Arbor House.

Legal Issues

Schimmel, D., & Fischer, L. 1987. *Parents, schools, and the law*. Washington, DC: National Committee for Citizens in Education.

Your child's school records. 1986. Washington, DC: Children's Defense Fund.

Math and Science

Carson, M.S. 1989. *The scientific kid: Projects, experiments and adventures*. New York: Harper Collins.

Gardner, R. 1989. *Science around the house*. New York: Simon & Schuster.

Paulu, N., & Martin, M. 1991. *Helping your child learn science*. Washington, DC: US Department of Education, Office of Educational Research and Improvement.

Shermer, M. 1991. *Teach your child math: Making math fun for the both of you*. Los Angeles: Lowell House.

Shermer, M. 1989. *Teach your child science: Making science fun for the both of you*. Los Angeles: Lowell House.

Skolnick, J., Langbort, C., & Day, L. 1982. *How to encourage girls in math and science*. Palo Alto, CA: Dale Seymour Publications.

Stenmark, J. K., Thompson, V., & Cossey, R. 1986. *Family math*. Berkeley, CA: Univ. of California.

Middle School

Ames, L. B. 1989. *Your ten- to fourteen-year old*. New York: Delacorte.

Baenen, J. 1991. *How to enjoy living with a preadolescent*. Columbus, OH: National Middle School Association.

Berla, N., Henderson, A. T., & Kerewsky, W. 1989. *The middle school years: A parent's handbook*. Washington, DC: National Committee for Citizens in Education.

Parent Involvement and Advocacy

Barth, R. S. 1990. *Improving schools from within.* San Francisco: Jossey-Bass.

Berla, N., & Hall, S. H. 1989. *Beyond the open door: A citizen's guide to increasing public access to local school boards.* Washington, DC: National Committee for Citizens in Education.

Bloom, J. 1992. *Parenting the schools: A hands-on guide to educational reform.* Boston: Little, Brown and Company.

Bloom, L. Z., Coburn, K., & Pearlman, J. 1975. *The new assertive woman.* New York: Dell Publishing.

Gensheimer, C. F. 1993. *Raising funds for your child's school.* New York: Walker and Company.

Henderson, A. 1987. *The evidence continues to grow: Parent involvement improves student achievement.* Washington, DC: National Committee for Citizens in Education.

Maeroff, G. 1989. *The school-smart parent.* New York: Henry Holt and Company.

Making sense of school budgets: A citizen's guide to local public education spending. Washington, DC: U.S. Department of Education.

Marburger, C. L. 1985. *One school at a time: School-based management, a process for change.* Washington, DC: National Committee for Citizens in Education.

Parents organizing to improve schools. 1985. Washington, DC: National Committee for Citizens in Education. (Available in Spanish.)

Schwartz, C. O. 1982. *How to run a school board campaign and win.* Washington, DC: National Committee for Citizens in Education.

Promoting School Achievement

Cutright, M. 1992. *Growing up confident: How to make your child's early years learning years.* New York: Doubleday.

Feiden, K., & Miller, R. 1989. *Parents' guide to raising kids who love to learn.* New York: Prentice-Hall.

Greene, L. J. 1991. *1001 ways to improve your child's schoolwork.* New York: Dell.

Rich, D. 1992. *MegaSkills: How families can help children succeed in school and beyond.* New York: Houghton Mifflin.

Wlodkowski, R. J., & Jaynes, J. H. 1991. *Eager to learn: Helping children become motivated and love learning.* San Francisco: Josey-Bass.

Public Schools

Fiske, E. B. 1991. *Smart schools, smart kids.* New York: Simon & Schuster.

Frith, T. 1985. *Secrets parents should know about public schools.* New York: Simon & Schuster.

Martz, L. 1992. *Making schools better.* New York: Times Books.

Townsend-Butterworth, D. 1992. *Your child's first school.* New York: Walker and Company.

What works: Research about teaching and learning. 1986. Washington, DC: U.S. Department of Education.

Zemelman, S.; Daniels, H.; & Hyde, A. 1993. *Best practice: New standards for teaching and learning in America's schools.* Portsmouth, NH: Heinemann.

Reading

Fox, B. J. 1989. *Rx for reading: How the schools teach your child to read and how you can help.* New York: Penguin Books.

Graves, R. 1987. *The RIF guide to encouraging young readers.* New York: Doubleday.

Kimmel, M. M., & Segel, E. 1991. *For reading out loud: A guide to sharing books with children.* New York: Dell.

Lipson, E. R. 1991. *The* New York Times *parent's guide to the best books for children.* New York: Random House.

Russell, W. F. 1992. *Classics to read aloud to your children.* New York: Crown.

Smith, C. B. 1991. *Help your child read and succeed.* Bloomington, IN: Grayson Bernard.

Trelease, J. 1989. *The new read-aloud handbook.* New York: Penguin.

School Problems

Heacox, D. 1991. *Up from underachievement: How teachers, students and parents can work together to promote school success.* Minneapolis: Free Spirit.

McEwan, E. K. 1992. *The parent's guide to solving school problems.* Wheaton, IL: Harold Shaw Publishers.

Vail, P. 1989. *Smart kids with school problems: Things to know and ways to help.* New York: Dutton.

Special Needs Students

Bain, L. 1991. *A parent's guide to attention deficit disorders*. New York: Dela-corte.

Bloom, J. 1990. *Help me to help my child: A sourcebook for parents of learning disabled children*. New York: Little, Brown and Company.

Greene, L. J. 1983. *Kids who hate school: A survival handbook on learning disabilities*. Atlanta: Humanics Limited.

Moss, R. A., & Dunlap, H. H. 1990. *Why Johnny can't concentrate: Coping with attention deficit problems*. New York: Bantam Books.

Novick, B. C., & Arnold, M. M. 1991. *Why is my child having trouble at school?* New York: Random House.

Shore, K. 1986. *The special education handbook: How to get the best education possible for your learning disabled child*. New York: Warner Books.

Silver, L. 1984. *The misunderstood child: A guide for parents of learning disabled children*. New York: McGraw-Hill.

Turecki, S. 1989. *The difficult child*. New York: Bantam Books.

Standardized Testing

Boehm, A. E., & White, M. A. 1982. *The parents' handbook on school testing*. New York: Teachers College Press.

McCullough, V. E. 1992. *Testing and your child*. New York: Plume.

Shore, M.; Brice, P. J.; & Love, B. G. 1992. *When your child needs testing*. New York: Crossroad Publishing.

Summer

Silver, S. 1990. *The smart parents' guide to summer camps*. New York: Farrar, Straus, & Giroux.

Ware, C. 1990. *Summer programs for teenagers*. New York: Arco.

Television

Lappé, F. M. 1985. *What to do after you turn off the TV: Fresh ideas for enjoying family time*. New York: Ballantine.

Roes, N. 1992. *Helping children watch TV*. Barryville, NY: NAR Publications.

Writing

Edwards, S. A., & Maloy, R. W. 1992. *Kids have all the write stuff: Inspiring your children to put pencil to paper.* New York: Penguin.

Graves, D., & Stuart, V. 1985. *Write from the start: How to tap your child's innate writing abilities.* New York: E. P. Dutton.

Wiener, H. S. 1990. *Any child can write.* New York: Bantam.

BOOKS AND MAGAZINES FOR CHILDREN

Books

The following are fiction and nonfiction books for children on school-related themes:

Starting School, by Janet and Allan Ahlberg (Viking), features typical school activities done during the first few months of school, with illustrations and large type.

Berenstain Bears Go to School, by Stan and Jan Berenstain (Random House), tells the story of Sister Bear's initial discomfort with school and her gradual adjustment.

Will I Have a Friend? by Miriam Cohen (Macmillan), is the story of a boy who is very nervous about his first day of school.

Alice Ann Gets Ready for School, by Cynthia Jabar (Little, Brown), also tells a story about a child who is beginning school.

Off to School, by Ann Schweninger (Viking), is about a child with first-day jitters.

Waiting for Mom, by Linda Wagner Tyler (Viking), is an amusing but reassuring book about a child who becomes worried when his mother is late picking him up after school.

Arthur's Teacher Trouble, by Marc Tolon Brown (Little Brown), is the story of a boy who is angry with all the schoolwork he is receiving but learns to work out his problems with the teacher.

Today Was a Terrible Day, by Patricia Reilly Giff (Viking), is the story of a second-grader who has reading and other school difficulties but eventually gains insight into his troubles.

Third Grade Is Terrible, by Barbara Baker (Dutton), reflects the concerns of many elementary students in its story of a girl who is separated from her best friend and also has to adjust to a strict and demanding teacher.

Winning of Miss Lynn Ryan, by Ilene Cooper (Morrow), tells of a girl who learns to deal with a teacher she wants to impress who plays class favorites.

It's George, by Miriam Cohen (Greenwillow), depicts a slow learner who has many special abilities and qualities, including being kind and thoughtful.

The Beast in Ms. Rooney's Room, by Patricia Reilly Giff (Dell), is the story of a boy who is retained in second grade but with time begins to enjoy academic and social success.

Don't Look at Me, by Doris Sanford (Multnomah), is a book about a child having difficulty learning who gradually gains self-acceptance.

Different Not Dumb, by Margot Marek (Watts), is about a boy who is self-conscious about his reading problem but learns techniques to achieve success in school.

Putting on the Brakes, by Patricia Quinn (Magination), helps children from 8 to 13 learn about attention deficit disorder.

Shelly, the Hyperactive Turtle, by Deborah Moss (Woodbine House), helps children in early elementary grades understand hyperactivity and what can be done to help.

Josh: A Boy with Dyslexia, by Caroline Janover (Waterfront), a story about a child with a reading disability, is for children from 5 to 12.

The Don't Give Up, Kid, by Jeanne Gehret (Verbal Images Press), is a book for children from 6 to 10 about a learning disabled child.

Living with a Brother or Sister with Special Needs: A Book for Sibs (University of Washington Press) is written by siblings of children with special needs for elementary schoolchildren.

My Brother, Matthew, by Mary Thompson (Woodbine House), describes what it is like to have a brother with special needs.

Trouble with School, by Kathryn B. Dunn and Allison B. Dunn (Woodbine House), looks at the problem of learning disabilities from both the parent and child perspective.

The School Survival Guide for Kids with Learning Differences, by Rhoda Cummings and Gary Fisher (Free Spirit), looks at ways of making learning easier and more fun.

School Power: Strategies for Succeeding in School, by Jeanne S. Schumm and Marguerite Radencich (Free Spirit), is intended to help children age 11 and over become better readers and develop better study habits.

The Gifted Kids Survival Guide, by Judy Galbraith (Free Spirit), comes in two versions: one for students 10 and under and one for students 11 to 18.

Fourth Grade Rats, by Jerry Spinelli (Scholastic), is a story of growing up and coping with peer pressure.

Search for Grissi, by Mary Francis Shura (Dodd, Mead), is the story of an 11-year-old girl who moves to a new community and struggles at first to make new friends and adjust to the changes.

Charlotte Cheetham: Master of Disaster, by Barbara Ware Holmes (Harper), is the story of a fifth-grade girl who attempts to gain peer approval by lying and exaggerating but instead gains only trouble.

Herbie's Troubles, by Carol Chapman (Dutton), depicts a 6-year-old boy's successful efforts to deal with a classmate who is taunting him.

King of the Playground, by Phyllis R. Naylor (Macmillan), is the story of a child who with the aid of his father learns to confront a bully.

Why Is Everybody Always Picking on Me? by Terrence Webster-Doyle (Atrium), provides children with guidance about handling bullies.

Latchkey Kid, by Irene Kleeburg (Franklin Watts), offers advice for children from 9 to 13.

On My Own, by Lynette Long (Acropolis), is a "survival" guide for children in self-care.

Queen of the Sixth Grade, by Ilene Cooper (Morrow), is the story of a girl who finds herself an outcast at school after an argument with another child.

My Life in 7th Grade, by Mark Geller (Harper & Row), deals with common adolescent concerns, including developing friends and making decisions.

Friends Are Like That, by Patricia Hermes (Harcourt), is about a 13-year-old girl divided between wanting to be popular and wanting to remain loyal to an old unconventional friend.

Middle School Blues, by Lou Kassem (Houghton Mifflin), features two 12-year-old girls who eventually learn to meet the challenges of middle school.

And the Other, Gold, by Susan Wojciechowski (Orchard/Watts), is about two girls dealing with the stresses of eighth grade.

Good-bye, Pink Pig, by C. S. Adler (Putnam), is about a child who retreats into fantasy because of problems adjusting to middle school but gradually learns to face the world and make decisions.

Hang on, Harvey! by Nancy Hopper (Dutton), is about an eighth-grade boy who must deal with bullies, girls, and demanding teachers.

Magazines

The following is a selection of magazines for children of different ages and interests. Additional information about these and other magazines can be found in the book *Magazines for Children,* by Selma K. Richardson, published by the American Library Association in 1991. Also review sample copies in your public library.

Boys Life
1325 Walnut Hill Lane
PO Box 152079
Irving, TX 75015
Published by the Boy Scouts, this monthly magazine has articles on outdoor life, sports, and recreation for youngsters from 8 to 18.

Chickadee and *Owl*
Young Naturalist Foundation
PO Box 11314
Des Moines, IA 50340
*These two magazines for children from 3 to 9 (*Chickadee*) and from 9 to 12 (*Owl*) stress science and nature.*

Cobblestone
Cobblestone Publishing
30 Grove Street
Peterborough, NH 03458
This history magazine devotes each issue to a different event or period in American history.

Cricket
PO Box 52961
Boulder, CO 80322
A literary magazine for children from 6 to 12, including both fiction and nonfiction. Sponsors art and writing contests.

Highlights for Children
PO Box 269
Columbus, OH 43272
A monthly magazine for children from 2 to 12 to help them develop basic skills and general knowledge through stories, crafts, and puzzles.

Humpty Dumpty and *Jack and Jill*
Children's Better Health Institute
PO Box 7133
Red Oak, IA 51591
*These two magazines for children from 4 to 6 (*Humpty Dumpty*) and 7 to 10 (*Jack and Jill*) emphasize themes of health, nutrition, hygiene, exercise, and safety.*

Kid City
Children's Television Workshop
PO Box 53349
Boulder, CO 80322
This monthly magazine for children from 6 to 10 has amusing articles on a range of subjects.

National Geographic World
National Geographic Society
PO Box 2330
Washington, DC 20077
This monthly magazine for children from 8 to 13 provides information about a wide range of subjects, including people, places, science, sports, and animals, and includes full-color photos.

Odyssey
Kalmbach Publishing Company
21027 Crossroads Circle
PO Box 1612
Waukesha, WI 53187
Articles on space exploration and astronomy for children from 8 to 14.

Ranger Rick
National Wildlife Foundation
8925 Leesburg Pike
Vienna, VA 22184
A monthly magazine for children from 6 to 12 on themes of nature, conservation, the outdoors, and the environment.

Sports Illustrated for Kids
Time Incorporated Magazine Company
PO Box 830609
Birmingham, AL 35283
A monthly magazine on sports for children from 8 to 13.

Stone Soup
Children's Art Foundation
PO Box 83
Santa Cruz, CA 95063–0083
A bimonthly magazine for children through age 13 featuring art and writing by children.

3-2-1 Contact
Children's Television Workshop
PO Box 53051
Boulder, CO 80322
A monthly magazine for children from 8 to 14 on science and technology topics.

Zillions (formerly *Penny Power*)
Consumers Union
PO Box 54861
Boulder, CO 80322
A Consumer Reports publication for children from 8 to 14 that gives advice about spending money and rates children's products.

GLOSSARY

Ability grouping. Dividing students into groups based on ability for teaching purposes. Often used synonymously with "tracking."

Achievement test. A test that measures what a student has learned in a specific area.

Acting out. Behaving in a socially inappropriate way.

Affective education. A program to help students understand and deal with their own and others' feelings as well as interact appropriately with others.

Annual goal. A statement in a special education plan describing what a student is expected to achieve in a specific area in one year.

Annual review. A review of a student's special education program that is required by federal law at least once a year.

Aptitude test. A test that measures a student's capacity for learning and is used to predict future performance.

Articulation disorder. A difficulty in speech pronunciation.

Assertive discipline. A formal and systematic program of classroom discipline used by many teachers.

At risk. Prone to having a problem.

Attention deficit disorder (ADD). A significant difficulty in focusing attention that interferes with academic performance.

Basal reader. An instructional reading book geared to a particular grade level.

Behavior modification. A system for eliminating undesirable behavior and promoting desirable behavior by modifying the events that precede or follow the behavior.

Bilingual education. An educational program for students for whom English is a second language in which instruction is provided in two languages. Students gradually receive increasing amounts of instruction in English-speaking classes.

Buckley amendment. Federal law that provides parents access to their child's school records, limits the release of these records to others, and allows parents to challenge the contents of the records. More formally called the Family Educational Rights and Privacy Act.

Classification. The process of determining eligibility for special education and assigning a term to a student describing the specific kind of educational disability.

Confidentiality. In the context of schools, refers to the obligation of educators not to share personal information about a student with other school staff unless those persons have a need to know the information.

Cooperative learning. A teaching method in which a small group of students of varying abilities work together on a classroom assignment and students are evaluated according to the group's performance.

Corporal punishment. The intentional infliction of pain to change a child's behavior.

Criterion-referenced test. A test that produces a specific profile of skills that a student has mastered and not mastered.

Cumulative record. The accumulated school records on a particular student.

Curriculum. The course of study for a particular subject.

Curriculum guide. A description of a course's goals and objectives, materials, methods of evaluation, and suggested lesson plans.

Decoding. The ability to translate written symbols into words.

Developmental delay or lag. A delay in the student's development of a skill or characteristic.

Due process. A system of procedures to ensure that individuals are treated fairly and have an opportunity to challenge decisions made about them.

Dyslexia. A learning disability marked by a difficulty in the understanding of language. Often used synonymously with "reading disability."

Early intervention. The provision of educational instruction to students with learning problems at an early age to avoid more significant problems in later years.

Educational disability. A specific cognitive, physical, or behavioral problem that interferes with the acquisition of academic skills.

English as a second language instruction (ESL). A program for students whose native language is other than English to help them develop proficiency in English. Students attend mostly English-speaking classes.

Evaluation. In the context of schools, usually refers to a battery of tests and other procedures given by a team of professionals to determine whether a student has an educational disability and requires special education.

Expulsion. The decision to exclude a student from a public school because of severe behavioral or disciplinary problems.

Fine-motor coordination. The ability to use small muscles to accomplish tasks requiring precision such as writing or cutting.

Freedom of Information Act. A federal statute that allows public access to governmental information and records.

Frustration level. The point of an academic task at which a student begins to experience difficulty. Instruction should be just below this level.

Gifted. Refers to an exceptionally bright student who may need specialized instruction to progress in accordance with his or her ability. Different districts use different criteria for determining giftedness.

Grade-level equivalent. A test score that refers to the grade level at which a student performs. A third-grade child who receives a 4.5 grade-level equivalent on a standardized math test is performing comparable to an average child in the fifth month (January) of fourth grade.

Gross-motor coordination. The ability to use large muscles in a coordinated, purposeful manner for such activities as running, throwing, and jumping.

Heterogeneous grouping. Teaching students of different abilities in the same group or class.

Higher-order thinking. Thinking skills that go beyond the learning of rote information to the understanding of ideas and concepts.

Home instruction. Temporary instruction at home provided by a certified teacher when a student's illness or injury prevents school attendance for a significant period.

Home schooling. The provision of a student's educational program at home by the parents or others. Must be approved by the local school district and meet state criteria.

Homogeneous grouping. Teaching students of similar ability in the same group or class.

Inclusive education. Instruction of educationally disabled students, even those with severe disabilities, in regular education classes. The student may receive help from special education personnel while in regular class.

Independent level. The highest level of an academic task that a student can perform independently.

Individualized education program (IEP). A written plan describing a specific educational program for an educationally disabled student.

Individualized instruction. Academic instruction that is tailored to a student's specific educational needs and learning style.

In-school suspension. A disciplinary measure in which a student is barred from attending regular classes but must remain in school under supervision and do assigned work.

In-service training. Provision of educational programs to school staff to keep them updated on new trends and information in their field.

Instructional level. The level at which a student should be taught an academic task.

Intelligence quotient (IQ). Score on an intelligence test for which 100 is the mean.

Intelligence test. A test used to estimate overall capacity for learning.

Invented spelling. Spelling of words as they sound by young children who are just learning how to read and write.

Language arts. Refers to subject involving use of language, including reading, writing, and spelling.

Latchkey child. A child who is home alone either before or after school on a regular basis.

Learning disability. A specific deficiency in the way a student takes in information that impedes mastery of specific academic skills. May be characterized by a significant discrepancy between measured intellectual ability and measured academic achievement that cannot be explained by emotional, environmental, or sensory problems.

Learning style. The specific ways that a student approaches a learning task.

Magnet school. A specialized school organized around a specific theme, designed for a specific kind of student, or characterized by a particular educational approach.

Mainstreaming. The placement of an educationally disabled student in a regular class.

Manipulatives. Concrete materials such as beads or sand used to convey academic concepts that may be hard for students to visualize.

Math anxiety. Anxiety engendered by math that may inhibit a student's ability to learn math and perform optimally on tests.

Mental age (MA). A form for expressing a student's performance on a test. A student who receives an MA of 7 years, 5 months performed comparable to an average student of that age.

Multisensory approach. An instructional approach in which a teacher uses more than one sense to teach a task (for example, having students spell words out loud and then write them).

Norm group. The group of children to whom your child is being compared on a standardized test.

Norm-referenced test. A test that yields a numerical score that allows comparison of a student's performance with that of other students of the same age or grade.

Out-of-school suspension. A disciplinary measure in which a student is temporarily barred from attending school because of a serious violation of school rules.

Paraprofessional. A person who assists a professional such as a classroom aide.

Peer teaching. The teaching of one student by another student.

Percentile rank. A test score that describes how well a child performed compared with other students in the norm group of the same age or grade.

Phonics. An approach to reading instruction in which students learn to sound out letters and combinations of letters.

Portfolio assessment. Evaluation of a student's performance based on a cumulative review of his or her work in the course.

Preacademic. Refers to basic skills that are necessary to the acquisition of more formal academic skills.

Public Law 94–142. The primary federal law that describes the obligations of schools with regard to educating students with disabilities as well as parent and student rights.

Pullout program. A program in which students are taken out of class for one or more sessions a week to see an educational specialist (for example, a remedial reading teacher).

Readiness test. A test that assesses the presence of basic skills that are necessary to learning a more complex set of skills.

Reading readiness. A level of skill development necessary to learn how to read.

Referral. A formal request for an evaluation to determine if a student is educationally disabled and in need of special education.

Related services. Support services needed by an educationally disabled student to enhance his or her school adjustment and performance (for example, counseling).

Reliability. The degree to which a test elicits consistent results over time and under various conditions.

Remediation. The process of strengthening areas of academic weakness.

Retention. The decision to have a student repeat a grade because of academic failure or deficiency.

School-based management. An approach to running a school in which parents and teachers join with the principal to make key decisions.

School phobia. An extreme reluctance to attend school that is often related to a child's difficulty in separating from his or her parents.

Screening. A brief assessment that identifies students in need of more in-depth evaluation.

Social promotion. Promoting a student to the next grade regardless of school performance.

Sound-symbol relationship. Understanding the sounds that correspond to letters and combinations of letters.

Special education. Specialized instruction for students with educational disabilities that is tailored to their instructional needs and learning style.

Speech therapy. Instruction and exercises provided by a speech language pathologist to correct a speech disorder or improve language usage.

Standardized test. A test with explicit procedures for administration and scoring as well as norms or average scores for comparison purposes.

Stanine score. Test scores ranging from 1 (lowest) to 9 (highest).

Structure. Provision of explicit and specific directions regarding the rules and routines of the classroom.

Sunshine law. A law that allows public access to the deliberations of or information generated by public agencies.

Test anxiety. Anxiety engendered by taking a test that may lessen performance.

Time out. Disciplinary measure in which a student is removed from contact with other students or the teacher for a short period and is not allowed to engage in any activity.

Tracking. Grouping students by ability for instructional purposes. Often used synonymously with "ability grouping."

Underachiever. A student who performs below his or her apparent academic potential.

Validity. The degree to which a test actually measures what it purports to measure.

Values education. The effort to help students consider and develop appropriate values through discussion and formal exercises.

Visual-motor integration. The ability to coordinate eye and hand movements, as illustrated by the copying of designs onto paper.

Vocational education. The provision of technical training to students to enable them to obtain skilled jobs upon graduation.

Whole language. An approach to reading and writing that stresses understanding over the sounding out of letters.

INDEX